Animals in Human Society

Amazing Creatures Who Share Our Planet

Edited by Daniel Moorehead

University Press of America,® Inc.
Lanham • Boulder • New York • Toronto • Plymouth, UK

Copyright © 2016 by University Press of America,® Inc.
4501 Forbes Boulevard, Suite 200, Lanham, Maryland 20706
UPA Acquisitions Department (301) 459-3366

Unit A, Whitacre Mews, 26-34 Stannary Street,
London SE11 4AB, United Kingdom

Library of Congress Control Number: 2015950959
ISBN: 978-0-7618-6676-3 (pbk : alk. paper)—ISBN: 978-0-7618-6677-0 (electronic)

∞™ The paper used in this publication meets the minimum requirements of American
National Standard for Information Sciences Permanence of Paper for Printed Library
Materials, ANSI/NISO Z39.48-1992.

I dedicate this book to a dear friend, Linda Kelly,
who taught me that animals know how to love unconditionally,
they love us humans much more
than we could ever love them although we try.
You have saved the lives of so many animals over the years
when others turned them away.
Many years ago you introduced me to sibling black cats,
I was hooked from that moment.
Thank you!!

Also, to all the different animals I have known and loved over the years.
I still miss each of you daily, terribly, but will see you all again,
I'm certain of it.

Then the LORD opened the mouth of the donkey, and she asked Balaam,
"What have I done to you that you beat me these three times?"
[29]"You have acted so willfully against me," said Balaam to the donkey,
"that if I only had a sword at hand, I would kill you here and now."
[30]But the donkey said to Balaam,
"Am I not your donkey, on which you have always ridden until now?
Have I been in the habit of treating you this way before?"
"No," he replied.

[31]Then the LORD opened Balaam's eyes, so that he saw
the angel of the LORD standing on the road with sword drawn;
and he knelt and bowed down to the ground.
[32]But the angel of the LORD said to him:
"Why have you beaten your donkey these three times?
I have come as an adversary
because this rash journey of yours is against my will.
[33]When the donkey saw me, she turned away from me these three times.
If she had not turned away from me, you are the one I would have killed,
though I would have spared her."

Numbers 22:28–33, New American Bible (Revised Edition)

Contents

Preface

Non-human animals (hereafter) animals are amazing creatures. Every day it is likely one can read, see, or learn about some remarkable accomplishment an animal has engaged in. However, we must not just recognize them for what acts of bravery they may have performed, their remarkable ability to search and rescue human beings, work as service animals, care for and grieve for their own kind in the wild, we must recognize them as amazing creatures simply because who they are.

Animals have demonstrated time and time again they possess far superior skills than those of humans, but it is unlikely that our society will fully recognize these facts. For example, humans have about 5 million scent glands whereas dogs have 125 million to 300 million (depending on breed), meaning their sense of smell is 1,000 to 10,000,000 times better than humans. Puppies are born deaf and usually cannot hear until they are about 21 days old. By the time their sense of hearing has developed, they can already hear 4 times the distance of a human with normal hearing. Dogs can hear higher pitched sounds and can detect a frequency range that far exceed those compared to a human. It is also known the cats can see much better at night than humans can.

Wild animals are amazing in their own right. They do what comes naturally to them. They hunt for food as a means for survival, not for pleasure. Humans invade their space by wanting to live in "nature" or among the "wild animals" and when an animal acts on instinct to protect their "own" or in search of food we blame the animal and rid "problem animals" from society by having them destroyed. Humans also have a fascination with attempting to domesticate wild animals and take them on as so called "pets," never a good idea. Humans often seek out wild or exotic animals to become "pets," not fully understanding the negative consequences that could transpire. Wild animals want and deserve to live in their natural habitat, humans should respect their space. It's vital as a society to realize that we share the planet with other animals and we must learn to co-exist.

It is my belief all animals were created by God. Animals and Humans were originally created to co-exist, but man chose to disobey God and the animals continue to suffer simply because their association with man. It is my belief that in the afterlife the "lion will lay down with the lamb," death will be no more, animals will co-exist as originally designed.

I cannot imagine life without animals, many hold a similar view, and therefore they need our protection. It's time we take animal interests and needs more seriously. I often ask my students if they have ever "stood up" for something meaningful to them at the risk of ridicule or embarrassment. Surprisingly, many say they have not. While I'm not surprised at their responses, perhaps it's time as a society generally, and educator's specifically, to bring animal issues to the forefront. Rescue and habitat loss may be a good place to begin?

The maltreatment, abuse, and neglect of innocent animals must cease. If we humans are the superior species as many would argue, why is so difficult to find alternatives for our food sources, discover new technologies to advance science without experimenting on animals, create new ways of recycling materials instead of continuing deforestation, continue to contaminate our waterways and drill for oil in protected areas where wildlife thrive?

The problem is, many people do not take animal interests or issues seriously. Much of society give no thought as to where their food (meat) comes from, how the animals suffer, and how the meat is processed. My students in my "Animals in Human Society" course often say they had no idea what really goes on with the animals when it comes to food production prior to taking the course. They also comment on how "awful" other animals are treated in the name of science. One goal of my course is to present the facts, and at the conclusion, it's really up to the students if they take what they learned and make any changes to better the lives of animals, the environment, and perhaps themselves by becoming better consumers. It's been suggested by well-respected physicians that a plant based diet is a much heathier than an animal based. I personally feel better eating a plant based diet and sleep better knowing that no animal suffered and died to feed my appetite.

As a "civilized" society we must recognize that animals are amazing creatures that share our planet and take into consideration their needs. There needs include to be loved, live free (wild animals need to be left in the wild), not forced to satisfy the "needs" or desires of humans, not to be experimented on, not live in factory farms and fed liquid diets, and realize they deserve our respect to be the creatures they are. We must recognize the variety of situations in which animals enhance and promote human health and well-being, something humans often take for granite.

As Marc Bekoff writes in "The Animal Manifesto" (2010) "if animals can think and feel" and we know they do, what would animals "think and feel about the ways humans treat them?" (p. 8). Bekoff (2010) writes that all animals share the Earth and we must coexist; animals think and feel; animals have and deserve compassion; connection breeds caring, alienation breeds disrespect; our world is not compassionate to animals; and acting compassionately helps all beings and our world (pp.8-9).

These ideas are not unreasonable, in fact, Bekoff's suggests it's "common sense," I would agree.

Acknowledgments

I want to thank my Lord and Savior Jesus Christ, to him be the glory.

Thank you to Ms. Nicolette Amstutz at University Press of America. She was terrific to work with, so very helpful and knowledgeable.

Thank you to Ms. Holly Buchanan at University Press of America, your attention to detail was fantastic. This project would not have been able to be completed without your commitment and dedication.

Thank you to my friend and colleague Dr. Robert Moore, chair of the sociology department at Frostburg State University who always encouraged me to do this project. He recommended University Press of America, as he had previously published two books with them.

Introduction

I often tell students in my "Animals in Human Society" course that we'll attempt to bring into the realm of sociological study the relationships that exist between humans and other animals. We will do this by exploring the social relationships between humans and animals and examine the social meanings which shape the role and status of animals in society and encourage personal reflection and discovery of the benefits of sustainable living.

In the course there are several very important goals I want them to learn. These goals consist of (1) understanding that our society places little to no value on animal interests, (2) explore the oppression of non-human animals, and consider the moral status and rights of animals in human society, (3) explore the oppression of nonhuman animals, and consider the moral status and rights of animals in human society; (4) explore and investigate the nature and forms of abuse/cruelty animals are subjected to through interdisciplinary inquiry spanning sociology, criminology, moral philosophy, and law; (5) study animal/human interaction in several major social institutions-family, health, politics, economy, religion, and sports; (6) examine several major philosophical positions about human social policy regarding the future of animal/human relations; (7) examine institutionalized forms of abuse in research, zoos, hunting, sport/entertainment and food production; (8) recognize the variety of situations in which non-human animals may enhance and promote human health and well-being, and (9) introduce students to the growing discourse surrounding "sustainability" and sustainable issues. Therefore, students emerge with a greater awareness of sustainable issues and the capacity to apply sustainable thinking elsewhere in their lives. Students come to understand the world as a series of dynamic and interrelated and interdependent processes – physical and social – and begin to identify and articulate some of the challenges as well as promises of moving toward a more sustainable world for both humans and animals.

The following chapter's emphasis the amazing creatures who share our planet and in some cases highlight the "brutal" side of our society with continuing the inhumane treatment of all types of animals. We must, as a civilized society take animal interests seriously and stop the abuse and cruelty towards all animals. Not only must we stop the inhumane treatment of animals for human interests, society must recognize that animals possess skills and abilities far exceeding that of humans. Perhaps the sad truth is, although some animals, amazing as they are will never be fully recognized for their abilities – those abilities their Creator instilled in them from the beginning of time.

Eleven authors affiliated with a variety of institutions such as Colorado State University; Frostburg State University; Michigan's Institute of Continuing Legal Education; Michigan State University; Michigan Veterinary Medical Association; University of Birmingham; University of California, Irvine; Salisbury University; Texas Woman's University.

The book may appeal to many different audiences, required and supplemental readings for courses relating to Animals and Society; for courses in Agricultural Science; Animal Behavior; Anthropology; Biology; Criminology; Deviant Behavior; Ecological Science; Environmental Science; Environmental Sociology; Geography; History; Humane Education; Natural Resources; Philosophy; Psychology; Religious Studies; Sociology; Social Problems; Social Work; Women's Studies; and Veterinary Medicine.

Although the book was written primarily for Academia, it may appeal to Animal Organizations, Government Agencies, Politicians at all levels, Environmental Organizations, and Grass Roots Activists.

Some authors have included their personal experiences in addition to their expertise in their chapter, relevant research is also included. The authors have attempted to present to the reader in a meaningful, responsible, and scholarly way what they believe to be the amazing creatures who share our planet and what role humans play in sharing the planet with other animals.

Chapter One

Ideology, Subjectivity, and Mind in Animal Models and Human Infant Research

Jessica Bell

INTRODUCTION

Nonhuman animal models (henceforth, "animal models") are scientific paradigms that use nonhuman animals to simulate human psychological, biological, and social processes or to investigate human disease. Animal models rest upon a Darwinian platform that has been a source of ideological contest for centuries. In Victorian England, both vivisectionists and anti-vivisectionists appealed to the evolutionary similarity between human and nonhuman animals to gain support for their cause (Mayer, 2009), and animal experimentation has been a source of persistent controversy (Michael and Birke, 1994). Although Darwin argued for *both* physical and mental continuity between humans and other animals, in scientific paradigms Darwinism has often been integrated with Cartesian ideology to produce the notion of physical continuity and mental discontinuity. Examining animal models of human psychological concepts provides the opportunity to explore the boundaries of human/animal and mind/body. Can animals be considered models of mind if they don't possess minds of their own? If so, how do scientists reconcile such an apparent contradiction? Are mind and body considered holistic in humans but discrete components in animals? Since language is a core mediator between ideology and scientific practices (Crist, 1999; Haraway, 1989), I use published scientific articles on four experimental paradigms to examine how discourse shapes the nature of human and animal minds. Multiple scholars have examined how social constructions of laboratory animals are created and maintained (Mayer, 2009; Phillips, 1994; Shapiro, 2002; Birke, 2003;

1

Lederer, 1992; Rader, 2004; Asdal, 2008). However, there are several limitations to that literature. The focus is primarily on biomedical research, although animals in psychological research are particularly interesting for examining issues related to mindedness. Also, there has been little attempt to compare the discourse used in nonhuman and human infant research paradigms. Human infants, like animals, cannot use human language to communicate their mental states; the relationship between their minds and their behaviors must be inferred. Juxtaposing animal research and human infant research reveals how methodological ideologies, presuppositions about mind and behavior, and discourses are shaped by the species of the experimental subject.

ANTHROPOMORPHISM AND ANTHROPODENIAL

A common theme in discussions of nonhuman animal mind is whether or not attributing particular cognitive capacities to animals is "anthropomorphism." Xenophanes first used the term anthropomorphism in 570 B.C.E. to criticize Homer's poetry for depicting gods as if they were people (De Waal, 1999). As gods were above humans and so clearly (to Xenophanes) ontologically different from humans, it was ridiculous to assume that gods would take human form. The negative connotations of anthropomorphism, and the implications of hierarchy (disbelief that animals could possibly be so like "higher up" humans) persist in contemporary conceptualizations of anthropomorphism.

There are two main forms of anthropomorphism: categorical and situational (Mitchell, 1997). Categorical anthropomorphism refers to inaccuracy in psychological characterization; categorical anthropomorphism assumes that an animal *cannot* possess a particular psychological characteristic. Situational anthropomorphism refers to inaccuracy in the psychological characterization of a particular behavior, even though the species may exhibit that psychological characteristic through another behavior. An example of situational anthropomorphism is interpreting a chimpanzee's threat gesture (which resembles a human smile) as happiness. If you say that one chimpanzee "loves" another, you could be accused of categorical anthropomorphism, since, according to some, only humans are capable of love. Most authors writing about "inappropriate" anthropomorphism in scientific paradigms are concerned with the categorical variety (Mitchell, 1997).

However, there are several problems with the notion of categorical anthropomorphism. First, it places all nonhuman animals, who possess a wide variety of cognitive and physiological characteristics, into a single category (Keeley, 2004). Second, it implies that we have positivistic knowledge about what animals possess, what humans possess, and where the line between the two lies. However, there is no clear and objective boundary between human and nonhuman animals; this boundary is a social construction contingent upon the cultural and historical context (Creager & Jordan, 2002; Noske, 1997). The historical development in Western culture of a clearly demarcated human-animal boundary is closely tied to mind-body dualism. Often traced to the 17th century philosophy of Descartes, notions of mind/body and human/animal dichotomies were themselves products of the scientific and religious culture of the period. Deacon (1997) asserts that the influence of the Christian Church was a primary influence on Descartes' notion of the uniqueness of human consciousness. Although anthropomorphism technically refers to the *misattribution* of human characteristics to nonhumans, it is often used more broadly to refer to the "fallacy" of describing animal behavior in intentionalistic terms, a remnant of the human/animal and mind/body dualisms of Descartes (De Waal, 1997; Spada, 1997).

The attempt to "guard" against anthropomorphism reached its zenith in the behaviorist paradigm, which sought to remove mentalistic terminology from descriptions of animal behavior. Behaviorism or neo-behaviorism is often justified by appeals to Morgan's canon, the methodological principle elaborated by the 19th century comparative psychologist C. Lloyd Morgan: "In no case may we interpret an action as the outcome of the exercise of a higher psychical faculty, if it can be interpreted as the outcome of the exercise of one which stands lower in the psychological scale" (Sober, 2005, p. 86). The position that assumes that mental operations in nonhuman animals are relatively simple is known as cognitive parsimony (De Waal, 1999). However, there are two major flaws in Morgan's canon. First, it looks at the relationships between species in terms of hierarchy ("higher" and "lower") despite the fact that Darwin emphasized branching, not hierarchy. Darwin so disagreed with the notion of "higher" and "lower" animals that he once wrote himself a note reminding himself to not mistakenly use those terms (Sober, 2005). Secondly, it overlooks the issues of anthropodenial and evolutionary parsimony (De Waal, 1999). Anthropodenial refers to the rejection of similarities between humans and other animals when in fact such similarities may exist. Whereas anthropomorphism refers to a Type I error (mistakenly detecting that an animal has mind when he does not), anthropodenial denotes a Type II error (mistakenly concluding that an animal does not have mind when he does). Evolutionary parsimony, also called cladistic parsimony, operates from the default position that closely related species are cognitively similar. Structuring a scientific paradigm under the assumption of evolutionary parsimony carries the risk of anthropomorphism, but cognitive parsimony carries the risk of anthropodenial. The fact that there is much concern about anthropomorphism but no mention of anthropodenial in Morgan's canon represents its (unscientific) bias towards human-animal mental discontinuity (Sober, 2005). The result of such bias has been the mechanomorphism of animals: the tendency to describe and conceptualize animals as machine-like (Spada, 1997; Crist, 1999).

THE MYTHS OF AN ATHEORETICAL PERSPECTIVE AND NEUTRAL LANGUAGE

Many have argued that using non-minded language to portray animal behavior is more objective than using minded language. However, this contention rests upon two myths: the myth of an atheoretical perspective and the myth of neutral language. The notion of objective or neutral language implies that the observer has no subjective point of view, a concept that Spada (1997, p. 40) refers to as "amorphism." Describing language as objective implies that it conforms to the real object of study. Nonhuman animals are not humans, but they are not machines either. Is using machine-like language any more "real" than using human-like language to describe animal behavior? Both rely on analogy to predict patterns of behavior and both are constrained by ideological frameworks. But to claim that one corresponds more "truly" to animal behavior is a fallacy. The myth of an atheoretical perspective has ideological and philosophical foundations relevant to the examination of animal agency, mind, and modeling. Haraway (1991), who calls the illusion that man can see everything from nowhere "the god-trick" (p. 189), links this myth to the ideology of humanism. Although "man" views himself as omnipotent, he is actually producing the world in his own image. To the humanist engaged in this act of production, the nonhuman becomes a mere tool for self-reflection or a vehicle for self-reproduction. The god-trick allows man to reproduce himself in nature while simultaneously remaining apart from it. The use of an "animal model" that reflects human biological or psychological processes while remaining unrepresentative of the animal himself is a prime example of the god-trick. This manner of approaching the world, in which everything is a resource for appropriation and self-reproduction, forces the world to become objectified, a thing rather than an agent. Therefore, what Haraway (1989) calls the "ideological fiction, and a powerful one" of the "detached eye of objective science" (p. 13) has important implications for animal mind and agency.

In explaining the myth of neutral language, Crist (1999) states that the language used to describe animal behavior has a direct impact on whether or not animal mind is "discovered" and perceived. For example, she argues that technical terms such as "innate releasing mechanism" in classical ethology and "maximizing fitness" in sociobiology represent a worldview in which sentience is at best unnecessary and at worst incompatible with describing animal behavior. She argues that technical language portrays behavior as something that happens *to* an animal, thus presenting the animal as an unminded object. Crist (1999) points out that, although the *intent* of such language may be objectivity, the use of these terms actually promotes a biased view of animal mind. However, Crist (1996, 1999) focuses exclusively on observational paradigms (ethology, sociobiology, and naturalism) and does not explore the language used in experimental paradigms that use nonhuman animals.

In their work on neuro-epistemology, the study of the nature and status of knowledge in the neurosciences, Mazabow et al. (2004) draw on Foucault in asserting that power and knowledge have a reciprocal relationship; "power produces knowledge... there is no power relation without the correlative constitution of a field of knowledge, nor any knowledge that does not presuppose and constitute at the same time power relations" (Foucault, 1977, p. 29). Mazabow et al. (2004) emphasize that discourse is a major mechanism through which the reciprocal relationship between power and knowledge is maintained. Once certain designations in language become widely accepted, the user of the language must generate ideas within the constraints of those designations. Experience and knowledge is structured to reflect the dominant discourse (and its accompanying ideology), which serves to reinforce the legitimacy of that dominant discourse. In addition to discourse, research paradigm choices such as the level of analysis, method of data collection, and what is considered data versus anomaly influence what type of information is found and legitimatized. Mazabow et al. (2004) note that knowledge about mind, an intangible and elusive concept, is particularly vulnerable to the replication of dominant ideology. Both the myth of an atheoretical perspective and the myth of neutral language reinforce the dominant ideology; the profusion of these myths renders the dominant ideology "what is" rather that "what may or could be."

DISCOURSE AND ANIMALS IN THE LABORATORY

Scientific practices and theories produce and are embedded in particular forms of narrative. As Haraway (1989) phrases it, "any scientific statement about the world depends intimately upon language, upon metaphor" (p. 4). Sociologists of science, in particular Latour (1987), discuss how the scientific paper can be considered a narrative rather than an "objective" report. Certain elements of the experimentation experience may be withheld from or altered in the scientific report. In their analysis of the "Methods" section of biomedical research papers, Birke and Smith (1995) find that euphemisms, omissions, and circumlocutions are used when describing both animal experimentation and animal death. For example, it is often unspecified whether an animal was alive or dead during a procedure. Although much detail is given about how measurements were taken, little detail is provided on what actually happened to the animal. Other rhetorical themes include using the passive voice while describing experiments and focusing on parts of the animal rather than the whole animal. In a similar vein, Durham and Merskin (2009) use discourse analysis to examine deliberations of an Institutional Animal Care and Use Committee (IACUC) at a public research university in the United States. The IACUC reviews proposed protocols for animal experimentations and has the ability to approve, revise, or reject protocols. Durham and Merskin (2009) find that members of the committee use passive verbs and a focus on parts of the animal (rather than the whole animal) to distance themselves from the procedures. In situations where experimenters had violated federal animal welfare regulations, the value of the animals are discussed in utilitarian terms; the death of the animal only becomes problematic if the data from the animal is unusable. Animals are also described as "giving their life" for research (Durham & Merskin, 2009, p. 243). This terminology portrays animals as voluntary agents and perpetuates an ideology of "false consciousness" (Durham & Merskin, 2009, p. 244). In other words, animals are given consciousness but it is an illusion produced to serve human ends. Providing further evidence that the discourse of science is tied to ideology and hegemony, Durham and Merskin (2009, p. 247) provide excerpts from interviews with scientists who attest to the cultural pressure to adhere to particular "rhetorical rules" when discussing animal research.

Multiple authors have explored the metaphor of "sacrifice" used prominently in scientific publications. For example, Lynch (1988) notes that this term is not just a euphemism but also serves a ritual and ideological purpose. It marks the transformation of a naturalistic animal that dies or is killed into an analytic object that is sacrificed for the "greater good." Animals who die before data can be collected or in ways that prevent the accumulation of data are not depicted as "sacrificed"; their deaths are meaningless and not given a term that involves ritualized meaning (Phillips, 1994). Arluke (1994) discusses how, according to Bakan (1968), sacrifice only serves its ritual meaning if the sacrificed is both distant from the sacrificer and also a part of the sacrificer's self. Consistent with this thesis, Arluke (1994) found that advertisements for laboratory animals represented animals as both inanimate products and consenting collaborators.

Another discursive theme that emerges in the scholarship of laboratory animals is the language of production. In his analysis of advertisements marketed at animal experimenters, Arluke (1994) notes that advertisers use language that indicates that animals are consumer goods that can be tailored into custom models to fit the needs of scientists. For example, one advertisement reads: "You can now opt for our standard model that comes complete with hair. Or try our new 1988 stripped down, hairless model for speed and efficiency" (Arluke, 1994, p. 148). Animals are transformed from natural beings that *reproduce* into objects that are *produced* (Arluke, 1994).

Discourse also has the ability to diminish or exacerbate objections to scientific practices. This is illustrated by Lederer's (1992) detailed account of the rhetorical strategies used by the editor of the leading biomedical research journal in the United States, *The Journal of Experimental Medicine*, from 1921 to 1946. These strategies included renumbering animal subjects in order to mislead critics about the number of animals used, removing any descriptive passages that indicated animal distress or resistance, using word substitutions such as "fasting" instead of "starving" or "hemorrhaging" instead of "bleeding" and referring to animals as "it" instead of "he/she." Since the historical and archival evidence indicates that these strategies emerged directly in response to the criticisms of anti-vivisectionists, Lederer (1992) concludes that these discursive strategies were motivated by political concerns rather than by the desire to be more "objective."

The literature on discourse and animals in the laboratory illustrates how ideology shapes social constructions of laboratory animals. However, there has been little work comparing the discourse used in nonhuman animal and human infant experimentation. A human infant, like a nonhuman animal, cannot use human language to communicate her mental state, and her mind and the relationship between her mind and her behavior must be inferred. Comparing nonhuman animal research and human infant research reveals how methodological ideologies, presuppositions about mind and behavior, and discourses are influenced by the species of the experimental subject.

SAMPLE

I examined a sample of published scientific articles on four experimental paradigms: 1) the rhesus monkey model of attachment developed by Harry Harlow, 2) the canine model of learned helplessness established by Martin Seligman, 3) the rodent model of pro-social behavior, and 4) human infant eye-tracking studies. Harry Harlow's work attempted to model human social deprivation and love through separating infant rhesus monkeys from their mothers. Infants were then exposed to various experiments. Some were provided with two different substitute mothers, one made of cloth and one made out of wire that gave milk, to measure the differential preference for contact comfort versus physical nourishment. Some were subjected to such apparatuses as the "well of despair" or "tunnel of terror" to examine early life social deprivation and/or depression. Martin Seligman's experimentation, which began with canines and then broadened to include rodents, strove to model human depression through creating learned helplessness in dogs. Dogs were placed into a restraining device and given painful, inescapable electric shocks. They were then placed into a "shuttle-box" where they again received painful shocks but where they had the ability to terminate the shocks by leaping from one end of the shuttle-box to another. The aim was to discover if the helplessness (or depression) learned in one environment would generalize to another environment. The rodent model of pro-social behavior uses multiple rodent species (rats, mice, and prairie voles) to measure how genes, hormones, and neuropeptides impact forms of affiliative behavior such as monogamy, parental care, and empathy. These studies are typically invasive, using genetic engineering or surgical intervention to alter a biological variable of interest and then examining the animal's organs post-mortem. However, one study included in this paradigm Bartal et al. (2011) used a non-invasive behavioral model. Infant eye-tracking studies provide human infants with various stimuli and then measure variables such as direction and duration of gaze; this paradigm is used to examine processes such as object perception, face perception, and categorization.

The four paradigms were selected to represent a diversity of academic disciplines and species of study. I chose these paradigms because they've been highly influential in their respective fields of experimental psychology (rhesus monkey and canine paradigms), social neuroscience (rodent model), and developmental psychology (eye-tracking paradigm). I selected ten influential scientific articles from each paradigm; influence was operationalized as number of citations on Google Scholar. A description of each paradigm was entered into Google Scholar. I then looked at the first ten pages of Google Scholar and selected the ten most cited articles. Books and book chapters were excluded from the analysis. For the first two paradigms, which are associated with particular researchers, I only included articles that were either a) authored or co-authored by the original author or b) authored or co-authored by a collaborator who had joint-published with the original author. With the unit of analysis the article, the total N was 40 articles (a full list of the articles is available from the author). The articles on the rhesus monkey model were published between 1959 and 2008, the articles on the canine model were published between 1967 and 1984, the articles on the rodent model were published between 1995 and 2011, and the articles on infant eye-tracking were published between 1977 and 2007.

CRITICAL DISCOURSE ANALYSIS

I used Critical Discourse Analysis (Fairclough, 1989) to examine the articles. A key concept in Critical Discourse Analysis is hegemony, the reproduction of oppression and power through ideological rather than coercive means. Hegemony produces "common sense in the service of sustaining unequal power relations" (Fairclough, 1989, p. 70). Common sense in the service of power refers to the way discourse can be used as a tool of legitimation and naturalization. The methodology of Critical Discourse Analysis (CDA) is outlined in Fairclough (1989). CDA involves the examination of formal features of vocabulary and grammar such as lexicalization (word choice), collocation (word placement), and nominalization (creating nouns from words that normally act as verbs). CDA also analyses how discourse yields particular presuppositions, frames, or schemata. Presupposition is when a person, in order to make sense of a grammatical sentence, must make certain assumptions that reinforce common sense in the service of power. For example, the sentence, "Even though she was married, Jane continued to work" presumes that women no longer work after they marry. This presumption reinforces the ideology that it is "normal" for women to cease working after marriage. Frames and schemata refer to the cognitive representations created by discourse. For example, referring to an animal as "it" or "that" creates a cognitive representation of the animal as an inanimate object. Finally, CDA examines how discourse relates to power relations, ideology, and societal struggles. This involves analyzing what patterns emerge in the discourse and how these patterns might perpetuate common sense in the service of power.

AGENCY AND SUBJECTIVITY

Congruent with previous work, I found that scientific articles on invasive animal experimentation selectively concealed human agency. Human agency was apparent in verbs that described intellectual processes. Authors wrote how "we reasoned" or "we achieved" (Maier et al., 1973, p. 591; Harlow and Suomi, 1974, p. 286). However, human agency disappeared in verbs that explained painful or invasive procedures. Young (2002, p. 19) noted that, "one hour after the 90-sec exposure, the brains *were harvested* and processed;" Maier et al. (1973, p. 589) discussed how "inescapable shocks *were administered* in the restraining tube." These phrases use the passive voice to remove the experimenter from the description. Nominalization was also used to remove human agency. Animals were characterized as "the isolates" (Harlow and Harlow, 1966, p. 266) or "pretreated with inescapable shock" (Seligman and Beagley, 1978, p. 534). This linguistic device conceals the fact that someone was responsible for isolating and shocking these animals.

Although both human and nonhuman animals were referred to as "subjects," the construction of their subjectivity was vastly different. The vast majority of sentences in articles about animal models had a specific behavior, effect, or brain region as the linguistic subject. If present at all, the animal was reduced to a prepositional phrase, a vehicle or site for the biological process or behavior but not the subject executing this process or behavior. For example, Insel (2010) noted that, "*The brain employs* specific receptors or cortical regions for processing social information" (p. 768). Other examples of this pattern included: "Once *the brain gathers* and processes social information, *it must decide* how to react to the situation" (Young, 2002, p. 20); "*Oxytocin facilitates* the formation of the mother-infant bond in sheep and stimulates nurturing behaviors in rodent females towards pups" (Young, 2001, p. 53); and "The *pattern appears* to be that of utilizing the partner or partners for bodily contact, and this *behavior tends* to become fixated" (Harlow & Harlow, 1966, p. 255). In all of the above examples, the subject is a biological or behavioral process. Removing the animal as the linguistic subject erases the animal's agency and subjectivity.

In contrast, papers on infant experimentation referred to the infant as the linguistic subject. For example, Johnson et al. (2003) stated that, "*infants perceived* continuity under less demanding conditions, when occluder size and occlusion time were reduced" (p. 10568). Other infant researchers wrote that, "*infants provided* evidence that they can rapidly develop expectations for visual events" (Haith et al., 1988, p. 474) and "*infants produce* a preponderance of retinocentric saccades" (Johnson et al., 2004, p. 198). The reason that infant subjectivity was more prevalent may be due to differences in how scientists interpret animal and human behavior.

MIND AND BEHAVIOR

The origin of behavior was described differently in human and animal research. Scientific discourse implied that infants *produce* behavior whereas behavior *is produced in* animals. Infant experimenters discussed how: "Six-month-old infants *produced* a reliably higher proportion of anticipations than did four-month-old infants" (Johnson et al., 2003, p. 10570); "We believe that infants *are motivated to develop expectations* for noncontrollable spatio-temporal events, because these expectations permit them to bring their visual behavior under partial internal control" (Hath et al., 1988, p. 467); and "There were nine coding areas to which infants *could direct* eye movements on each trial" (McMurray & Aslin, 2004, p. 219). This language conveys the notion that behavior originates from within the infants and that the infants are in charge of their own behavior.

In contrast, nonhuman animal research often portrayed the *experimenter*, not the animal himself, as the producer and director of animal behavior. For example, Maier (1984, p. 443) wrote that, "Many of the behavioral and physiological changes that are seen in the subjects that are not *provided with the behavioral coping response* could be viewed as adaptational adjustments to a situation in which behavioral coping fails" and Seligman and Beagley (1975) discussed how, "*we produced in the rat* the behaviors characteristic of learned helplessness in the dog" (p. 540). Nonhuman animals that have not yet been experimented on are often referred to as "naïve" (see for example Maier and Seligman, 1976). Like the metaphor of "sacrifice" mentioned earlier, this word has particular connotations. "Naivety" insinuates that the animal enters the experimental paradigm without prior knowledge or skills. The connotation is that the experimenter, not the animal, produces the behaviors of interest.

Consistent with the schema of animal behavior as product, the discourse of animal experimentation often used terminology reminiscent of the production and marketing of consumer goods. For example, Suomi and Harlow (1969) discussed the reasons for switching from the experimental technique of maternal isolation to the "pit of despair" apparatus in terms of speed and standardization: "these isolation techniques were *relatively slow in pathology production* and created a greater variance in behavior syndromes that was desired" (p. 248). Young (2002) wrote that, "The *amenability* of rodent models for genetic and pharmacologic manipulations make them valuable *tools* for preclinical studies to examine the basic neurobiology of social behavior" (p. 24). Other articles mentioned the utility, Young et al. (2011); efficiency, Maier & Seligman (1976); reliability, Maier & Seligman (1976); and convenience, Maier et al. (1973) of using particular animals or apparatuses to produce desired behaviors. The insinuation is that animal behavior is a product that should be controllable (by the experimenter, not the animal) and able to be replicated on demand. However, describing animal behavior in this way makes animal mind superfluous.

The relationship between mind and behavior was also represented differently between human and nonhuman paradigms. In human infants, mind and behavior were seen as inextricably linked. For example, Senju and Csibra (2008) described how infants "*preferentially* orient towards the source of these signals, sometimes responding to them by smiling" (p. 670). In all the studies on infants, looking time was an index of preference. This is important because, while duration of gaze is a behavioral construct, preference is a mental or cognitive construct. The merger of the two indicates that an infant's behavior is taken as evidence of her mind. In other words, the Cartesian separation of mind and body is absent. Behavioral constructs are seen as reliable indexes of mindedness. For example, Sobel and Kirkham (2006) wrote that, "Infant researchers have provided robust evidence through both eye-tracking and habituation (looking time) paradigms that young infants can *predic*t the outcome of a ball's partially hidden trajectory, *perceive* object unity under conditions of occlusion, *display* their understanding of the continuity principle, and *reason* about fully hidden objects" (p. 1108). In contrast, behavior and mind are seen as discrete categories in nonhuman animal subjects; one is not viewed as implying the other. This is demonstrated by how, in animal research, behavioral terms were used to qualify emotional and mental terminology. The implication is that animals display behavioral forms of mental states that are separate from, and lower than, the "true" mental states experienced by humans.

QUALIFIED AND ABSOLUTE DESCRIPTORS

In the animal paradigms, a common discursive strategy was to alternate between absolute and qualified emotional and mental descriptors. This strategy was absent from human infant research. By absolute descriptors, I mean a relatively simple descriptor that is meant to represent a concept, such as "depression." By qualified descriptors, I refer to a phrase that limits or modifies the meaning of another word or phrase, such as "depression-like." Qualified descriptors do not simply represent a concept. They simultaneously represent and alter a concept. Examples of qualified emotional and mental terminology from the sample included "anxiety-related behavior" (Bosch and Neumann, 2008, p. 17139), "depressive-like despair activity" (Suomi et al., 1976, p. 110), "affectional patterns" or "affectional systems" (Harlow, 1960, p. 676), and "behavioral depression" (Suomi, 1997, p. 174). Even when an article portrayed a phenomenon as inherently and necessarily psychological, behavioral qualifications were still used. For example, Maier (1984) asserted that coping is a necessarily psychological phenomenon, but then stated that animals "cope behaviorally" (p. 443). By adding qualifiers such as "behavior" or "system" to mental and emotional concepts, these authors imply that animals are experiencing a behavioral or mechanistic version of the mental, human version of these concepts.

Rewording and skepticism quotations were also used to simultaneously represent and qualify the mentality and emotionality of nonhuman animals. Rewording involved using both a "behavioral" and a "mental" term for the same concept. For example, Suomi (1997) referred to animals first as exhibiting "behavioral expressions of fear and anxiety" and then as being "shy and withdrawn" (p. 173). Peterson and Seligman (1983) talked first of "an expectation of response-outcome independence" and then of "a 'belief' in helplessness" (p. 106). Placing quotation marks around a word allows an author to simultaneously make use of a word while communicating skepticism that the word is correct or meaningful (Fairclough, 1989). Authors working with animal paradigms frequently used mentalistic or emotional terminology to describe animals but then introduced skepticism quotes around these terms later in the text. References to animals as neurotic, Maier & Seligman (1976); fearful, Maier & Seligman (1976); frustrated, Maier & Seligman (1976); hopeless, Seligman & Maier (1967); anxious, Suomi (1997); and despairing, Suomi et al. (1976) were all introduced with skepticism quotes but then used without qualification later in the texts. It is possible that experimenters tried to distance themselves from anthropomorphism by problematizing (through skepticism quotes) the notion that animals were experiencing states such as despair and neurosis. This is a strategy meant to maintain the human-animal boundary. However, by then using those same words without skepticism quotes, the experimenters were emphasizing and making use of human-animal similarity.

I argue that the vacillation between qualified and absolute descriptors of emotional and mental states serves two ideological purposes. The first is that it creates a distinction between "behavioral" and "mental" manifestations of such phenomena as love, fear, anxiety, depression, frustration, and stress. Although the scientific community has largely rejected Descartes' notion of mind/body dualism, the shadow of this Cartesian concept persists in nonhuman animal research. This remnant of Cartesian ideology allows for the creation of a "behavioral depression" that is different from mental depression. This reinforces the ideology that there is a fundamental difference between humans and animals and that, in animals, behavior is distinct from mind. This leads to the second ideological purpose, which is to problematize the use of emotional and mental language to describe animal behavior while still relying upon such language to justify the experimental paradigm. Since the experimental designs I examined specifically aim to model human psychological concepts, it is not surprising that experimenters must use cognitive and emotional terms. However, acknowledging animal mind could lead to ethical questions that threaten animal experimentation. Therefore, the discourse grants animals mind, but only skeptical or behavioral "versions" of mind.

Discourse that alternates between qualified and absolute descriptions of mental states positions nonhuman animals in the gray area between subjectivity and objectivity. The ambiguous subject-object identity of laboratory animals emerged frequently in the discourse of animal experimenters. For example, authors used both objective ("it") and subjective ("he/she") pronouns in reference to animals. Maier and Seligman (1976) wrote, "If the dog is given inescapable shock in the shuttle box and then required to press panels with *its* head to escape in the hammock, *he* is still helpless" (p. 8). Harlow and Harlow (1966) discussed how, "We believe that these negative responses of the mother assist the infant in gradually breaking *its* dependency relationship to *her*" (p. 245). Although most of the articles use objectifying descriptions of animals, subjective language occasionally breaks through. For example, Bosch and Neumann (2008), in discussing a study on rats, used the term "mother-child interactions" once in their article (p. 17143). Scattered sparsely through Harlow's articles, which heavily objectify monkeys, are references to monkeys as "unhappy and ill at ease" (Harlow, 1960, p. 684), exhibiting "forgiveness" (Harlow and Suomi, 1970, p. 166) and "sentient and intelligent" (Harlow, 1960, p. 680). These types of references are far and few between, but they should not be written off as accidental. They represent the way in which mentalistic terms are sometimes the most parsimonious and informative way to explain animal behavior.

AN OUTLIER

One article, Bartal et al. (2011) on nonhuman animals was quite different discursively than the others. Probably not coincidentally, it was also the only nonhuman animal study in the sample that did not rely on invasive or pain-inducing procedures. This study, which measured if rats would choose a food reward over helping a trapped cage-mate, consistently portrayed rats as linguistic subjects and intentional producers of their own behavior. For example, Bartal et al. (2011) noted that "the most parsimonious interpretation of the observed helping behavior is that *rats free* their cage mate in order to end distress, either their own or that of the trapped rat" (p. 1430). The authors also concluded that, in freeing a fellow rat, the experimental rats were engaging in "deliberate, goal-directed action" (Bartal et al., 2011, p. 1428).

IDEOLOGIES OF FUNCTIONALISM AND HUMANISM

The aim of Critical Discourse Analysis is to expose the implicit ideology that underlies discourse. When ideology is latent, it produces common sense in the service of power. The ideology is simply the *way things are*, not the way *things are viewed*. The majority of the articles on animal models in this study implicitly promote the ideologies of functionalism, humanism, and species-ism, although these terms and ideas are not explicitly mentioned. Although some would argue that the authors of these articles are simply being "objective," the comparison with scientific articles on human infants makes clear the falsity of this claim.

Functionalist theory argues that mental states are constituted by their causal relationships to sensory stimulations, other mental states, and behaviors (Reus and Olivier, 2007). In other words, what is defined as "a mental state" does not depend on its constitution but rather the role it plays in a system. Unlike behaviorists, who attempted to expunge references to psychology in favor of inputs and outputs, functionalists use mental terminology such as "intentions." However, Reus and Olivier (2007) argue that functionalism is actually a form of neo-behaviorism. They note that, "the words that, in everyday language, refer to *qualia* [the subjective character of conscious experience] are present in functionalist texts, but the realities they refer to have been eliminated. Sentient experience per se has been disposed of, as a reality of the world existing independently of the relations it can have with other events" (Reus & Olivier, 2007, p. 13). In other words, sentience becomes an epiphenomenon, a byproduct of neural effects that plays no causal role in behavior.

Although functionalism allows the attribution of mind to nonhuman animals, mind is redefined to produce a "concept of consciousness from which all consciousness is expunged", so that is cannot be said that animals prefer one state of 'mind' over another" (Reus & Olivier, 2007, p. 14). Functionalism is neo-Darwinian in that it sees the main aim of consciousness as the reproduction of the organism. However, when combined with a culturally conditioned notion of a human-animal cognitive boundary, this can lead to the assertion that the evolutionary or mental "program," not the animal himself, possesses the agency. Although "program" replaces the behavioral discourse of "instincts," the functionalist viewpoint still suggests that nonhuman animals "provided with such a consciousness are actually just mechanical automata" (Reus & Olivier, 2007, p. 19). This functionalist notion of animal mind has real implications for the treatment and welfare of animals. Reus and Olivier (2007) provide an example of a committee charged with evaluating the pain caused to ducks through the force-feeding used in *foie gras* production. The committee determines that "pain" in animals cannot be considered "suffering" but can only be discussed in terms of nociception, "the sensory modality specific to the processing of the signal that are triggered by potentially tissue-damaging stimuli" (Reus and Olivier, 2007, p. 25). Seeing conscious experience as only part of a system leads to the disregard of what we ordinarily classify as "conscious experience," though such skepticism is rarely if ever applied to human experience. The discourse used in the nonhuman animal paradigms reflects a functionalist ideology in that it a) uses mentalistic terminology while removing the realities these words refer to and b) represents animal sentience as playing no causal role in behavior. The discourse creates a qualified and diminished version of animal mind, a "behavioral mind" of sorts, in which animal agency and sentience are unnecessary.

Humanist ideology also informed the scientific paradigms in the sample. As Shapiro (2002) notes, much of modern science can be considered "scientific humanism" since its ideology is often grounded in the humanistic philosophy of the Enlightenment. A basic tenet of humanism is that individuality requires rationality and that only human beings are rational; in the humanistic tradition, animals are dominated by instincts and are not autonomous agentive beings (Shapiro, 2002). Descartes contributed to humanism the notions of human/animal and mind/body dichotomies. Humanism also entails seeing the environment (and other species) as mere tools for the self-reflection and self-reproduction of the human race (Haraway, 1989). This allows "man" to reproduce himself in nature while also remaining separate from nature. The entire concept of the "animal model," in which an animal exists merely to reflect human processes, is a humanistic paradigm. The animal research paradigms I examined also perpetuate tenets of humanist ideology by endorsing a) mind/body dualism and b) the notion that animals are mechanical vehicles of behavior rather than conscious producers of behavior.

CONCLUSION

The fact that methodological ideologies, presuppositions about mind and behavior, and discourse differed so strongly between the human infant and nonhuman animal paradigms illustrates the speciesist bias in studies of other minds. As mentioned, concern about anthropomorphism that ignores the risk of anthropodenial represents a nonscientific bias based purely on ideology and tradition. Ideology and tradition are also behind the speciesist bias in representations of mind. Other scholars have drawn attention to the parallels between nonhuman animals and non-linguistic human groups and the need for consistency in how we think about these groups. For example, in political philosophy, ethical and philosophical paradigms developed for non-linguistic humans have also been applied to nonhuman animals (Donaldson & Kymlicka, 2011). Donaldson and Kymlicka (2011) demonstrate how moving away from rationalist interpretations of agency (the prevailing view of humanism) allows both marginalized humans and nonhuman animals to express their agency. I argue that researchers examining psychological phenomena should think critically about how implicit ideology shapes their perceptions of other minds. Latent ideological assumptions may preclude the discovery of other minds and prohibit the expression of non-traditional agency.

Note: Throughout the paper, the italicized emphasis is mine.

REFERENCES

Arluke, A. (1995). We build a better beagle. *Qualitative Sociology, 17*(2), 143–158.

Asdal, K. (2008). Subjected to Parliament: The laboratory of experimental medicine and the animal body. *Social Studies of Science, 38*(6), 899–917.

Bakan, D. (1968). *Disease, pain and sacrifice*. Chicago, IL: University of Chicago Press.

Bartal, I. B. A., Decety, J., & Mason, P. (2011). Empathy and pro-social behavior in rats. *Science,* 334, 1427–1430.

Birke, L. (2003). Who-or-what is the laboratory rat (and mouse)? *Society and Animals, 11*(3), 207–224.

Birke, L., & Smith, J. (1995). Animals in experimental reports: The rhetoric of science. *Society and Animals, 3*(1), 23–42.

Bosch, O. J., & Neumann, I. D. (2008). Brain vasopressin is an important regulator of maternal behavior independent of dams' trait anxiety. *PNAS, 105*(44), 17139–17144.

Creager, A. N. H. & Jordan, W. C. (2002). *The animal-human boundary*. Rochester, NY: University of Rochester Press.

Crist, E. (1996). Naturalists' portrayals of animal life: Engaging the verstehen approach. *Social Studies of Science, 26,* 799–839.

Crist, E. (1999). *Images of animals: Anthropomorphism and animal mind*. Philadelphia, PA: Temple University Press.

Deacon, J. W. (1997). *The symbolic species: The co-evolution of language and the human brain*. London, England: Penguin.

De Waal, F. B. M. (1997). Foreward. In R. W. Mitchell, N. S. Thompson, & H. L. Miles (Eds.), *Anthropomorphism, anecdotes and animals* (xiii-xix). Albany, NY: State University of New York Press.

De Waal, F. B. M. (1999). Anthropomorphism and anthropodenial: Consistency in our thinking about humans and other animals. *Philosophical Topics, 27*(1), 255–280.

Donaldson, S. & Kymlicka, W. (2011) *Zoopolis: A political theory of animal rights.* Oxford: Oxford University Press.

Durham, D., & Merskin, D. (2009). Animals, agency and absence: A discourse analysis of institutional animal care and use committee meetings. In S. E. McFarland & R. Hediger (Eds.), *Animals and agency: An interdisciplinary exploration* (229–247). Boston, MA: Brill.

Fairclough, N. (1989). *Language and power.* London, England: Longman.

Foucault, M. (1977). *Discipline and punish.* New York, NY: Pantheon.

Haith, M. M., Hazan, C., & Goodman, G. S. (1988). Expectation and anticipation of dynamic visual events by 3.5-month-old babies. *Child Development, 59*(2), 467–479.

Haraway, D. (1989). *Primate visions: Gender, race and nature in the world of modern science.* New York, NY: Routledge.

Haraway, D. (1991). *Simians, cyborgs, and women: The reinvention of nature.* New York, NY: Routledge.

Harlow, H. F. (1958). The nature of love. *American Psychologist, 13,* 573–685.

Harlow, H. F. (1960). Primary affectional patterns in primates. *American Journal of Orthopsychiatry, 30*(4), 676–684.

Harlow, H. F., & Harlow, M. (1966). Learning to love. *American Scientist, 54*(3), 244–272.

Harlow , H. F., & Suomi, S.J. (1970). Nature of love: Simplified. *American Psychologist , 25* (2), 161–168.

Harlow, H. F., & Suomi, S.J. (1974). Induced depression in monkeys. *Behavioral Biology, 12,* 273–296.

Harlow, H. F., & Zimmermann, R. R. (1959). Affectional responses in the infant monkey. *Science, 130*(3373), 421–432.

Insel, T. R. (2010). The challenge of translation in social neuroscience: A review of oxytocin, vasopressin, and affiliative Behavior. *Neuron,* 65, 768–779.

Johnson, S. P., Amso, D., & Slemmer, J. A. (2003). Development of object concepts in infancy: Evidence for early learning in an eye-tracking paradigm. *PNAS, 100*(18), 10568–10573.

Johnson, S. P., Slemmer, J. A., & Amso, D. (2004). Where infants look determines how they see: Eye movements and object perception performance in 3-month-olds. *Infancy, 6*(2), 185–201.

Keeley, B. L. (2004). Anthropomorphism, primatomorphism, mammalomorphism: Understanding cross-species comparisons. *Biology and Philosophy, 19,* 521–540.

Latour, B. (1987). *Science in action.* Milton Keynes, UK: Open University Press.

Lederer, S. E. (1992). Political animals: The shaping of biomedical research literature in twentieth-Century America. *Isis, 83,* 61–79.

Lynch, M. E. (1988). Sacrifice and the transformation of the animal body into a scientific object: Laboratory culture and ritual practices in the neurosciences. *Social Studies of Science, 18,* 266–269.

McMurray, B., & Aslin, R. N. (2004). Anticipatory eye movements reveal infants' auditory and visual categories. *Infancy, 6*(2), 203–229.

Maier, S. F. (1984). Learned helplessness and animal models of depression. *Progress in Neuro-Psychopharmacology and Biological Psychiatry, 8*(3), 435–446.

Maier, S. F., Albin. R. W., & Testa, T. J. (1973). Failure to learn to escape in rats previously exposed to inescapable shock depends on nature of escape response. *Journal of Comparative and Physiological Psychology, 85*(3), 581–592.

Maier, S. F., & Seligman, M. E. P. (1976). Learned helplessness: Theory and evidence. *Journal of Experimental Psychology, 105*(1), 3–46.

Mayer, J. (2009). Representing the experimental animal: Competing voices in Victorian culture. In S. E. McFarland & R. Hediger (Eds.), *Animals and agency: An interdisciplinary exploration* (pp. 184–205). Boston, MA: Brill.

Mazabow, M., Burke, A. & Stuart, A. (2004). Neuro-epistemology: A post-modernist analysis of the neuro-sciences. *Health SA Gesondheid, 9*(2), 54–66.

Michael, M., & Birke, L. (1994). Enrolling the core set: The case of the animal experimentation controversy. *Social Studies of Science, 24,* 81–95.

Mitchell, R. W. (1997). Anthropomorphism and anecdotes: A guide for the perplexed. In R. W. Mitchell, N. S. Thompson, & H. L. Miles (Eds.), *Anthropomorphism, anecdotes and animals* (pp. 407–428). Albany, NY: State University of New York Press.

Noske, B. (1997). *Beyond boundaries: Humans and animals*. Buffalo, NY: Black Rose Books.

Overmier, J. B., & Seligman, M. E. P. (1967). Effects of inescapable shock upon subsequent escape and avoidance responding. *Journal of Comparative and Physiological Psychology, 63*(1), 28–33.

Peterson, C., & Seligman, M.E.P. (1983). Learned helplessness and victimization. *Journal of Social Issues, 2*, 103–116.

Phillips, M. T. (1994). Proper names and the social construction of biography: The negative case of laboratory animals. *Qualitative Sociology, 17*(2), 119–142.

Rader, K. (2004). *Making mice: Standardizing animals for American biomedical research, 1900–1955*. Princeton, NJ: Princeton University Press.

Reus, E., & Olivier, D. (2007). Mind-matter for animals matters: Science and the denial of animal consciousness. *Between the Species, VII*, 1- 26.

Seligman, M. E. P. (1972). Learned helplessness. *Annual Review of Medicine, 23*, 407- 412.

Seligman, M. E. P., & Beagley, G. (1975). Learned helplessness in the rat. *Journal of Comparative and Physiological Psychology, 88*(2), 534–541.

Seligman, M. E. P., & Maier, S. F. (1967). Failure to escape traumatic shock. *Journal of Experimental Psychology, 74*(1), 1–9.

Senju, A., & Csibra, G. (2008). Gaze following in human infants depends on communicative signals. *Current Biology, 18*, 668–671.

Shapiro, K. (2002). A rodent for your thoughts: The social construction of animal models. In M. J. Henninger-Voss (Ed.), *Animals in human histories: The mirror of nature and culture* (pp. 439–469). Rochester, NY: University of Rochester Press.

Sobel, D. M., & Kirkham, N. Z. (2006). Blinkets and babies: The development of causal reasoning in toddlers and infants. *Developmental Psychology, 42*(6), 1103–1115.

Sober, E. (2005). Comparative psychology meets evolutionary biology: Morgan's canon and cladistic parsimony. In L. Daston, & G. Mitman (Eds.), *Thinking with animals: New perspectives on anthropomorphism* (pp. 85–99). New York, NY: Columbia University Press.

Spada, E. C. (1997). Amorphism, mechanomorphism, and anthropomorphism. In R. W. Mitchell, N. S. Thompson, & H. L. Miles (Eds.), *Anthropomorphism, anecdotes and animals* (pp. 37–49). Albany, NY: State University of New York Press.

Suomi, S.J. (1997). Early determinants of behavior: Evidence from primate studies. *British Medical Bulletin, 53*(1), 170–184.

Suomi, S. J., Collins, M. L., Harlow, H. F., & Ruppenthal, G. C. (1976). Effects of maternal and peer separations on young monkeys. *Journal of Child Psychological Psychiatry, 17*, 101–112.

Suomi, S. J., & Harlow, H. F. (1969). Apparatus conceptualization of psychopathological research in monkeys. *Behavior Research Methods and Instrumentation, 1*(7), 247–250.

Young, K. A., Gobrogge, K. L, Liu, Y., & Wang, Z. (2011). The neurobiology of pair bonding: Insights from a socially monogamous rodent. *Frontiers in Neuroendocrinology, 32*, 53–69.

Young, L. J. (2001). Oxytocin and vasopressin as candidate genes for psychiatric disorders: Lessons from animal models. *American Journal of Medical Genetics, 105*, 53–54.

Young, L. J. (2002). The neurobiology of social recognition, approach and avoidance. *Biological Psychiatry, 51*, 18–26.

Chapter Two

Institutionalizing Animal "Subject" Protection in Research

Erin M. Evans

The outcome of the great struggle no one at this moment can foresee. Is it possible that Force, governed by ambition, is henceforth to hold in its grasp the destiny of nations? We cannot believe it.

—Albert Leffingwell, 1914

INTRODUCTION

The animal advocacy movement is more diverse than militants throwing blood on fur coats, or little old ladies dressing their cats in sweaters and Halloween costumes. Although the movement certainly has these characters, who play important roles, there are also professional lobbyists in Washington DC, academics who campaign for cageless eggs on their campuses, and bioethicists who have made their life's work studying the ethics of animal research. The following narrative describes how activists gained political recognition for animals used in research, representing one component of this complicated movement.

There are several books on the history of animal rights in the U.S. (Beers, 2006; Carbone, 2004; Finsen & Finsen, 1994; Guerrini, 2003; Guither, 1998; Jasper & Nelkin, 1992). The following offers a more narrow focus on how demands to protect animals in research became "institutionalized." By "institutionalization" I mean how the issue of animal protection in research went from being ignored by power holders, like politicians, to being established in federal policy. This institutionalization eventually created bureaucratic structures that regulated animal research by federal agencies, and eventually mandated committees within the local research institution to oversee animal use.

External oversight of research facilities includes federal agencies like the Animal and Plant Health Inspection Service (APHIS). Internal oversight includes campus veterinarians and Institutional Animal Care and Use Committees (IACUCs) that now must approve all research projects involving animals within facilities that receive funding from the federal government. This system is deeply flawed, as advocates continue to point out, and this narrative does not praise this often times frustrating bureaucracy. My intention is only to describe the long road activists travelled to make animals politically important.

In narrowing the focus I explain how the movement slowly gained access to decision making in federal policy, and how the movement was forced to sculpt demands to maneuver the state and federal legislative processes at opportune times. Activists made vivisection an issue of political importance by engaging with a variety of strategies and tactics. Large organizations repeatedly tried to get policies passed on the city, state, and federal level, while also using a variety other tactics to gather public sympathy and elevate the social status of animals. These tactics included service work with homeless animals, public events like parades and pet shows, letters to the editor, peaceful demonstrations, disruptive protests, and militant direct action. The following history will end with the more important question to activists in the field: Does this political maneuvering result in policies that create obstacles for further change, or do policy reforms crack the walls of animal research, allowing activists to keep chipping away? Are policy reforms stumbling blocks, or are they stepping stones?

I use a theoretically grounded historical narrative to show how activists forced the state to consider animals, and to eventually incorporate a system of protection that is similar to that of humans (Stark, 2012). The opportunity to use political structures to influence regulatory oversight of research on the city, state, and eventually federal level explains the mobilization and timing of these policies (Kitschelt, 1986; Kolb, 2007; Meyer, 1990). While the way the movement had to sculpt their demands to fit legislative constraints explains the content of the Animal Welfare Act (Wisler & Giugni, 1996). The organizational division of labor, whereby the movement splintered into a variety of groups with varying goals, strategies, and tactics, may explain the successful passage of the policy, but more importantly it explains the ongoing persistence of the movement (Gamson, 1990; Meyer, 2012; Rohlinger & Quadagno, 2009).

In the following I will show how social movement organizations sought out and utilized political opportunities to access scientific laboratories by repeatedly trying to change legislative structures on the city, state, and federal level. As the movement blossomed conflict over the appropriate demands activists should make for animals created exponential splintering of organizations over time. The division of labor helped maintain a multi-tactical front that pushed for a variety of demands, including establishing institutional protection within laboratories.

As opposed to weakening the movement the splintering of organizations increased the "strategic capacity" of the movement as a whole. "Strategic capacity" is used in social movements' literature to capture the resourcefulness and ingenuity of single organizations (Ganz, 2000). As I will show, resourcefulness and ingenuity may not be deliberate, but may still result from the natural proliferation of movement organizations. I employ "strategic capacity" to capture how the movement's internal conflict and splintering fostered a strong multi-tactical force that eventually established regulatory oversight animal use in laboratories, and also an extra-institutional force that uses disruptive tactics to maintain more contentious pressure.

Throughout the following narrative I refer back to the three causal explanations that explain the passage of the AWA, its content, and the consequent persistence of the movement: 1) political opportunities, 2) institutional selectivity, and 3) inter-organizational division of labor. I will conclude by asking whether institutionalization of animal protection through the AWA could foster or block activists' access into research facilities as law enforcement, and how regulatory oversight may influence a "welfare culture" in science.

THE BEGINNING(S):
ANTI-VIVISECTION BEFORE THE 20TH CENTURY

Some of the first recorded criticisms of animal use focused on experimentation (Guerrini, 2003; Guither, 1998; Rollin, 2002). In antiquity philosophers like Epicurus and Plutarch encouraged the public to consider the interests of animals. In fact, Plutarch refused to ingest medicine if it had been tested on animals. Aristotelians, Platonists, Neo-Platonists, and the Stoics all debated the moral status of animals (Sorabji, 1993). Because of the drastic differences in context and time one cannot define these thinkers as "welfarists" or "abolitionists," but it is clear that ideologies supporting the liberationist foundations of the current animal rights movement are not unique to the 19th century. The other common thread through history is that advocates for animals all vie for the same constituency with the same basic demand: to make the interests of nonhuman animals matter. For this reason I refer to the movement and the actors therein universally as the Animal Advocacy Movement. Although this assertion is highly controversial to activists and Animal Studies scholars (Francione, 1996) the history of the movement will show how distinct components of the movement worked as a functioning family of activists and organizations.

In the 17th century public figures in Europe questioned the belief that animals were machine-like automatons. Well-known scientists spent much effort defending their belief that animals' reactions to pain were not suffering, but rather instinctual responses that were purely physiological. Documented examples of painful experiments animals endured without anesthesia are plentiful, and horrific (Guerrini, 2003). The issue of animal suffering encompassed much public debate in this era. Criticisms animal experimentation in the U.K. were a foundation for the early sprouting of the movement in the U.S. (Beers, 2006; Guerrini, 2003). I highlight only the most important interactions between activists in the U.S. and U.K., as well as important differences between the development of federal policies in England and the U.S. Mostly I am interested the movement's trajectory at the establishment of the first organization in the United States by Henry Bergh: The ASPCA in 1866.

The ASPCA is the longest standing animal protection organization in the U.S., and was integral to making animal research a publicly important issue. Henry Bergh founded the ASPCA in New York City primarily as an organization for working animals and stray animals. Bergh was an extremely formidable presence whose confidence was at least partly due to his higher-class status in society. His passion for animal protection went beyond the typical pamphleteer or public speaker, and included publicly confronting owners of horses who beat and overworked their horses in the streets, and other brazen actions. Bergh argued that activists should not wait for the media's attention but rather hijack it through provocative direct actions that highlighted their agenda. He fast became famous (and infamous) for instigating daylong traffic jams on the city's busiest thoroughfares as he ordered freight drivers to unhitch weary horses and passengers to dismount from overloaded omnibuses. (Beers, 2006, p. 62)

These actions were not limited to horses, but also cattle and even sea turtles used for food. The ASPCA dealt with animal issues such as urban wildlife, food animals in transport, and exotic "pets," but most of the organization's energy and resources eventually focused on dealing with dogs and cats as companion animals. Their involvement in the issue of animals in research emerged because of an intersection of issues, between research and companion animals. This intersection also instigated the first major organizational division of labor in the campaign targeting vivisection.

Scientists in the U.S. used a variety of means to acquire shelter animals for experimentation, including breeding, pet theft, and importing from other countries. Finding enough animals for research was a consistent problem for scientists, especially those using monkeys, dogs, and cats. Free animals were difficult to come by, and purchasing them was too expensive given the unrestrained nature of research that killed so many of the "subjects." In the late 1800s and early 1900s there were no restraints on how scientists acquired animals, especially dogs and cats. During this time when the foundations of anatomy were still being established, finding appropriate models for research was not an issue. Scientists sought out the cheapest animals that suited their area of research. Nonhuman primates were expensive because of importing costs; dogs and cats were more suitable for issues of anatomy and surgical training than rodents because of their size. The issue of acquisition, and the use of shelter dogs and cats, eventually inspired Caroline Earle White to start the American Anti-Vivisection Society in 1883. This began the splintering of organizations based on ideological conflicts surrounding welfarist versus abolitionist goals.

In the late 1800s Bergh and ASPCA were heavily involved in the issue of cruelty in animal research, but he was only against experiments that didn't use of anesthesia. This may have been a public relations strategy to maintain support, but some activists were frustrated at this moderate stance in the face of unrestrained experiments. As Beers (2006) describes, during this time period Caroline Earle White became involved in the animal research issue because of an upsetting interaction she had with a scientist in Philadelphia in 1871. At this time women were the majority of rank and file activists in the movement, but were not allowed to head formal organizations. White was a prominent activist who was outspoken on behalf of dogs and cats, but was barred from heading any of the organizations she founded. While working at the Women's Branch of the Society for the Prevention of Cruelty to Animals (WPSPCA), which she cofounded, White was approached by S. Weir Mitchell, a local physician. He approached her about acquiring stray animals from their shelter for research. The thought of homeless dogs and cats being used for research appalled White deeply.

The incident prompted her to travel to Europe and meet Francis Power Cobbe, a famous and influential antivivisectionist in England. Cobbe urged White to form a strong and uncompromising front against vivisection (Beers, 2006). White eventually formed the American Antivivisection Society (AAVS) in 1883, a group that remained staunchly abolitionist even during times when public support of science was at its strongest. This division of labor between organizations helped maintain a strong front against vivisection. Both the welfarist and abolitionist fronts maintained pressure on the scientific community during times of strong mobilization for the entire movement, such as the early 1900s, and during times of low public support for animal protection in research, such as during the Great Depression and following the discovery of germ theory.

While the AAVS and other abolitionist groups worked against science specifically, the ASPCA, Anti-Cruelty Society, Massachusetts Society for the Prevention of Cruelty to Animals (MSPCA), and other moderate groups maintained a more moderate stance and stoked public esteem and sympathy for companion animals using education tactics. During times of low public support for companion animal issues, using education and service work helped the movement influence public opinion towards animals in a way that was vital to future legislative efforts.

Research using animals was often publicly visible and well known in the early 1800s in the U.S., but esteem for the animals used was not high enough to spark the same criticism as in the England and other European countries. In England, the first federal legislation passed to protect animals in laboratories was the Cruelty to Animals Act of 1876, which required licensing and inspections of all research by the Home Secretary. This legislation was a stark compromise compared to the bill introduced by the antivivisection movement. The original legislation proposed banning all vivisection that would not produce immediate medical benefit, and banning the use of all dogs and cats. At this time the antivivisection movement was strong; even Queen Victoria wrote letters to the parliament during the bill's deliberation condemning of vivisection as "evil" (Guerrini, 2003). The legislation that passed was a major compromise, but compared to the U.S. it was a major political change. In the U.S. the first federal policy regulating any aspect of animal research would not occur for about 90 years.

In the U.S. dogs and cats became more widely accepted as household companions and elicited widespread public sympathy in the early to mid-20th century. Until then only the elite in cities had the luxury of keeping either animal as pets, including hounds kept for hunting. (It should be noted that families running farms in rural areas also kept dogs and cats as pets, but since the movement kept their public activities within major cities the influence of rural populations is not as relevant to this history.) Packs of stray dogs that roamed the streets of New York City in the early 1900s were a public safety issue. In a random sample of 10% of *New York Times* articles from 1900 to 1930, more than a quarter of the articles about the ASPCA emphasized the danger of stray dogs and cats, including a rabies epidemic and attacks on children. The nuisance of stray dogs and cats lessened because of local shelter organizations that emerged in the late 19th and early 20th century. The ASPCA's model for dealing with stray and unwanted animals diffused to these local organizations, such as the Massachusetts Society for the Prevention of Cruelty to Animals (1868), the Humane Society for the Promotion of Animals Welfare (1883), and the Animal Rescue League of Boston (1889).

These local organizations all worked to remove stray animals from streets and taking on unwanted animals. A few organizations, like the MSPCA and its founder George T. Angell, also became involved in the antivivisection movement. As dogs and cats became less of a nuisance, their status as household companions continued to build. More people adopted dogs and cats as "pets" and their public image slowly improved. Coverage in the *New York Times* increasingly highlighted topics like children learning to care for dogs, or ensuring the safety of animals in extreme heat in the early 20th century.

"Service organizations," such as the ASPCA, elevated social status of animals through this service and through public relations tactics over a long period of time.[1] Organized efforts to regulate animal research through policies that were state based began in the United States in the late 1800s. Abolitionists at this time did not trust scientists, even when regulated, and did not support efforts to create laws they thought ultimately legitimated animal research (Beers, 2006; Leffingwell, 1914). (This perspective has changed very little in the abolitionist faction of the movement.) During campaigns to regulate vivisection abolitionist groups like White's AAVS engaged in public relations campaigns against animal research that resulted in an ongoing war of rhetoric between activists and scientists (Beers, 2006; Conn & Parker, 2008; Keen, 1912; Leffingwell, 1914; Munro, 2002). Activists accused scientists of hiding behind a guise of human medical advancement. They claimed that scientists engaged in experiments that provided very little benefit while inflicting intense suffering on animals. For instance, John Call Dalton, an American physiologist, defended animal research in 1875, saying that great advances in knowledge of physiology resulted from vivisection. He could not say the same for specific and practical human medical advances resulting from these great advances (Taber, 1903).

Depending on its leadership and on the political opportunities they were pursuing, the ASPCA vacillated between abolitionist efforts and compromise with the animal research. For instance, with the approval of their late founder and president, Bergh, the ASPCA introduced a bill in New York State in 1880 calling for complete abolition of medical experiments using animals. It was quickly rejected. Later in the mid-1900s the ASPCA acquiesced to surrendering animals to laboratories for research, which reflects how drastically the organization changed its stance. Despite this the ASPCA remained vigilant presence throughout this period in efforts to establish regulatory oversight of animal research. State based efforts emerged across the country in varying forms, resulting in some victories banning dissection in elementary schools in Massachusetts in 1894.

The small victories in elementary schools should not be dismissed because of the rippling effect it created on a local grassroots level (Beers, 2006). Neither should the failed state-wide efforts, nor the abolitionist efforts by activists who thought moderate policy reforms would be toothless compromises. While moderate organizations and activists gained visibility through both failed attempts at policy change, and through successful efforts to ban required dissection in elementary schools, abolitionists pushed hard against vivisection and exerted a tremendous amount of pressure on scientists who used animals. The successful mobilization against dissection demonstrates how activists used *any and all* political opportunities, including compromising their demands to make gains.

The institution of scientific research was too strong to relent to policy efforts seeking abolition. The movement shifted its goals strategically, and included the issue of research using children to utilize a concurrent campaign against human vivisection on children and vulnerable adult populations. (I will describe the bridging to human vivisection in the next section.) While moderate organizations sought out institutionalization of animal protection in elementary schools and in state-wide campaigns, radical organizations exerted more intense pressure on scientists through the use of graphic imagery and hostile attacks on scientists (Beers, 2006; Guerrini, 2003). While some policy efforts failed, abolitionists remained vigilant and strong, as they had not exerted energy on the failed policy efforts.

The pressure that scientists felt is evidenced by their reaction, both through pamphlets published by animal researchers who had been attacked (Keen, 1912), and by the proceedings of House of Delegate proceedings of the American Medical Association (Association, 2013). The American Medical Association was established specifically to maintain the legitimacy and autonomy of scientists against both legislative efforts and abolitionist efforts by the movement. In the minutes from delegate meetings of 1896 through the early 1900s there is consistent reference to the "Antivivisection agitators" and the need to protect scientific autonomy through both public relations campaigns and through legislative protection.

The effort that elicited the first big reaction from scientists in this period was a coalitional strike in 1896. A bill was proposed to the U.S. Senate calling for a federal mandate to regulate research through a nonmedical commission. The coalition was led by the SPCAs and the Womens' Christian Temperance Union's Department of Mercy that worked against vivisection. This bill received widespread support, including six Supreme Court justices, but was eventually stalled by a contextual event, the Spanish-American war in 1898. Public and political attention was diverted. During this time the scientific freedom side mobilized, and when bills were introduced on the state level in New York, Pennsylvania, and Massachusetts in 1901 they were ready to block the efforts (Beers, 2006; Guerrini, 2003; Keen, 1912).

The animal justice movement at this time was strong enough to attack scientists and their cruel practices from multiple angles. Although the splintering of the movement was not a deliberate move to create a strong multi-tactical front, and despite the contentious infighting that accompanied these splits, this kind of atomization of the movement created a diffused force that scientists felt and feared. The combination of accessing political opportunities, molding demands to fit institutional boundaries, and an inter-organizational division of labor carried the movement into the legislative burgeoning of the 20th century.

EARLY 20TH CENTURY:
THE BUILD UP TO THE ANIMAL WELFARE ACT

In 1901 the state legislature in Massachusetts held hearings regarding two bills introduced by the MSPCA and other groups on behalf on children's protection. The bill regarding animal protection was house bill 856, and demanded the following changes that would have increased protection of animals in laboratories. These welfare demands have persisted through the 20th century, and to the present.

- That no experiment shall be conducted unless it is directly relevant to saving or prolonging human life or alleviating human suffering.
- Only graduates of medicine shall conduct animal experiments and procedures, and no students will be present to the experiments.
- All animals shall be anesthetized to prevent their feeling pain.
- All animals shall be killed at the conclusion of the experimental procedure.
- Officers of the humane society (MSPCA) shall be permitted unannounced entrance to laboratories where animal research is held, and violators of the above regulations shall have fines not exceeding $300 levied against them by the society officers.

None of these demands have been met in full through federal legislation, and the last demand that officers of an autonomous animal protection organization have access to research facilities on a free basis has not been met in any form. This demand reflects the important issue of access, and how activists have never been granted access to animals used in research in any form. Over time activists sculpted the above demands to fit the limited political opportunities presented, which included institutions and a broader culture that was fierce in protecting the autonomy of science.

Scientists have comprised the opposition, or countermovement, to animal protection in research since the beginning of these organized efforts. As seen in archives documenting testimony to the Massachusetts state legislature in 1901 (Ernst, 1902), as well as House of Delegates proceedings of the American Medical Association from 1894 to the present (Association, 2013), *the two primary defenses against increased animal regulations have not changed, at all, in over 100 years*. House bill 855 passed and regulated human vivisection; Bill 856 did not pass and would have regulated animal vivisection with the provisions I presented above. Bill 855 received little critique, but 856 received testimony from researchers across the country, coordinated by Harold C. Ernst, a researcher in bacteriology at Harvard Medical School. I draw from the Massachusetts testimonies because they were used for state efforts, and reflect the views of 30 prominent scientists from that time period. These testimonies were collected by Ernst and used as a pamphlet and rhetorical tool to legitimize scientific freedom. The testimonies in this collection resonate strongly with more recent pro-research literature, media interviews with scientists, and conference proceedings. They also resonate with my interviews of more than 30 professionals involved in research using animals, wherein every researcher and administer I interviewed employed the two primary defenses.

From these 30 testimonies there were two bases of defense, with variations on how they were used. These defenses were 1) that regulatory oversight of animal protection was obstructive to medical progress, and 2) that this oversight was unnecessary because animals were adequately protected already. The testimonies claimed that internal regulatory oversight within most laboratories prevented abusive practices, and because data is compromised when animals endure unnecessary suffering there was an inherent incentive for scientists to vie for animals' welfare. These two defenses are the primary institutional boundaries that activists confronted when seeking legislative protection, and the compromises made in legislative process reflect how activists molded their demands to fit within these boundaries. Activists gained federal oversight by maneuvering this institutional selectivity—self-regulation and scientific autonomy—with each future effort to pass federal legislation.

The issue of self-regulation and scientific autonomy is pivotal. It is unclear whether the provivisectionists use internal forms of regulation to thwart animal advocates, or as a genuine response to successful mobilization against completely unregulated vivisection. By "internal forms" and "self-regulation" I mean a model of regulatory oversight where research institutions establish committees of scientists and administrators from within that institution to approve research projects. I will explain the development of these internal committees, but it is important to highlight how they could reflect cooptation of the movement, or incorporation of movement demands for recognition of animal interests. Historical accounts from Animal Studies scholars and historians who are critical of reforms portray this move as a method of cooptation, while those who are sympathetic to reforms portray this as a genuine effort to incrementally eliminate cruelty in research.

In 1908 the American Medical Association formed the Council on Defense of Medical Research (CDMR), which spearheaded a campaign to neutralize antivivisection efforts (Association, 2013). One method to do so was to create an internal review of laboratories, which eventually resulted in the first "Guidelines for Laboratory Animal Care." Some animal advocates claim that these forms of internal regulatory oversight neutralized the movement, but in reading the council's reports these standards seem to have been established because they thought the inconsistencies in internal regulations for animal care were problematic. In the AMA reports officials recognized there was abuse. When this is juxtaposed against the coinciding movement to regulate human vivisection it is possible to see these standards as a starting point to substantive change in animal research, instead of an obstacle. As I will show regulatory oversight of human subject research is parallel to that of animal subject, the differences are in degrees.

Human subject regulation occurred earlier, and stronger, but structurally the two realms of experimentation are virtually identical. Animal activists constructed their demands to fit the boundaries of scientific self-regulation and maintaining medical progress, in doing so they created in-roads towards establishing policy. In the following section on human and animal protection, I will show how the organizational division of labor allowed for moderates to bridge their grievances to those against human vivisection, while abolitionists continued to expose abuse and exert constant pressure on scientists.

COMMONALITIES IN HUMAN
AND ANIMAL SUBJECT PROTECTION

The history of human subject protection is, obviously, rich (Stark, 2012). Here I will only emphasize how the structures and models for oversight of human subject research are virtually identical to those for animal subject protection, with important differences in the amount of autonomy scientists are afforded.

As the status of dogs and cats improved, their use in research became a more important issue. The American Anti-Vivisection Society (1883) and The New England Anti-Vivisection Society (1895) were relatively small organizations, but their influence grew as dogs and cats became more beloved as companion animals. The American Humane Association (1877) grew increasingly influential because they also vied for children's protection. This provided a bridge between the animal advocacy movement and the movement against human vivisection, and for reforms of human subject research.

In the early 20th century abuses to orphaned and sick children, cognitively challenged adults, and prisoners in the name of science came under scrutiny. It should be noted that in Europe vulnerable people were used from as early as the 1600s, but these experiments were conducted as therapeutic procedures, not research. For instance, in 1667 Jean-Baptiste Denis transfused sheep's blood into a young man suffering from a fever, with positive results until the second transfusion. The young man, and others who underwent the same procedure, suffered from what we now know is hemolytic reaction (Guerrini, 2003). At this time blood transfusions from animal to animal and animal to human were all the rage, and when conducted on sick people the results were recorded in publications such as *Philosophical Trans-*

actions (King, 1666). (At this time philosophy and medical sciences were intertwined.)

I use this very early example to illustrate how human experimentation was also experimental therapy, and this ethical dilemma has persisted until the present. Early scientists and physicians were using any method possible to uncover the mysterious workings of the healthy body and of the diseased body, but their choice of vulnerable people violated ethical conduct. Their pursuit then, and now, is an entanglement of curiosity, utilitarianism, benefi-cence, and widespread panic. In the early 20th century physicians and law-yers who were exposed to the atrocities caused by unrestrained experimenta-tion formed the Vivisection Reform Society (VRS). VRS was not abolition-ist, but was critical of research on humans and animals that involved pain and did not directly benefit the patient. The Society focused primarily on human vivisection. Their literature details the use of humans by experimenters in research that was painful and served only to satiate the scientist's curiosity.

> They defined "human vivisection" as "the practice of subjecting human be-ings, men, women and children, who are patients in public charitable institu-tions, hospitals or asylums, to experiments involving pain, distress, mutilation, disease or danger to life, for no object connected with their individual benefit, but for scientific purposes." (Taber, 1903, p. 3)[2]

In their pamphlet, "Illustrations of Human Vivisection," they pull details of gruesome experiments conducted on vulnerable people from established medical journals, books, and hospital records. All of the sources they used came from the targeted scientists. In one section on experiments with poison, they pulled an article from the *American Journal of Medical Sciences* detail-ing experiments where two poisonous substances, atropia and morphia, were given to American soldiers.

> The experiments which we shall now relate *(sic)* were most of them made upon soldiers who were suffering from painful neuralgic diseases, or from some cause entailing pain. In some cases, however, convalescent men were the subjects of our observations, but in no instance were they allowed to know what agents we used, or what effects were expected...Some were suffering from neuralgia, and some were men in very fair health. (Taber, 1903, p. 5)

The pamphlet also details early inoculation experiments where healthy children were deliberately exposed to other children suffering from scarlet fever or foot and mouth disease, or had substances infected with these dis-eases (they did not know of bacteria or viruses at this time) put into wounds in their skin. These experiments are described as the dangerous products of the curious scientist, but in retrospect we know that these experiments were the preliminary stages of vaccinations. The ethical dilemma is that the patients could not consent, but contrary to the portrayal of the mad scientist, these early experiments were a part of the path towards inoculations (Guerrini, 2003).

What comes out in the pamphlet, and in the movement for regulation of human subject research, is how the issue of informed consent was central to mobilization for human subject protection (Stark, 2012). The VRS highlights how scientists preyed upon vulnerable people, especially orphaned children, for experimentation. Whether or not these experiments resulting in helpful data for future medical advancements, the violation of that vulnerability is emphasized in this literature to induce anger towards and fear of the mad scientist. The issue of informed consent is where protection of humans and protection of animals diverges in the content of regulation. It is impossible for an animal to consent, but scientists were successful in convincing the public and politicians that research using live subjects was necessary for medical advancement. Animal advocates were bound to welfarist measures if they wanted to secure protective policy.

The VRS emphasized that reform to the unjust practices of human vivisection required four events: 1) investigation of human vivisection and exposure to the public, 2) that investigation of the "relation existing between human vivisection, and the vivisection of animals as now carried on in this country," 3) that leading medical associations in the US must oppose human vivisection and "stamp the human vivisector with ignominy and disrepute", and 4) that state and national legislation should ban all human vivisection (Taber, 1903). This strategy, and these four tactics, resonate strongly with the campaign against animal vivisection, as does their repeated disclosure that the practices they oppose do not provide medical benefit. This is one of the political opportunities that animal advocates seized upon: bridging their movement to human protection.

The campaign against abuse in human experimentation is enmeshed with the campaign against animal abuse in research, and therefore it is useful to juxtapose policy reform that has occurred for animals against that for human subjects. In doing so I establish some comparative leverage of types of institutionalization and the resulting regulatory oversight. It highlights which policy reforms have provided substantial changes in the ways researchers use their subjects, and which maintain scientific autonomy in animal research and allow researchers to carry on their experiments without meaningful intervention.

As I discussed, early responses from the scientific community to the antivivisection movement show that the defenses used by scientists in the early 20th century are identical to those used now (Conn & Parker, 2008; Ernst, 1902; Keen, 1912). What is more interesting is that in early literature published by scientists they make references to both human vivisection and animal vivisection, and defend the practices of scientific curiosity on both using similar rationale. It should be mentioned that the mechanisms of attack against antivivisectionists' are also familiar; they are "hysterical," that they want to thwart any scientific progress, are not intelligent enough to interpret scientific papers, and that they lie about the abuses they expose. The two primary mechanisms used to legitimize vivisection of animals is also present for vivisection using humans. Again, one is that the experiments provide valuable medical knowledge. The other mechanism is more interesting because it may indicate a small amount of change in regulatory oversight of animal research from the early 20th century to today.

This other defense is that laboratories already comply with regulations on animal and human protection. The internal structures of protection of animals are intertwined with those of humans. For animals, the terms of these regulations used in the early 1900s also mirror those in place currently. In a pamphlet published by the American Medical Association in 1912, a self- described "vivisector," Dr. William Keen, responds to hate mail he received from the pubic following an article he published in the *Ladies Home Journal* wherein he defended animal vivisection. He states five rules that were "in force in practically all American laboratories of research" (Keen, 1912, p. 12). These rules include 1) that stray dogs and cats acquired by the laboratory would be held for a certain period and returned to owners if claimed, 2) that animals would be housed comfortably, including proper food and sanitation, 3) that all operations on animals would be approved by the director of the laboratory, 4) that animals would be anesthetized appropriately, and 5) that animals would be killed painlessly, and that "exceptions to this rule will be made only when continuance of the animal's life is necessary to determine the result of the experiment" (Keen, 1912, p. 13). He does not explain the sources of these rules, or the institutions that are bound to follow them, but he does mention the Rockefeller Institute, which was a laboratory that adhered to NIH structures of regulatory oversight.

The NIH established internal structures for animal protection before they established any for human protection (Stark, 2012). This insight is important to contextualizing the content and effect of animal protection regulations. It is also important for showing how activists used any available political opportunity to pursue increased protection for animals. In pursuing these opportunities, activists had to mold their demands so they did not overtly violate the autonomy of scientists or impede scientific progress. The internal review committee was a model that allowed oversight of scientists while not overtly violating these two values. The NIH is a federal agency that funds external institutions, like universities, for research that will benefit medical advancement, and it also runs its own research facilities. These internal facilities are located in Bethesda, Maryland. In the mid-20th century when the NIH was considering how to establish regulatory oversight of research it funded, they used their own system of internal oversight of animal research as a model

(Stark, 2012). Several scientists and administrative professionals were elected to committees to review and revise new research designs, most of which involved animals.

This model of internal self-regulation was mandated for all institutions that received NIH funding. They were, and are, called Institutional Review Boards (IRBs). Many research institutions had these kinds of internal review boards. The prototype institutional boards inside the NIH and other institutions were not given the explicit purpose of animal protection, but when animal experiments came under scrutiny these boards were used to defend their procedures (Association, 2013; Conn & Parker, 2008; Ernst, 1902; Keen, 1912). This model embodies the primary institutional constraint that advocates for human subject and animal subject research had to negotiate when fighting for protection: scientific autonomy. As Stark (2012) discusses, administrators had to negotiate a balance between scientific autonomy and oversight.

Scientists argued that they needed autonomy and freedom to conduct research. Freedom allowed them the spontaneous creativity to construct experiments and to make changes to them spur of the moment when an unexpected finding appeared. Scientists contended that autonomy allowed them to quickly conduct experiments and find data that would allow for creating antidotes and cures for voracious diseases (Ernst, 1902). Epidemics like influenza and influenza ravaged populations of people. The public's fear allowed scientists a great amount of power because they were the gatekeepers of knowledge and possible cures. But when atrocities committed against vulnerable groups were exposed this caused an equal amount of fear in the public, the fear of the "mad scientist" (Guerrini, 2003). Similar to the animal advocacy story, the plight for oversight of human subject research was galvanized following exposure of atrocities committed against people in the name of scientific advancement.

The story of human subject protection is important for two reasons. First, animal advocates maneuvered the framing of their campaign to align with human protection. Framing is a technique for creating meaning out of a movement's grievances and demands (Snow, 2009). Activists may adjust how they present their issues to resonate with the public more strongly, and induce public sympathy (Benford & Snow, 2000; Ferree, 2003). Throughout the 20th century the animal advocacy movement adjusted their frames in various campaigns in any attempt to make animal protection an important issue to the public. This is a common strategy for activists (Evans, 2010).

Extending the vivisection frame to humans exemplifies animal activists' seizure of any available political opportunity to put animal protection on the public agenda. As this historical narrative progresses we will also see how this opportunity also constrained activists during the federal legislative process. I will describe how the internal regulatory structures of the NIH were prototypes of the structures established by the 1985 Animal Welfare Act. These regulatory structures were established for human subject research in their strongest form following exposures of atrocities in the 1970s, like the Tuskegee project.

In the next section I will describe the types of institutional provisions that animal advocates received from the early 20th century to the present, and show how the establishment of bureaucracies to oversee animal research mirrors those for human protection, including the self-regulatory nature. What I will focus on are the mechanisms of access afforded to animal advocates for some issues (humane officers), but not others (laboratory use). The mechanism of access that is different is the jurisdiction afforded to humane officers, who are able to levy fines, press charges, and confiscate personal property (animals are legally objects) when laws are broken. Animal advocates started fighting for this kind of jurisdiction within animal laboratories in the first legislative efforts in the late 1800s but have yet to gain it.

EARLY 20TH CENTURY:
ANIMAL PROTECTION LAW AND TYPES OF ACCESS

There were members of moderate organizations who were anti-vivisectionists, but because of two major issues organizations like the ASPCA and the Humane Society of the United States (HSUS) did not take an abolitionist stance. Scientists, politicians, and much of the public believed (and still believe) that vivisection was integral to medical improvements. Medical successes like the discovery of germ theory and of antibiotics increased the public's esteem and trust in scientific exploration. The fear of disease and the collective memory of fatal epidemics and pandemics created a "boogey man" of anti-vivisection: without animal research all medical progress will stop (Beers, 2006). The controversy made some organizations afraid to take an anti-vivisectionist stance, even if their leaders were against animal research. This is one reason some moderate organizations were not publicly against vivisection. The other reason was simply because some leaders also believed that vivisection was a necessary evil.

So far the histories of the animal justice movement have largely overlooked one important component of the controversy over the effectiveness of policy gains. As discussed before, reformers in the late 1800s worked on the state level to implement anti-cruelty statutes, and were generally successful, but the enforcement thereof was ambiguous. This meant that anti-cruelty laws had no teeth, and were therefore only symbolic. This is the same argument against animal protection laws in research. The ASPCA, and other SPCAs, took to the streets to enforce these laws themselves. Those prototypical "humane officers" acted as the eyes for law enforcement, and reported violations to the official authorities.

In New York the state conferred authority to enforce these anti-cruelty statutes to the ASPCA, and with this power activists like Henry Bergh arrested offenders and brought them to court using this newfound jurisdiction. Although the courts initially reacted with skepticism, this jurisdictional anomaly diffused through the states over time. By providing a service to the city and state government, autonomous organizations like SPCAs and Humane Societies were legitimized as animal authorities, and eventually given the power to levy fines and press charges against offenders as police officers would. These movement actors had a form of jurisdiction over the public realm, and over time had jurisdiction over residences where abuse was reported.

Businesses regulated by the federal government had inspections and oversight by people within the relevant federal agency, not humane officers from autonomous organization. This access to federally unregulated animal use, but lack of access to federally regulated animal use, is a key juxtaposition that illuminates why the movement has made great gains on behalf of companion animals, but not animals used in food, entertainment, or research.

The ASPCA continued to be a major player in the introduction of legislation relevant to animals in research. Its loose stance on vivisection was a strategic move to establish legitimacy and clout in the campaign to regulate vivisection, while at the same time retain their more moderate membership. In 1911 the Bayne bill was introduce in the New York legislative. Although in a 1908 *NYT* article a spokeswoman for the ASPCA stated that experimentation was necessary, in 1911 it was quoted in the *New York Times*, "The worthlessness and inhumanity of the majority of experiments to which animals are subjected is beginning to impress itself more and more on the public mind, and must ultimately result in the restrictive legislation which humanity demands" (*New York Times*, March 3rd, 1911, Proquest ID 106782084).

The Bayne Bill would have given the ASPCA and other licensed organizations the right to inspect laboratories; it was defeated fairly quickly. Scholars claim that the antivivisection movement demobilized between 1915 and the 1950s (Finsen & Finsen, 1994; Jasper & Nelkin, 1992; Turner, 1980). In her history of the animal justice movement in the U.S., Diane L. Beers isolates four reasons given for this demobilization: 1) ideological cleavages between moderates and radicals disrupted cohesion of the movement, 2) major leaders of the movement died, including Henry Bergh and Caroline Earl White, 3) medical advances gave power to science, allowing them to quash critics easily, and 4) World War I, World War II, and the Great Depression absorbed the energy of most movements in this time (Beers, 2006, p. 140). But Beers found ample evidence that the movement actually shifted to educational tactics during this time, and that the antivivisection movement blossomed during this time. Not only did membership in major organizations such as the AAVA grow, both abolitionist and welfarist organizations that focused on vivisection proliferated during this time.

I also found evidence of this in newspaper articles through this time period as well. During this time public opinion towards scientists and their treatment of animals shifted dramatically. This could be related to movement activity, or the general shift in public opinion towards science following the atrocities like those committed by scientists in Nazi Germany, but those shifts are political opportunities that would become important to the movement's future efforts.[3] In the early 20th century activists set the public and political stage for gaining welfare reform that would institutionalize protection of animals used in research.

THE ANIMAL WELFARE ACT

Four decades after the failure of the Bayne bill in 1911, the next legislative effort related to animal experimented that garnered mass media attention was the Metcalf-Hatch Act in 1952. Preceding the Metcalf-Hatch Act, laboratories reported having issues acquiring animals for research, resulting in publicly scorned behavior like pet theft. The Metcalf-Hatch Act gave the state the right to seize animals from shelters for experimental purposes. It was introduced and passed without any resistance from the ASPCA, and the organization suffered intense public scrutiny for not doing so. According to one *New York Times* article, the ASPCA said it did not resist the bill because of ongoing lobbying and coalition building to gain inspection access to laboratories.

In the long explanation of why it did not oppose passage of the law, the board of managers of the society held it could do more to help and protect animals under the provisions of this law, when experimental laboratories are opened to our unannounced inspection, than we could do before its passage when experiments on animals were carried on behind doors closed to us (*New York Times*, June 21, 1952 "Law Test Dropped by Animal Society").

The Bayne Bill was introduced 1911, and more than four decades later, the movement was still fighting for access to laboratories. They were willing to acquiesce to seizure of shelter animals to gain access to the autonomous and protected realm of science.

The ASPCA was only one organization involved in the ongoing effort to gain access to laboratories. In 1966 the movement finally gained a degree of access after a high profile case of a stolen dog. Both activists and scientists tell the same story about the formation and passage of the initial 1966 Animal Welfare Act (Carbone, 2004). Animal advocacy organizations, like the Humane Society of the United States, ASPCA, and the American Anti-Vivisection Society lobbied for protective oversight both statewide and federally throughout the 50s and early 60s before a compromised bill finally passed in 1966 (Becker, 2009). By the early 1960s animal advocacy organizations primarily publicized the problems and abuses associated with pets stolen for scientific research. The issue was galvanized following the "dognapping" of a Dalmatian named "Pepper" and an undercover investigation of dealers who stole pets and sold them to laboratories.

Following a story published in *Sports Illustrated* in 1965 about Pepper's theft and death inside of a laboratory, there was a prolific public outcry. Pictures from inside dilapidated dealer facilities were disseminated to the public in another expose in *Life* magazine in 1966, with the title "Concentration Camps for Dogs." The magazines reported receiving more letters about this issue than they did about the civil rights and the war in Vietnam (Carbone, 2004; Kreger, 1996). The story attached to the 1966 passage of the Laboratory Animal Welfare Act is that the public exposure of a "dognapping," caused Congress to finally pass the Animal Welfare Act. This is, of course, only part of the work that went into the first federal law to regulate animal use in research.

"Pepper's" story is reflected in the content of the Animal Welfare Act. The bill that passed looked different from the one initially proposed by advocacy organizations, mainly in that it lacked any access to laboratories or regulation over care of animals or the act of vivisection. Following the exposes on stolen pets, the Act only regulated the acquisition of dogs and cats used for research by establishing a licensing program for both dealers and laboratories. Again we see how the institution of science was closed off to any violation of autonomy or to any impediments to research. And we see how the reformist activists adapted to these closures by molding their demands to successfully seize upon a powerful public outcry.

There were several reforms between 1966 and 1985 that increased standards for animal care, but did not regulate the use of animals during research. The 1985 Improved Standards for Laboratory Animals amendment (ISLA) is, by far, the most far-reaching amendment. It was the first to establish a bureaucracy of oversight of the process of animal research. Previous regulatory oversight did not intrude on actual vivisection, but rather regulated housing, acquisition, and animal care. This shift from regulating "animal care" to regulating "animal use" is pivotal in the trajectory of oversight, and highlights the importance of types of institutionalization and access given to advocates (Carbone, 2004).[4] The catalyst for the 1985 amendment were two undercover exposes attained by the radical flank of the movement, reflecting how an inter-organizational division of labor persisted and factored into welfare reform. The radical flank factored into this reform even when they did not want to.

The ASPCA and other organizations started fighting for legislative access to laboratories in the early 1900s. They finally succeeded with the 1985 ISLA, eight decades later. This access was highly bureaucratized and only allowed access to approved government officials, not independent advocates. Again, this legislative change was accompanied by two highly publicized exposes, one of extreme abuse of primates at Silver Spring laboratory by Dr. Edward Taub, and one of equally abusive conditions of baboons at a separate laboratory at the University of Pennsylvania.

The Silver Spring case was the first major expose by the group, People for the Ethical Treatment of Animals (PETA). Alex Pacheco, the co-founder of the group, started working undercover in Edward Taub's laboratory in 1981. Following major abuses he documented of primates in the facility, involving amputation experiments of rhesus and macaque monkeys, Pacheco alerted authorities and the monkeys were seized. This would eventually be the first animal cruelty case heard by the United States Supreme Court, and actions by the Animal Liberation Front (ALF) increased simultaneously. The ALF is a clandestine organization of loosely networked cells that use militant direct action to expose abuses, rescue animals, attain records, and economically sabotage their targets. In 1980 there was one documented ALF action targeting animal research, in 1984 there were twelve. Both animal advocates and freedom of research advocates state that this amendment was driven by movement activity related to undercover exposes and graphic images that were disseminated to the public (Association, 2013; Conn & Parker, 2008).

During these abolitionist actions reformist organizations were pursuing increased protection under the Animal Welfare Act. The Animal Welfare Institute was integral to this process. Christine Stevens worked closely with laboratory veterinarians, politicians, scientists, and activists in pursuing policy reform. Robert Dole was a personal friend, and during the public outcry following the two exposes and the court battles following, she worked with him and other Congress people on the 1985 amendment. The 1985 Improvement of Standards for Laboratory Animals (ISLA) established standards for the socialization of primates and exercise of dogs, and mandated all institutions receiving federal funds to establish committees that were responsible for reviewing all research protocols. Of course, what defines "socialization" and "unnecessary" are largely self-regulated.

These committees are called Institutional Animal Care and Use Committees (IACUCs), and they are modeled the same as Institutional Review Boards (IRBs) that oversee human subject research. Since the 1985 amendment the AWA has been amended another three times, but all of these have, again, only tweaked the scope of protection and rules for transport of animals in labs.[5] Both the researchers and activists describe ISLA as the most significant change to the AWA, although activists find major flaws in its enforcement. The major flaws relate to scientific autonomy, and how these committees embody self-regulation and a lack of access to the actual process of scientific experiments using animals. IACUCs, like IRBs, are comprised of fellow researchers, campus veterinarians, and one outside individual who is usually loosely affiliated with the research institution. None of the members are from animal advocate organizations, and inspections of the facilities are kept to only federal agency employees and IACUC members. This reflects how reformist activists sculpted their demands to not violate scientific autonomy, thereby adhering to institutional selectivity and constrained political opportunities.

THE 21ST CENTURY:
CHIMPANZEES AND ABOLITIONIST CHANGE

The AWA had few major changes between the implementation of ISLA and 2011, but two other major shifts occurred. With the invention of transgenic mice, much of the research that used dogs, cats, and other "higher" species shifted to using mice. This increased the use of mice dramatically, and decreased the use of other species.[6] In 2011 the National Institutes of Health (NIH) commissioned a study by the Institute of Medicine (IOM) to review the ethical basis of using chimpanzees in research. Part of the IOM's recommendations, which in turn became NIH policy in funding research, stated that existing chimp research could only proceed in cases where there was "acquiescence" to the procedures. Not only did the NIH place a moratorium on funding new research using chimps, it also retired most of the chimps under federal control, and are discussing them as sentient beings. The NIH regulations on chimpanzee use shows that this status change is institutionalized in an agency of the federal government.

I am conducting further research examining whether changes like the AWA and the moratorium on chimp research provide substantive protection or are simply symbolic. The National Institutes of Health is an important source of funding for researchers, so their decisions will influence the direction of animal research in substantial ways. Activists celebrated the NIH's retirement of federally owned chimpanzees, and their refusal to fund new research. There are many more chimps still used in research, not to mention the drastic increase in rat and mouse use, but activists celebrated the moratorium as a major incremental and abolitionist gain the in fight against animal experimentation. They celebrated it as a movement success, not a reformist success.

Even adamant abolitionists like Tom Regan and Gary Francione believe that "it is perfectly consistent with the philosophy of animal rights to take a gradual approach… as long as the steps that need to be taken are abolitionist in nature" (Guither, 1998, p. 194). What about the increase in the use of mice that may follow the abolition of chimp research? And what about the out-sourcing of chimp research to other countries that may increase following this moratorium? Without a closer examination of how these regulatory changes impact the intended target, researchers, one cannot make assertions either celebrating or condemning legislation governing animal research.

CONCLUSION

This historical narrative highlighted how the animal justice movement seized political opportunities to pursue their legislative demands on the city, state, and federal level. It also highlights how the movement had to sculpt their demands to fit the selectivity of the institutions with which they interacted. They did this by, first, bridging their movement with the movement to regu-late human subject research, and thereby created bureaucratic regulatory structures within institutions that were the same for humans and animals. Second, they sculpted their demands to fit the type of galvanization that pushed their legislation through. This is shown in how they fit the initial AWA to deal only with the issues made public, that being the acquisition of dogs used in research, and then creating committees to regulate animal use of dogs and primates following the exposes of Silver Springs and the University of Pennsylvania. The opportunities afforded to advocates allowed for only a certain amount of regulation, which has questionable effects.

The history of the movement also shows how organizations divided ideo-logical, strategic, and tactical labor to pursue their goals. As opposed to characterizing this as disrupting the cohesion of the movement, we should acknowledge that this kind of splintering is inevitable. We should examine this splintering analytically, instead of thinking in terms of "what if?" Histor-ical evidence shows that the movement persisted through difficult periods, like during major Wars and economic downturns, and that this persistence may be due to how some factions of the movement will fare these periods more successfully.

For instance, by providing a public service in the very early days of the movement, the ASPCA eventually gained a type of institutional access that is unique to animal advocacy, law enforcement by humane officers through levying fines, confiscating animals (legally private property), and pressing charges as police officers would. Another example of an ideological, strate-gic and tactical division of labor is the splintering of the movement into abolitionist and militant organizations, who engaged in uncompromising and publicly visible campaigns against vivisection. These representatives, who engaged in undercover exposes and militant direct actions, exerted an urgent type of pressure on researchers and legislative decision-makers that partly facilitated the passage of the Animal Welfare Act.

The struggle to elevate the status of animals requires using any and all means possible. As opposed to seeing internal conflict as toxic and demoralizing, we should take a step back and see how the movement has blossomed into an effective bicycle, with spokes connecting the diverse actors to the core that is animal advocacy.

REFERENCES

Association, A. M. (2013). House of Delegates Proceedings Archives. Retrieved from http://ama.nmtvault.com/jsp/browse.jsp?useDefault=true&sort_col=date&collection_filter=House+of+Delegates+Proceedings.

Becker, G. S. (2009). *The Animal Welfare Act: Background and selected legislation.* Washington, DC: Congressional Research Service.

Beers, D. L. (2006). *For the prevention of cruelty: The history and legacy of animal rights activism in the United States.* Athens, OH: Swallow Press/Ohio University Press.

Benford, R. D., & Snow, D. A. (2000). Framing processes and social movements: An overview and assessment. *Annual Review of Sociology, 26,* 611–639.

Carbone, L. (2004). *What animals want: Expertise and advocacy in laboratory animal welfare policy.* New York, NY: Oxford University Press.

Conn, P. M., & Parker, J. V. (2008). *The animal research war.* New York, NY: Palgrave MacMillan.

Ernst, H. C. (Ed.). (1902). *Animal experimentation: A series of statements indicating its value to biological and medical science.* Boston, MA: Little, Brown, and Company.

Evans, E. (2010). Constitutional inclusion of animal rights in Germany and Switzerland: How did animal protection become an issue of national importance? *Society & Animals, 18*(3), 231–250.

Ferree, M. M. (2003). Resonance and radicalism: Feminist framing in the abortion debates of the United States and Germany. *American Journal of Sociology, 109*(2), 304–344.

Finsen, L., & Finsen, S. (1994). *The animal rights movement in America: From compassion to respect.* New York, NY: Twayne Publishers.

Francione, G. (1996). *Rain without thunder: The ideology of the animal rights movement.* Philadelphia, PA: Temple University Press.

Gamson, W. A. (1990). *The strategy of social protest* (2nd ed.). Belmont, CA: Wadsworth Publishers.

Ganz, M. (2000). Resources and resourcefulness: Strategic capacity in the unionization of California agriculture, 1959–1966. *American Journal of Sociology, 105*(4), 1003–1062.

Guerrini, A. (2003). *Experimenting with animals: From galen to animal rights.* Baltimore, MD: Johns Hopkins University Press.

Guither, H. D. (1998). *Animal rights: History and scope of a radical social movement.* Carbondale and Edwardsville, IN: Southern Illinois University Press.

Jasper, J. M., & Nelkin, D. (1992). *The animal rights crusade: The growth of a moral protest.* New York, NY: Free Press.

Keen, W. W. (1912). The influence of antivivisection on character. In H. O. M. Collections (Ed.), *Duke University.* Chicago: American Medical Association. King, E. (1666). [Works].

Kitschelt, H. P. (1986). Political opportunity structures and political protest: Anti-nuclear movements in four democracies. *British Journal of Political Science, 16,* 57–85.

Kolb, F. (2007). *Protest and opportunities: The political outcomes of social movements.* Chicago, IL: University of Chicago Press.

Kreger, M. (1996). *Forward.* Paper presented at the Animal Welfare Act: Historical perspectives and future directions, symposium proceedings, Riverdale, MD:

Leffingwell, A. (1914). *An ethical problem or sidelights upon scientific experimentation on man and animals.* New York, NY: G. Bell and Sons, LTD.

Meyer, D. S. (1990). *A winter of discontent: The nuclear freeze and American politics*. New York, NY: Praeger.

Meyer, D. S. (2012). National human rights institutions, Opportunities, and activism. In R. Goodman, & T. Pegram (Eds.), *Human rights, state compliance, and social change*. New York, NY: Cambridge University Press.

Munro, L. (2002). The animal activism of Henry Spira (1927–1998). *Society & Animals, 10*(2), 173–191.

Rohlinger, D. A., & Quadagno, J. (2009). Framing faith: Explaining cooperative conflict in the U.S. conservative Christian political movement. *Social Movement Studies, 8*(4), 341–358.

Rollin, B. E. (2002). Ethics, animal welfare, and ACUCs. In J. P. Gluck, T. DiPaquale, & F. B. Orlans (Eds.), *Applied ethics in animal research: Philosophy, regulation, and laboratory applications*. West Lafayette, Indiana: Purdue University Press.

Snow, D. A. (2009). Framing processes, ideology, and discursive fields. In D. A. Snow, S. A. Soule, & H. Kriesi (Eds.), *The blackwell companion to social movements* (pp. 380–412). London, England: Blackwell Publishing.

Sorabji, R. (1993). *Animal minds & human morals*. Ithaca, New York: Cornell University Press.

Stark, L. (2012). *Behind closed doors: IRBs and the making of ethical research*. Chicago, IL: The University of Chicago Press.

Taber, S. R. (1903). Illustrations of human vivisection. In V. R. Society (Ed.), *History of medicine collection*. Duke University.

Turner, J. C. (1980). *Reckoning with the beast*. Baltimore, MD: The John Hopkins University Press.

Wisler, D., & Giugni, M. (1996). Social movements and institutional selectivity. *Sociological Perspectives, 39*(1), 85–10.

NOTES

1. Examples of these articles are available from the author upon request.

2. Given this statement of definition, I should mention that I use the same term interchangeably with "animal research." "Vivisection" means dissection of a living body, but because there is no comparable term for the deliberate endangerment of life of an animal or human subject, this term is used in this dissertation. In the following chapters I will discuss the deeper meanings of this word, and how scientists eventually rejected it as a term for the research they do with animals. But for clarification when I use this term it means the *deliberate endangerment of the subject's life, or infliction of pain or suffering, for experimental or research purposes*.

3. Figures of these trends in public opinion are available upon request to the author.

4. During this time the market burgeoned with books on animal ethics, such as Peter Singer's hugely successful book, *Animal Liberation*. For the purpose of this brief history I focus on organizational work on animal research and legislation.

5. The AWA was expanded to also cover other animal industries, like roadside zoos and dogfighting, but I am leaving this out of the project so I can focus on animal research.

6. All of these statements are relevant only to federal funded research. Contract animal testing laboratories are not obligated to abide by Guidelines established by the NIH, and are not obligated to report on the number of rodents, farm animals, or birds they use. They are also not obligated to establish IACUCs. Records from these private organizations are highly flawed all together. Tables and figures are also available by request to the author.

Chapter Three

Considering the Emotional Support Animal

The "Pharmaceuticalization" of Companion Animals

Andrea Laurent-Simpson

INTRODUCTION

In the midst of the decade's long social construction of the service animal, a new type of assistance animal has appeared. Because research has shown animals, especially dogs, to provide psychological benefits to their owners (Folse 1994; Krause-Parello 2008; Sanders, 2000), emotional support animals (ESA) have become the latest attempt to lay claim to the therapeutic benefits of canine companionship and assistance. While ESA's are companion animals that prescriptively provide support and comfort to their human partners; Tedechi et al. (2010), they differ significantly from service animals. According to the Americans with Disabilities Act, an ESA does not have to be a dog, but rather, can be any range of animals, including guinea pigs and pot-bellied pigs (Bourland 2009). Indeed, an ESA can simply be one's pet.

This chapter will examine two areas. First, the institution of medicine has become a social agent responsible for constructing everyday life as healthy or ill (Zola 1972). However, Conrad (2005) has argued that this trend has shifted over to a shared responsibility between doctors, pharmacies, managed care plans, and the individual consumer. In the process, the pharmaceutical companies have managed to construct illness as something that must be treated via pharmaceutical intervention (Abraham 2010). This process of "pharmaceuticalization" combined with Conrad's new conceptualization of medicalization means that patient consumers proactively look for drug interventions that will cure their self-labeled "illness." Patient consumers, wise to the health benefits of their furry friends, lobby their doctors for an ESA prescription, and then turn to their companion animals for therapeutic benefit in a manner reminiscent of pharmaceutical intervention. Second, the public perception of ESA guardians as either legitimately in need of this type of therapy or as opportunists seeking a venue with which to gain acceptance of their companion animals becomes a possible arena of contention. Here, ESA owners pit their diagnoses against public perception that may be suspicious of their motivations for having an ESA present in the first place.

SERVICE DOGS

The history of assistance animals in the United States is a relatively new development over the past 100 years. Animals used to assist humans first appeared in World War I as a way to locate wounded soldiers in the middle of combat (Tedeschi, Fine, & Helgeson, 2010). This skill would soon alert people like Dorothy Harrison Eustis, who founded The Seeing Eye Dog in 1929, to the fact that canines could be good companions for the blind, guiding them away from danger as assistance (Tedechi, et al., 2010). Service dogs especially began being used in subsequent decades as animals capable of assisting with a wide range of disabilities.

The 1970's saw the development of the service dog by Canine Companions for Independence. These dogs were specifically trained to support people with disabilities in activities with which they struggled on a daily basis. Socialization and training was in-depth and time consuming, with the average training program, puppy to client, taking in excess of 16 months (Tedechi, et al., 2010). Services could include anything from picking up dropped items to turning lights off and on to actually pulling owners out of their beds in an emergency. In 1977, Dogs for the Deaf began training service canines that would specifically assist those that could not hear with daily activity. This application of service dogs was so successful that the organization began training dogs to assist individuals with autism; Tedechi, et al. (2010), although this program has recently been placed on hold due to finding suitable rescue animals fit autism spectrum disorder individuals.

PSYCHIATRIC SERVICE DOGS

Recently, another branch of service dog specialty has emerged in the form of psychiatric applications. Founded on literature that finds canines to provide insulation from anxiety while reducing the number of psychotropic drugs necessary; Tedechi, et al. (2010), these particular canines are being trained to assist in the amelioration of anxiety, paranoia, and even compulsive behaviors. Psychiatric service dogs (PSD's) require a different type of training from that of a seeing eye dog or dog for the hearing impaired requires. Because these animals work to alleviate symptoms, their training tends to be focused more on advanced obedience training that enables them to assist in ameliorating panic attacks, remembering medication, searching rooms for intruders to ease PTSD symptoms, or waking up a partner experiencing major depression, for example (Froling, 2003). As with other service dogs, they are also trained to avoid barking behaviors, mitigate any aggressive tendencies, and avoid intrusive sniffing into the personal space of others (Froling, 2003).

Because service animals assist the disabled, the Americans with Disabilities Act of 1990 (ADA) defined service animals as *dogs* that are "individually *trained* (emphasis added) to do work or perform tasks for people with disabilities" (DOJ, 2011). From a federal standpoint, this particular legislation allowed people with disabilities to bring their service animals into public places that would otherwise not allow animal access. Indeed, the ADA is what allows physically or mentally disabled Americans to enter restaurants, grocery stores, and libraries with their service animal without repercussion from the proprietor. The ADA also provides the legislative structure that requires reasonable housing accommodations for the disabled, including the use of service dogs on rented property.

EMOTIONAL SUPPORT ANIMALS

In the midst of the decade's long social construction of the service animal, a new type of assistance animal has appeared. Because research has shown animals, especially dogs, to provide psychological benefits to their owners (Folse, 1994; Krause-Parello, 2008; Sanders, 2000), emotional support animals (ESA's) have become the latest attempt to lay claim to the therapeutic benefits of canine companionship and assistance. Unlike guide dogs and psychiatric service dogs, ESA's are companion animals *without formal service training* that provide support and comfort to their human partners (Tedechi, et al., 2010). For example, Folse, Minder, Aycock, and Santana (1994) experimentally demonstrated that loneliness, anxiety, and depression could be abated in college students with the introduction of animal-assisted therapy. Furthermore, in her study of older females, Krause-Parello (2008) found that there was a mediating effect between loneliness and general health, suggesting that the human-animal bond provided therapeutic psychological effects. Kidd and Kidd (1994) found that the homeless, a population riddled with both psychological and physical disability, perceived their animals as important sources of companionship, friendship, and love. Such characteristics of that human-animal bond provided support for the idea that pets can reduce the sense of loneliness (Kidd & Kidd, 1994).

While ESA's are companion animals that provide support and comfort to their human partners; Tedechi, et al. (2010), they differ significantly from the service animals described above. According to the ADA, an ESA does not have to be a dog, but rather, can be any range of animals including guinea pigs and pot-bellied pigs (Bourland, 2009). Indeed, an ESA can simply be one's pet. The most important distinction between ESA's and service animals such as guide dogs or psychiatric service dogs is that an ESA has received no formal training to complete their status. Furthermore, because the ADA requires service animals to have been individually trained to meet their specific client's needs, an ESA is not covered as a reasonable accommodation for disabled people (Bourland, 2009). However, nuances of Section 504 of the Rehabilitation Act of 1973 combined with that of the Fair Housing Act Amendments of 1988 (FHAA) suggest that ESA's should be allowed as a reasonable accommodation for those that have either a mental or physical disability.

Receiving the designation of ESA for one's animal does require a prescription from a qualified medical professional. However, beyond this particular distinction, it is relatively easy to obtain (or simply claim one's own pre-existing pet as) an ESA. Doing so enables a wide range of those suffering from mental ailments such as anxiety or depression to demand that landlords with "no pet" policies allow them residence (Bourland, 2009) under the auspice of the FHAA and Section 504 legislations and multiple case law precedence.

Additionally, ESA's have increasingly been allowed access into the main cabin of major airlines under the umbrella of the Air Carrier Access Act, which dictates that emotional support animals will be allowed on board provided that the human partner has a prescription from a medical professional. Very recent rulings by the U.S. Department of Housing and Urban Development have even constrained college residence halls and dormitories from disallowing ESA's providing the student has a medical prescription for the animal's presence (Grieve, 2014).

THESIS

In the vein of Conrad's (2005) "shifting engines of medicalization," I first explore the idea of ESA's as evidence of the trend to self-medicalize the human condition as a way to escape the social notion that the human life should constantly be happy (Dworkin, 1991). The Western idea that daily social life should be "healthy" and free of negative emotions leads to the medicalization of daily life (Zola, 1972). A subsequent search for treatment of those problems has arisen alongside the patient consumer as a powerful source of discourse regarding what kind of treatments may be prescribed. I discuss the importance of the proliferation of medical knowledge to the general public as a way in which those that are emotionally distraught self-diagnose and then seek treatment.

Then, building on Abraham's (2010) concept of pharmaceuticalization, I argue that classifying the companion animal as an ESA increasingly changes and "pharmaceuticalizes" it, transforming the social construction of the animal from that of pet to that of embodied psychiatric therapy. This is an important distinction, because when a patient chooses to label their animal with ESA designation, they are not just socially trading off the invisibility of emotional disability for that of visible treatment. They are also choosing to forfeit the unseen nature of their disability in exchange for tolerance of the visible consequences of their emotional disability, such as "underperformance" in a society whose value system demands success.

MEDICALIZATION AND THE ESA

The broad spectrum that defines the emotional support animal and the relatively easy means of obtaining one means that the population of emotional support animals has exploded in recent years within the United States. While there is no federal regulation or service registry that requires official counts of ESA's, some online ESA registry services do keep track of clients. In 2012 alone, the National Service Animal Registry registered approximately 7,000 ESA's, up four times what it had been in 2008 (Teitell, 2013). In contrast, official service dog statistics, also cataloged by registries not affiliated with the federal government, reveal a total U.S. service dog population of around 20,000 of which 10,000 have been designated guide dogs for the visually impaired (American Humane Society, n.d.). Numbers like this suggest that ESA's are rapidly climbing in presence and may have even surpassed the total U.S. service dog population already.

This begs the question: what is driving this increasing registration of ESA's? To date, virtually nothing has been published in the mass media involving ESA's. While there are just a very few news articles discussing ESA's, there are even fewer new media sources with which to tap. Indeed, new media seems to be limited to a handful of lawyers overtly advertising their services to ESA owners that have been refused housing and an occasional blog discussing one's own ESA. What does seem to be present on the Internet is any number of businesses purporting to diagnose illness for and/or register one's ESA.

The peer-reviewed literature examining ESA's is even starker. Other than a few legal journal entries examining the interpretation of federal law regarding ESA's, there is very little other research on ESA's in general, let alone how their proliferation might exhibit a type of "pharmaceuticalization" of the companion animal. A theoretical exploration of Zola's medicalization thesis provides a sociological lens with which to consider the ESA.

Zola's (1972) medicalization thesis claims that the institution of medicine has gained the power to determine both acceptable behaviors as well as acceptable interpretation of those behaviors. As such, Zola argued that medicine has become an agent of social control, defining everyday life experience within the constraints of "healthy" and "ill" labels. Of course, as Zola points out, the medicalization process ultimately destigmatizes human and social problems. This in turn, according to Parson's (1951) "sick role" theory, relinquishes the patient from "healthy" social expectations as they work to recover from their illness. Ultimately, the patient assumes responsibility for maintaining self-health and holds self-accountable for that very expectation. It would seem that it is this self-responsibility that eventually undergirds the possibility of the patient consumer to consider ESA's as prescribed therapy. Not only would a psychological diagnosis release those suffering from depression or anxiety from the expectations required of healthy people, the prescription of an ESA would make that diagnosis more visible to the public. This, in turn, would ease the experience of social judgment concerning the presence of the animal in areas traditionally reserved for humans.

However, the trend of advertising psychiatric diagnoses on websites promoting paid registration of ESA's suggests that the agent of diagnosis is now co-shared by both patient and practitioner, rather than only the practitioner, as Zola theorized. This practice is not surprising given that a "shift" in medicalization has apparently moved the authority involved in medicalization from that of the medical professional to a shared process involving both patient and doctor (Conrad, 2005). Conrad (2005) argues that this shift is a result of commercial interests emanating from the pharmaceutical industry, managed care, and increasing empowerment of the consumer patient. Indeed, one of the driving forces behind this shift has come from several decades of pharmaceutical advertising to prospective patients as a means of bolstering that industry's profit margin. Donohue (2006) argues that, arising from the patient rights movements of the 1970's, the direct-to-consumer advertising strategies of pharmaceutical companies provided a key component of the present trend of both self-help and self-treatment. Certainly, the earliest of the direct-to-consumer campaigns compelled patients to approach their physicians with possible ailments as well as solutions to the problem. And this is exactly what is happening when patient consumers search online for psychiatric help and ESA prescriptions.

The influence of the pharmaceutical industry on patient care in the United States cannot be understated as an impetus for self-diagnosis and demands for prescription intervention as a means for the patient to maintain the responsibility for self-health that Zola (1972) claimed was resultant of medicalization. Indeed, Abraham (2010) argues that the growth in pharmaceutical markets has resulted from social construction demanding that behavioral or bodily conditions be treated via pharmaceutical intervention. Using medicalization and pharmaceuticalization as theoretical foundations, I argue here that companion animals, while clearly not biopharmaceutical entities, are increasingly being recognized for their health benefits in a manner reminiscent of pharmaceutical intervention. As a result, many consumer patients, looking for a cure to their ills that fits into their daily, self-labeled "sick" identities, may turn to their companion animals for support. When it is realized that, unlike an ingested drug, the therapeutic benefits of pets cannot possibly transcend all public spatial boundaries, the patient turns to ESA designation in order to legally legitimize companion animal presence in a more consistent manner. This in turn allows the patient consumer a constant "dose" of companion animal therapy.

Indeed, the increasing number of ESA registrations may highlight a trend of the over medicalization of anxiety and sadness. Parker (2007) argues that the Diagnostic and Statistical Manual - III (DSM-III) approach to depression encompasses so many types of sadness that psychologists actually medicalized universal "sadness" in addition to actual pathological depressive disorders. Activity such as crying and feeling sorry for oneself have both become symptomatic of the minor depressive diagnosis of dysthymia, a "medical" condition requiring mental health treatment (Parker, 2007). Examining a more recent version of the DSM-IV, Aragones, Pinol, and Labad (2006) found in a cross-sectional study of Spanish primary care patients that primary care physicians over diagnosed depression at a rate of 26.5%. This suggests that, while there may be valid cases of pathological sadness or life debilitating anxiety, the diagnosis of such could be becoming far too prevalent to classify such emotional states as anything other than the human condition. In an effort to ease the patient's own perceived anxieties, the question remains as to whether or not flippant misdiagnoses and subsequent prescription of ESA's (discussed below) is contributing to the over medicalization of these disorders.

PHARMACEUTICALIZATION AND THE ESA

Discussing Zola's original medicalization thesis, Conrad (2005) noted that most research in this vein focused on one of three entities: the authority of the medical profession, social movement and interest group activities, or specific professional activities that broadcast the legitimacy of medicine over alternative methods. However, the bureaucratization of managed care as a means of controlling costs emerged alongside a decreasing trust in physician care on the part of the general public (Conrad, 2005). Ultimately (though a bit simplistically here), this led to the emergence of the patient as a consumer of sorts that had choices not only of which insurance policy to use, but also which doctor to "hire" for service.

Also important in Conrad's (2005) argument is the idea that the pharmaceutical industry has led the charge with disease definition as a way to bolster profits. As a result, both consumer initiated and market mediated forces serve to usurp physician power over health and put that power in the hands of both of these emerging entities. Both self-treatment and self-diagnosis as trends in the patient consumer have emerged out of the now decades old practice of direct-to-consumer advertising (DTCA) engaged in by the pharmaceutical industry (Donohue, 2006). DTC campaigns socialized patients that they were no longer simply responsible for maintaining the "healthy" label. Rather, patients could now bring up their ailments with physicians alongside their own treatment options (Donohue, 2006). To some degree effectively subjugating the physician to middleman, patient consumers have become quite vocal in the patient-doctor relationship as to what they "have" and how they want to be treated for it. Indeed, Zola's (1972) original thesis that the physician practiced social control via deciding what he wanted to treat has virtually disappeared in an era of the self-informed patient.

Abraham (2010) argues that the power of the pharmaceutical industry to usurp the medical profession has allowed it to "invent, develop, and sustain markets for whole classes of drugs." This coupled with the proliferation of drug company DTCA examined by Donohue (2006) and the rise of the informed (often by pharmaceutical companies) consumer encourages the average person to direct the medical gaze inward in the search for any issue that could be bettered by not only drugs, but medical therapy in general. Angell (2004) notes that it is this advertising that actually persuades people to believe that they may need treatment for certain ailments that may have actually been invented by the pharmaceutical industry. Ultimately, Abraham (2010) argues that this process of "pharmaceuticalization" is one in which any bodily or mental condition can be relegated to a need for drug intervention, by patient, doctor, or both.

While ESA's are not pharmaceutical in nature, they do serve a similar function to that of drugs in a culture that seeks to alleviate the bodily and mental states that pharmaceuticalization promises to assuage. Witz (2013) notes that the patient consumer search for ESA prescriptions has become so common, that some mental health professionals are advertising their diagnostic services online in an attempt to attract business that would result in the prescription of ESA's. Airlines are seeing increasing levels of ESA's traveling in the cabin, uncaged and free of charge with their owners (Witz, 2013). Concomitantly, landlords are increasingly seeing more and more renters present ESA certification in order to override "no pet" policies (Teitell, 2013).

Griffis (2013) notes on her blog that she travels with her Schnauzer-Yorkie mix because of debilitating depression and anxiety that led her to abandon her "permanent address" and travel the world. Luna, an ESA, helps her avoid the anxiety and depression with which she once struggled. As such, Griffis contends that her ESA is a trained therapy dog with ESA papers. That the dog is with her constantly as a sort of security blanket working to mitigate the stress and strain of unhappiness and anxiety is reminiscent of what Dworkin (2001) refer to as the medicalization of unhappiness.

In his critique of the DSM, Dworkin (2001) claimed that the DSM actually encourages physicians to diagnose emotions such as unhappiness in ways that would include minor sadness characteristic of non-pathological, everyday life. Highlighting the diagnoses, for example, of minor depression or Depressive Disorder - Not Otherwise Specified, Dworkin further critiques the profession for its "(they) almost do" practices. That is, mental health professionals seem increasingly willing to diagnose based on patients "almost" fitting the current DSM criteria. This, of course, opens up the door even more so for loosely applied, online diagnoses that may make it easier to obtain an ESA.

Work on the sociology of stress confirms the tendency of mental health professionals to use the DSM in a manner that encourages higher diagnoses of stress related disorders (Horowitz, 2007). Horowitz (2007) notes that non-disordered people can be distressed in the face of negative social outcomes such as job stress. He contends, however, that the habit of providing these patients with a pathological diagnosis does nothing but transform normality into pathology. Coupling the DSM flaw of ease of diagnosis with that of patient self-diagnosis makes it clear that those who wish to receive treatment for something have a good shot at achieving that goal simply by going to the physician.

As a result, the drive of those seeking to establish an ESA registration is symptomatic of what Barker (2008) notes to be the practice of patients seeking "physician compliance" in order to self-medicalize ailments. The ease with which Dworkin (2001) claims this can be accomplished on the mental health profession side implies not just medicalization of sadness, but an over medicalization of these moods by patient consumers demanding diagnoses that may not be appropriate. Indeed, self-diagnosis and demand for treatment has become so common that physicians are now being trained on how to partner with patient perception of diagnosis as a means to make a final diagnosis. Henghan et al. (2009) suggest that doctors presented with self-diagnosis follow steps that include the initiation of diagnosis by patient, followed by physician refinement of that diagnosis to ultimately lead to a final diagnosis. Goyder, McPherson, and Glasziou (2010) caution that this consistent approach is imperative as the trend of patients desiring a diagnosis for normal physiological processes increases.

But how does the medicalization of unhappiness (and thus the overmedi-calization of sadness), especially via self-diagnosis, point to a metaphorical "pharmaceuticalization" of companion animals? While "registration" of ESA's is not necessary and, in fact, likely a waste of money, diagnosis and prescription for the animal is absolutely necessary in order to obtain ESA privileges to housing and airline travel. The practice involving the registra-tion of ESA's is so widespread that there is a robust competition on-line for consumer patients seeking prescriptions for and registrations of ESA's. A Google search for ESA registration resulted in at least six different sites dedicated to registering an animal, such as ESA Registration of America and RegisterServiceDogs.com. Many ESA registration sites conveniently offered psychological evaluation and prescription to its clients or at least guidance on how to obtain a prescription, if needed.

Goyder et al. (2010) warn doctors that self-diagnosis is often wrong, underscoring the importance of continued medical vigilance in even the knowledge laden patient consumer. Yet, there are websites offering psycho-logical services and subsequent prescriptions for ESA's, all done via the convenience of online technology. Offering up prescriptions for ESA's is "pharmaceuticalization" of the companion animal in its most logical sense. Given the increasing frequency of such treatment, especially via online regis-tration services, the ESA now literally embodies the companion animal as a pharmaceutical-like strategy to alleviate social and behavioral symptoms of often over diagnosed problems.

LEGITIMATE NEED OR OPPORTUNISM?

The presence of ESA registration sites is duplicitous in nature. First, their success seems indicative of the empowered patient that is seeking informa-tion regarding, in this case, ESA treatment. The proliferation of registrations (Teitell, 2013) implies that patients are getting prescriptions, and thus treat-ment via ESA's, for ailments that are minor enough that they can be diag-nosed by a medical professional via Skype (Witz, 2013). If this is true, then evidence of the overmedicalization of general affective states likely derived from social conditions may be apparent in the rapidly increasing number of ESA registrations occurring.

Second, there is the chance that the rapidly increasing numbers of ESA's are a result of people that have realized they can game the ESA system in an effort to escape "no pet" landlord policies as well as fly their companion animals in coach or even first-class comfort of an airline. In fact, many people that find themselves in an ever-increasing presence of ESA's may be more prone to believe that this is what is occurring rather than a true increase of depressive and anxiety disorders in ESA populations (Teitell, 2013). As a result, a backlash among the general public against ESA's and their caretakers is gaining steam, regardless of how legitimate one's need may be for such therapy (Teitell, 2013).

CONCLUSION

It is obviously difficult to explore this phenomenon with any depth at all unless future research examines ESA's and their guardians. Indeed, there are multiple avenues of interest in this particular area. First and foremost, it seems apparent that ESA's are being pharmaceuticalized by their keepers in an attempt to either assuage the daily symptoms of living or to illegitimately ensure the rights and privileges to ESA's embodied in a true mental disorder diagnosis. Research must endeavor to fetter out which types of ESA caretakers are using the system and how this is affecting social perceptions of the pharmaceuticalization of companion animals. Following that lead, other research must consider the effect that both legitimate and opportunist usage of ESA's has on the overmedicalization of affective states that are normal to human life. If, as lay people are increasingly believing, it comes to light that ESA's are overwhelmingly being used by patient consumers that simply purchase a "diagnosis" and ESA treatment plan for convenience, then future directions may need to explore the repercussions of sacrificing one's "healthy" label in order to have the constant presence of their companion animals.

Ultimately, the transformation of the pet from that of companion animal to that of embodied psychiatric therapy deserves further exploration. In fact, ESA's may be evidence that the medicalization of everyday life has made an intuitive jump from over diagnosis of the human condition to that of an "every diagnosis." That is, if the everyday companion animal of post-industrial, American society can now be claimed to also embody legitimate psychological therapy (and not simply opportunistic ventures), then much less stands in the way of finding that the some Americans are transforming themselves into patient within the confines of their own homes–literally medicating with animal companionship.

REFERENCES

Abraham, J. (2010). The sociological concomitants of the pharmaceutical industry and medications. In C. Bird, P. Conrad, A. Fremont, & S. Timmermans (Eds.), *Handbook of medical sociology* (6th ed.). (290–308). Nashville, TN: Vanderbilt University Press.

American Humane Society. (n.d.). U.S. pet (dog and cat) population fact sheet.Retrieved from http://www.americanhumane.org/assets/pdfs/pets-fact-sheet.pdf.

Angell, M. (2004). Excess in the pharmaceutical industry. *Canadian Medical Association Journal, 171*(12), 1451–1453.

Aragones, E., Pinol, J., & Labad, L. (2006). The over diagnosis of depression in non-depressed patients in primary care. *Family Practice, 23*(3), 363–368.

Barker, K. (2008). Electronic support groups, patient consumers, and medicalization: The case of contested illness. *Journal of Health and Social Behavior, 49*(1), 20–36.

Barsky, A. & Borus, J. (1995). Somatization and medicalization in the era of managed care. *Journal of the American Medical Association, 274*(24), 1931–1934.

Bourland, K. (2009). Advocating change within the ADA: The struggle to recognize emotional-support animals as service animals. *University of Louisville Law Review*, 197.

Conrad, P. (2005). The shifting engines of medicalization. *Journal of Health and Social Behavior, 46*(1), 3–14.

Donohue, J. (2006). A history of drug advertising: The evolving roles of consumers and consumer protection. *The Milbank Quarterly, 84*(4), 659–699.

Dworkin, R. (2001). The medicalization of unhappiness. *Public Interest, 144*, 85–99.

Goyder, C., McPherson, A., & Glasziou, P. (2010). Diagnosis in general practice: Self-diagnosis. *British Medical Journal, 340*(7739), 204–206.

Grieve, K. (2014). Reasonable accommodations? The debate over service and emotional support animals on college campuses. Retrieved from https://www.naspa.org/rpi/posts/reasonable-accommodations-the-debate-over-service-and-emotional-support-ani.

Griffis, G. (2013). Gigi who? *The Ramble* blog. Retrieved from http://gigigriffis.com/to-sum-myself-up/.

Folse, E., Minder, C., Aycock, M., & Santana, R. (1994). Animal-assisted therapy and depression in adult college students. *Anthrozoos, 7*(3), 188–194.

Froling, J. (2003). Service dog tasks for psychiatric disabilities. Retrieved from http://www.iaadp.org/psd_tasks.html.

Heneghan, C., Glasziou, P., Thompson, M., Rose, P., Balla, J., Lasserson, D., Scott, C., & Perera, R. (2009). Diagnosis in general practice: Diagnostic strategies used in primary care. *British Medical Journal, 338*(7701), 1003–1006.

Horowitz, A. (2007). Transforming normality into pathology: The 'DSM' and the outcomes of stressful social arrangements. *Journal of Health and Social Behavior, 48*(3), 211–222.

Kidd, A. & Kidd, R. (1994). Benefits and liabilities of pets for the homeless. *Psychological Reports, 74*, 715–722.

Krause-Parello, C. (2008). The mediating effect of pet attachment support between loneliness and general health in older females living in the community. *Journal of Community Health Nursing, 25*, 1–14.

Parker, G. (2007). Is depression over diagnosed? Yes. *British Medical Journal, 335*(7615), 328.

Parsons, T. (1951). Illness and the role of the physician: A sociological perspective. *American Journal of Orthopsychiatry, 21*(3), 452–460.

Sanders, C. (2000). The impact of guide dogs on the identity of people with visual impairments. *Anthrozoos, 13*, 131–139.

Tedeschi, P., Fine, A., & Hegelson, J. (2010). Assistance animals: Their evolving role in psychiatric service applications. In A. Fine (Ed.), *Handbook on animal-assisted therapy: Theoretical foundations and guidelines for practice* (3rd ed.). (421–438). London, England: Academic Press.

Teitell, B. (2013, September 18). Service dogs barred, doubted, and deeply treasured. *The Boston Globe*, Retrieved from http://www.bostonglobe.com/lifestyle/2013/09/18/the-growing-number-dogs-assisting-people-with-invisible-conditions-causing-conflict-and-some-cases-confrontation/igPnUBYHa97K07ccBGJJVJ/story.html.

Vuckovic, N. (1999). Fast relief: Buying time with medications. *Medical Anthropology Quarterly, 13*(1), 51–68.

Witz, B. (2013, November 16). Emotional support, with fur, draws complaints on planes. *The New York Times*, p. A-1.

Zola, I. (1972). Medicine as an institution of social control. *The Sociological Review, 20*(4), 487–504.

Chapter Four

Human Supremacy, Post-Speciesist Ideology, and the Case for Anti-Colonialist Veganism

Corey Wrenn

INTRODUCTION

Nonhuman Animal[1] rights theory has long been divided in regard to the degree to which moral concern should be extended to other animals (Rollin, 2006). While many see little conflict with Nonhuman Animal use, others reject it completely in favor of liberationist, vegan, and anti-speciesist goals. Increasingly, many attempt to locate a moral middle ground and support the growth of "humane"[2] Nonhuman Animal agriculture systems or the maintenance of "symbiotic" relationships. This division over moral inclusion is a troubling one for those animals facing extreme violence and violation. For these communities, institutionalized oppression has long since reached crisis levels: more than 65 billion Nonhuman Animals were killed for human consumption in 2013 alone (Food and Agriculture Organization of the United States). This number does not include the millions of other animals killed by vivisection, homelessness, and "hunting," or the billions of animals also pulled from the oceans as food or "bycatch." Given the staggering level of violence committed against other animals, the belief that use and death are not present harms for other animals represents a problematic ideology that protects systemic discrimination against nonhuman communities.

This paper first argues that use and death do indeed constitute a harm, therefore, no amount of "humaneness" or institutional reform could make the consumption of a Nonhuman Animal ethically permissible. It is further argued that veganism best realizes the human moral obligation to Nonhuman Animals because it recognizes nonhuman personhood and right to life. Ending the exploitative use and killing of Nonhuman Animals is the most pressing concern for vegan ethicists, but a post-liberation society will entail further conflicts in regard to human use and Nonhuman Animal autonomy. This paper contributes to the dialogue of human-nonhuman relationships by extending the vegan ethic to include an ongoing commitment to repairing Nonhuman Animal communities devastated by human colonialism and imperialism. The project of human supremacy has subsumed Nonhuman Animals into systems of oppression that would continue to cause suffering and harm even in post-liberation vegan world. Therefore, a policy of noninterference is not recommended. Oppressive relationships with Nonhuman Animals (that is, continued human use) should cease, but a major component of dismantling oppression is the engagement of restorative work. Human aid workers and allies should take care not to reinstitute a pattern of colonialism by interfering with the independence of Nonhuman Animals and the particular cultures of their various species groups and ecosystems.

THE PROBLEM WITH CONSUMPTION

At least since the inception of welfare efforts in Western nations of the 19th century, some humans have been working to increase the political recognition of Nonhuman Animals as objects of moral concern. Following many years of advocacy and reform, the public may subsequently be under the impression that violence against other animals has either been eradicated or is in the process of elimination. Certainly, the state, industries, and elites that benefit from speciesism will have an interest in facilitating this societal attitude (Wrenn, 2013). As a consequence, the consumption of Nonhuman Animals may be justified or permitted under the influence of this post-speciesist ideology. Attitude research indicates that humans are opposed to violence against other animals, but most are unaware of the continued suffering involved with institutionalized use (Prunty & Apple, 2013). This false consciousness regarding the status of other animals is likely a result of industry's advertising power, as well as its tremendous influence over the state and media (Nibert, 2013). The welfare approaches favored by large, professionalized non-profits may also be warping public awareness (Wrenn, 2013). Post-speciesist ideology presents a major impediment to social justice efforts because it masks continued human supremacy. Just as many white-identified Americans can point to highly paid athletes of color and Barack Obama's presidency as evidence of "post-racism," so can humans point to the proliferation in "humane" products as evidence of "post-speciesism."

If it is recognized that there are no defensible grounds for excluding Nonhuman Animals from the moral community (Rollin, 2006), it would follow that humans ought to extend equal consideration to other animals

(Francione, 2000). According to Francione, the principle of equal consideration means taking the interests of other animals seriously. That is, instead of
offering birds slightly bigger cages as reformist approaches may attempt,
humans are obliged not to cage them at all. Humans cannot claim to *seriously*
care about the suffering of Nonhuman Animals, nor can humans insist that
other animals matter morally, if oppressive behaviors like eating hamburgers,
drinking cows' milk, and visiting "zoos" are considered permissible. Francione's (2000) notion of equal consideration recognizes that Nonhuman Animals, like humans, have a morally significant interest in avoiding suffering.
This position presupposes that being used as a resource inherently entails
unnecessary suffering. Therefore, extending moral concern to Nonhuman
Animals will necessitate that their flesh, excretions, and labor no longer be
consumed. It is argued that using Nonhuman Animals as resources, fatally or
not, constitutes harm to these individuals who have an interest in not experiencing exploitation or suffering.

The notion that *all* use is harmful to Nonhuman Animals is admittedly
contentious. Yet, even those uses which do not entail *direct* harm to other
animals (like the consumption of corpses that are the result of automobile
collisions or natural death) still perpetuate the notion that Nonhuman Animals are nonpersons, objects, and consumable resources. Just as most humans would not eat human "road kill" or recently deceased companion animals (because they continue to be viewed as *persons*, not objects), anti-
speciesist humans would not think to eat the bodies of deers[3] (or any other
species traditionally viewed as consumable) who have died accidentally or
by natural causes.

The preservation of Nonhuman Animal corpses for display "taxidermy" is
similarly objectifying. While not all "taxidermy" patrons are "hunters" and
many "taxidermists" work with the bodies of Nonhuman Animals who have
died naturally or by accident, the practice reduces Nonhuman Animals to
resources of human pleasure and amusement. Alternatively, the taxidermy of
human bodies is often met with disgust and is generally considered immoral.
Indeed, it is regularly the stuff of horror movies. Even displaying the preserved remains of very ancient humans creates moral unease, with some
scholars insisting that deceased humans have the "right" to remain undis-
turbed (Bahn, 1984). Persons with privilege (namely, Western white men of
means) have historically exploited the remains of vulnerable groups to their
advantage, but legal reforms that reflect moral developments have begun to
curb this practice (Highet, 2006). The understanding is not that dead persons
have actual rights that can be infringed, but rather that the deceased bodies
represent *persons* and a moral society should treat those persons with some
amount of reverence (unless the person gave consent to dissection, organ
donation, etc. prior to death). The intention of upholding the "rights" of dead
persons is also a matter of respecting the cultures and communities they are

connected to. Western science has been responsible for a considerable amount of post-mortem colonization, extracting countless Egyptian mummified corpses and other bodies from nonwhite, developing countries for research and display in Western laboratories, classrooms, and museums. Western imperialism allowed for this looting as well as the systematic objectification of vulnerable cultures, and human imperialism seems to have accomplished the same with vulnerable nonhuman species. The display of Nonhuman Animal bodies for the human gaze is relevant to animal ethics specifically because it reinforces human supremacy. Nibert (2002) notes that viewing countless dead and mounted Nonhuman Animal bodies in human institutions normalizes oppression and hierarchies of power. It is "[. . .] yet another powerful socialization device about the role of devalued others in society" (p. 216), and it "[. . .] objectifies and demonizes[4] other animals and promotes anthropocentrism [. . .]" (p. 217). The use of Nonhuman Animal bodies thus continues to represent and reinforce the systemic oppression of other animals. The consequences of this superficially nonviolent use works to protect the normalcy of explicitly violent use.

Another argument that is frequently raised in discussions over the morality of human-nonhuman relationships is the one made in favor of "pet-keeping." However, seemingly symbiotic relationships with other animals are also problematic. Many view the inherently paternalistic relationship between humans and companion animals as a mutually beneficial relationship (Scully, 2002; Winograd & Winograd, Forthcoming), but this belief obscures and naturalizes structural discrimination. Hall explains, "Domestication of animals into pets not only takes these animals out of their own world and puts them into our houses and businesses, but physically alters them so that they, like domesticated cattle, are forever exiled from their free-living state" (2010, p. 192). Companion animals are both legally and socially considered consumable items. Dogs, cats, horses, and others are purposefully bred into existence for human enjoyment. While some may seek to treat companion animals well, it remains that they are their property (Francione, 2000). This means that humans can create a considerable amount of suffering for their companions that is well within legal limits, including, but not limited to, tail docking, ear cropping, rape and forced pregnancy (otherwise known as "breeding"), genetic manipulation that leaves animals susceptible to painful physical and mental illnesses and premature death, "breaking" (forcing animals to accept a bridle, saddle, pack, and/or "rider"), surrendering animals to "shelters" (many of which utilize lethal means for managing the facility's intake), or simply giving them away, abandoning them, isolating them, exposing them to the elements, and separating them from their family members or friends. Companion animals are maintained in a state of constant dependence: they rely on their human "owners" to feed them, water them, shelter them, and provide them with adequate stimulation, protection from harm, and necessary medical care. Domestication ensures that most companion animals are no longer capable of surviving without human interference. The institution of domestication (or what Nibert (2013) calls "domesecration") is itself a form of systematic oppression. It puts Nonhumans within the full control of humans for the benefit of humans. Given the inescapable power dynamics that structure the society in which most animals inhabit, "mutually beneficial" relationships of this kind inevitably work in the service of human supremacy.

DEATH AS A HARM

In regard to the *direct* consumption of Nonhumans (that which necessitates their death), whether or not death is recognized as a harm to Nonhuman Animals is critical to moral decision-making. Rollin explains that life itself is evidence to the importance of continued interest in living: "If being alive is the basis for being a moral object and if all other interests and needs are predicated upon life, then the most basic, morally relevant aspect of a creature is its life. We may correlatively suggest that any animal, therefore, has a right to life" (2006, p. 110). Yet, this right to life is sometimes questioned based on a Nonhuman Animal's possession of cognitive abilities. The argument that death is not a harm for Nonhuman Animals is generally based on an animal's ability to be forward thinking with categorical desires. Cigman (1981) emphasizes that the awareness of death is particularly important: "To be a possible subject of misfortunes which are not merely unpleasant experiences, one must be able to desire and value certain things. [...] the radical and exclusive nature of the transition from life to death must be understood" (p. 150-151). Theoretically, then, a painless death would not be a harm to Nonhuman Animals if it could be scientifically demonstrated that these animals cannot conceptualize death. However, even for those Nonhuman Animals who may not be able to conceptualize their long-term future possibilities, they do indeed, regardless of awareness, possess long-term *possibilities*. In this sense, Cigman's notion of capacity could be understood as potential. Both Nonhuman Animals *and* human animals, for the most part, possess potential (Regan, 2004). Furthermore, the proposed inability to conceptualize long-term possibilities is not unique to Nonhuman Animals; it also applies to mentally disabled and very young humans. Francione (2000) adds that the theoretical reliance on an animal's capacity to forwardly think is speciesist. This is because necessitating such a requirement for moral inclusion reflects the epistemological limitations of humans. These barriers will prevent an accurate understanding of what death truly means to other animals. This human limitation should not be equated with a disinterest in continued life for other animals.

Even those theorists who seek to incorporate the diverse experiences of the animal kingdom can be limited by human supremacist values. While Regan recognizes death as a harm to Nonhuman Animals, he does not go so far as to equate a nonhuman life with that of a human (Regan, 2004; Rudavsky, 2009). Regan's notion of comparable harm argues that two harms are comparable when they detract equally from each individual's welfare, or from the welfare of two or more individuals. Harm experienced by Nonhuman Animals, he argues, is not comparable to that experienced by humans because of variations in awareness and potential. However, if it is recognized that there are no defensible grounds for excluding Nonhuman Animals from the moral concern that humans enjoy, it follows that the privilege afforded to human life would be contrary to the principle of equal consideration. Likewise, if death is a harm for Nonhuman Animals and death is also a harm for the human, equal consideration is necessitated; both humans and other animals would have an interest in avoiding death. The process of assigning degrees of harm based on subjective human assumptions which suppose that death is somehow more a harm to humans promotes a post-speciesist ideology. That is, this theoretical process utilizes the presumption that speciesist discrimination has been addressed in order to excuse continued speciesist discrimination. It is a moral negotiation which obscures an unequal relationship that protects human interests above all others. Because human privilege is engaged for the power to define worth, harm, and right to life for vulnerable Nonhuman Animals, this process protects human supremacist social relations.

As a result of human supremacist influences on Nonhuman Animal ethics and post-speciesist ideologies that perpetuate the notion that Nonhuman Animal use does not necessarily entail suffering, there is a widespread societal belief that humans can consume other animals without causing them harm. Singer theorizes that death (and presumably use in general) is not a moral wrong if it is accepted that the Nonhuman Animals who are impacted lack self-consciousness, lead a pleasant life, are not members of an endangered species, are killed painlessly, and do not cause duress to others by dying (1993, p. 133). This is an idealized scenario that does not currently exist, and, for a number of reasons, cannot practically be achieved without the realization of science fiction imaginaries. For the present time, it is not feasible to rear and slaughter a Nonhuman Animal for human purposes without undermining some aspect of their telos. For instance, agricultural practices ensure that family structures will be disrupted, causing significant duress to others. The millions of mother cows who bellow for days at the loss of their calves in the dairy industry exemplify this trauma. At the very least, the eventual death necessitated for consumption is a harm if it is accepted that, as Rollin argues, the state of being alive inherently entails a desire to stay alive, and, as Francione argues, humans are not able to fully comprehend the subjective experiences of other species and are subsequently unable to make accurate determinations about nonhuman awareness of the self or death.

The desire for pleasurable consumption and freedom from the uncomfortable feelings roused by cognitive dissonance ensures that this idealistic conception of a happy life and happy death is perpetuated at the societal level. Consumers and Nonhuman Animal rights advocates alike can become preoccupied with alleviating the many moral aversions identified by Singer's idealized scenario to the detriment of anti-speciesism efforts (Francione, 1996). Post-speciesist ideology occupies the human imagination and subsequently obscures the fundamental moral inconsistency of Nonhuman Animal use. It is likely that a narrow focus on Singer's unachievable vision may prevent any serious consideration of the oppressive reality faced by Nonhumans used as resources. Rachels (2008) warns that welfare reforms normalize the violence in human relationships with other animals, thus distracting from the systemic oppression imposed on them:

> It is true enough that, if you are opposed to cruelty, you should prefer that the meat-production business be made less brutal. But it is also true that, if you are opposed to cruelty, you have reason not to participate in social practices that are brutal as they stand. As it stands, meat producers and consumers cooperate to maintain the unnecessary system of pig farms, feedlots, and slaughterhouses. Anyone who finds the system objectionable has reason not to help keep it going. The point would be quickly conceded if the victims were people. (p. 263)

The position that Nonhuman Animals could theoretically be violated, used, killed, and consumed in a manner that protects the desires of oppressors without posing harm to the oppressed is a position that works in the service of human supremacy. As it is a decidedly more radical and transformative approach, the vegan position is subsequently overshadowed by the powerful and alluring claimsmaking of speciesist institutions and their nonprofit allies. Because veganism calls for the complete cessation of Nonhuman Animal consumption and thus requires a commitment to significant attitude and behavior changes (changes that are not required by the "humane" use perspective), it is more easily dismissed as utopian or impractical.

While Singer protects the possibility of using vulnerable bodies for the benefit of those in power so long as that use is done "humanely," he also argues that humans should ideally avoid consumption: "In any case, at the level of practical moral principles, it would be better to reject altogether the killing of animals for food, unless one must do so to survive. Killing animals for food makes us think of them as objects that we can use as we please" (1993, p. 134). Much of Singer's work explores the root issue of Nonhuman Animal objectification and subjugation, however, he continues to stand as a major proponent "humane" speciesism, legitimizing it as an ethical alternative to veganism (Singer & Mason, 2006). Francione counters that use is incongruent with a full recognition of Nonhuman Animal interests:

> [. . .] we could, of course, treat animals "better" but that, apart from the economic realities that militate against such improved treatment, to improve animal treatment would be no different from enacting a rule that it is better to beat slaves less often. We would still be treating animals as things because we would be denying the application of the principle of equal consideration to animal interests. (Francione, 2000, p. 149)

The rising popularity of "humane" Nonhuman Animal products does not indicate progress towards liberation; rather, *it indicates further entrenchment of oppression*. Indeed, this oppression becomes even more insidious and impermeable, as it is normalized as something that is "natural" and mutually beneficial to humans and nonhumans alike. As Adams (2003) notes, it is this notion of pleasurable consumption—that Nonhuman Animals (and other vulnerable groups like women) are happy to service their oppressors—that makes oppression a formidable force. When oppressed groups are understood to be complacent in their oppression and are also thought to benefit from the system of inequality, challenging the system becomes especially difficult. For example, pornography has become mainstream under the protection of post-feminist ideology. The result being that the human imagination has been shaped to accept exploitative and violent sexual relationships as desirable, while female victims are framed as "porn stars" with lucrative careers who "enjoy what they do." Likewise, the mainstreaming of violence against animals and post-speciesist ideology shapes the human imagination about willing Nonhuman Animal victims on idyllic farmlands with caring "farmers" and full bellies. Structures of oppression are normalized and romanticized when the victims of oppression are painted as beneficiaries. Modifying and reforming consumption practices generally works to reduce the moral awareness. A more appropriate fulfillment of humanity's moral obligation to other animals will entail the disruption of these ideologies and a restructuring of the systems they protect.

VEGANISM AS A SITE OF RESISTANCE

Veganism is an ethical alternative to the idealized human/nonhuman relationship of oppression which entails an abstinence from Nonhuman Animal products. Wherever possible, vegans do not consume any animal-derived product in any form; this includes food, clothing, toiletries, etc. ("Vegan Society," n.d.). Veganism is more than a diet or a lifestyle, however. It also exists as a political resistance to human supremacy (Torres, 2007). Veganism is differentiated from vegetarianism, as vegetarianism seeks only to exclude the flesh of other species from the human diet and is limited in its aim to eliminate non-food Nonhuman Animal products from consumption patterns (i.e. "leather" and mainstream toiletries which contain slaughterhouse renderings). Furthermore, dairy and egg industries enact comparable levels of structural violence on nonhuman species (Singer & Mason, 2006). In effect, vegetarianism as a political position fails to address the human supremacist projects of consumption and use. Vegans also reject "organic" and "humanely-raised" Nonhuman Animal products, as consuming these products necessitates the objectification, use, and harm of other animals.

Because veganism is a form of protest, it generally entails a challenge to the exploitation of Nonhuman Animals in any situation. This protest includes resistance to rodeos, circuses, experimentation, and sometimes domestication for companionship. This protest is often intersectional as well. Most vegan ethicists, advocates, and organizations recognize that there is a connection between the consumption of Nonhuman Animal products (including "humanely-raised" or "organic" products) and the detrimental impacts on the environment, human health, and human justice (speciesism is thought to be entangled with sexism, racism, classism, etc.) (Nibert, 2013). It should be clarified that several variations of vegan protest exist across cultures and movements. Veganism is sometimes promoted as a diet, while at other times it exists as a religious artifact. However, ethical veganism as a means of resisting oppression is perhaps the variation that is most relevant to extending justice to vulnerable groups,[5] both human and nonhuman. In particular, veganism prioritizes the interests of Nonhuman Animals as persons who are worthy of justice, equality, and liberty. According to this anti-oppression vegan ethic, implementing a moral obligation to other animals would necessitate a cessation in their consumption by humans. The consumption of Nonhumans, be it literally in the form of flesh or secretions or indirectly through fashion, experimentation, or amusement in the form of "pets," zoos, rodeos, etc., is neither necessary nor morally consistent with the principle of equal consideration. If it is understood that death and use is harm to Nonhuman Animals, veganism is necessary for accurately recognizing them as objects of moral concern. Practically all Nonhuman Animal use can be reduced to matters of pleasure or convenience, and neither of these privileges constitutes sufficient reason to deny Nonhuman Animals moral consideration (Francione, 2000). Even instances of Nonhuman Animal use that are justified as necessary (e.g. vivisection for scientific advancement[6] or killing and consumption in survival situations) are nevertheless in violation of equal consideration and reflect human supremacist interests. If a Nonhuman Animal is used because that species wields less social power and is thus vulnerable to exploitation, this is speciesism. In other words, while human oppression of other animals is often justified for a number of reasons ("humane" use, "symbiotic" use, "necessary" use, comparable lack of awareness, etc.), when humans engage their social power to subjugate other animals and specifically take advantage of their nonhuman status in the process, they engage speciesism and human supremacy.

It is worth considering that Nonhuman Animals also commit acts of violence, use, and consumption against other animals. However, these behaviors do not represent oppression in the sociological sense because they are not enacted as an act of *structural* discrimination. In other words, Nonhuman Animals do not have the political capability of building a social structure that benefits them and systematically disadvantages other species. They are primarily at the whim of human activities, evolution, and circumstance. Consider, for instance, that many communities of color engage violence or prejudice against one other, but no community of color wields the social power necessary to engage institutional oppression as whites can and do. Indeed, much intra-racial violence is a result of social inequality perpetuated by white supremacy. Black-on-Black killing in impoverished urban areas, for example, is not an exercise in Black oppression, but rather a reaction to environmental stressors and disruptions related to a white supremacist society that underserves and exploits Black communities. These include, but are not limited to, segregation, poverty, unemployment, absent social services, and police harassment. This is not a society built by Blacks to serve Black interests; therefore, Black-on-Black violence cannot be understood to be institutionalized. Rather, it is a consequence of white oppression.

Likewise, humanity exists as an oppressing class that enacts institutionalized violence on vulnerable Nonhuman Animal communities, meaning that the human exploitation of nonhuman communities is generally not a true matter of survival or necessity, but a matter of systemic privilege. Humans do not need to use Nonhuman Animals, but do so because human supremacy allows for the practice as a means to grow and protect their privilege. As a result, intra-species violence taking place within nonhuman communities is strategically subsumed within human supremacist ideologies: Nonhuman Animals kill each other, so it is excusable for humans to kill other animals as well. Just as intra-racial violence is frequently referenced as a means to obscure the role of white supremacy, intra-species violence is used to normalize or naturalize violence in the animal kingdom, thus absconding the project of human supremacy from moral investigation. Vegans will recognize this logic in the diversionary tropes that point to lions killing gazelles, predatory food chains, and the "circle of life." That is, instead of addressing the presence of structural discrimination which works in the favor of oppressing classes, the focus is displaced on non-structural violence enacted by individuals of the oppressed classes. Again, these acts are related to survival or as a reaction to environmental stress, but they are nonetheless highlighted to the effect of protecting systems of inequality. While it may be true that lions kill gazelles, humans are not obligate carnivores. Nor is the lion's survivalist predation comparable to the systemic destruction of billions of cows, chickens, pigs, sheep, and fish to produce unhealthy convenience foods.[7]

THE ROLE OF VEGANISM
AND HUMAN ALLIES POST-LIBERATION

It has thus far been argued that all human use of Nonhuman Animals is, to some extent, problematic in that it supports a system of human supremacy. For instance, consuming "road kill" and naturally expired Nonhuman Animal corpses may not constitute a harm to those individuals who are consumed, but it does constitute a harm to Nonhuman Animals as a group. Even if consumption were to take place completely free of individual suffering, the persistence of consumption as an acceptable practice to impose on vulnerable populations would speak to the maintenance of a speciesist system of oppression. I have introduced veganism as a political resistance to this speciesist oppression. Specifically, I have framed this protest as one that recognizes human violence against other animals as a structural phenomenon. It also rejects the possibility of reforming or humane-washing use, as it continues to serve human interests. "Humane" reforms function primarily to assuage human discomfort (an added value that is routinely capitalized on by industries and non-profits). However, this absolutist position certainly leaves room for many questions in regard to how a societal restructuring would ideally be achieved and what the end results might look like. If all use is problematic, what will be the future of human-nonhuman relationships?

Donaldson and Kymlicka (2011) argue that a major failing in Nonhuman Animal liberation efforts is that vegan activists insist that the human relationship to other animals should be one of non-interference. That is, there should be no relationship at all. It is unclear, however, if this mindset is actually indicative of prominent vegan discourse. For instance, Hall's theory of Nonhuman Animal rights prioritizes autonomy and freedom: "It's about simply letting them be," and "[. . .] letting them thrive on their own terms in untamed spaces" (2010, p. 14). Yet even Hall's strict "hands off" approach to human-nonhuman relations recognizes the importance of building a "hospitable world" (p. 257), a project that will necessitate some amount of prosocial interference. Most individuals go vegan because they have a deeply felt appreciation and concern for Nonhuman Animals (Cron & Pobocik, 2013; Haverstock & Forgays, 2012; Hussar & Harris, 2010), and it is not the case that many believe that Nonhuman Animals should be freed and then subsequently abandoned. The public support of many "wildlife" rehabilitation centers that offer assistance to non-"game" species like vultures, squirrels, and opossums lends some evidence to this attitude. The popularity of trap-neuter-release programs and the tendency for caring individuals to feed and supervise feral cat colonies also speaks to this disinterest in abandoning free-living Nonhuman Animals in need.

While it may be inaccurate that vegan abolitionist theory is one of separation without interference, it is true that a meaningful position will need to acknowledge Nonhuman Animals as communities within a human-dominated society and should seek to accommodate this vulnerability. Hall makes clear that the ideologies of domination must be disrupted before any form of meaningful Nonhuman Animal autonomy can be achieved: "Without a whole paradigm shift, animal rights means nothing" (2010, p. 2013). Donaldson and Kymlicka (2011) suggest that one way to accomplish this is to conceptualize Nonhuman Animals as *citizens*. Depending on their species and domestication status, they may be categorized as sovereign free-living persons, migrants who inhabit human spaces, or full citizen persons if they are domesticated. As citizens, Nonhuman Animals would be retained within humanity's political sphere of moral obligation. Indeed, a vegan ethic would be ineffective if it should advocate for the liberation of other animals only to ignore their subsequent fate. A similar failing is evidenced in the aftermath of African American emancipation. Without addressing the persistent consequences of generations of colonization and bondage, liberation without continued structural assistance seriously inhibits African American access to equal opportunities. True civil rights require more than physical freedom; continued assistance and political recognition will be necessary. Therefore, vegan ethics are concerned specifically with Nonhuman Animals as victims of human oppression. Liberated and autonomous animals are still victims of this oppression if they are denied the assistance they need to thrive. Active efforts to combat the negative impact of colonization, domestication, and systemic violence will also be necessary to assist future generations who will also experience lingering and cumulative disadvantages. As Hall suggests, humans should "let them be" and work to end speciesist oppression. However, full autonomy should not also entail erasing Nonhuman Animals from humanity's political sphere, as this could leave them vulnerable and short-changed.

As members of a moral community, humans should also be obligated to provide services to Nonhuman Animals who may require assistance even if the need is unrelated to a legacy of human supremacy. I have argued that use entails harm, and this includes interfering with free living animals to suit human needs or domesticating them. Suffering is a harm for Nonhuman Animals, as is their death, even when not directly imposed by human activity. Allowing Nonhuman Animals to suffer and die is still failing humanity's moral obligation to them. With human privilege comes responsibility. Therefore, humans remain obligated to act as allies for other animals where appropriate and with respect for Nonhuman Animal autonomy.

Mitigating situations of conflict will be particularly challenging in a post-liberation landscape. The ability to decide which instances of Nonhuman Animal suffering and death are most important (particularly within a carnivorous ecosystem) will ultimately reflect human privilege. How the influence of human supremacy might be overcome in human relationships with other animals will be difficult even within a vegan framework. I suggest that anti-racist discourse might be useful to this conundrum. Many vulnerable human populations suffering from centuries of colonization are struggling to overcome the legacy of domination and become self-sufficient in their efforts to better their situations. Western whites are largely responsible for the litany of social, economic, and political problems facing communities of color, thus, to some degree, it is Western whites who must work to dismantle their oppressive actions and assist people of color in their fight for justice and freedom. However, social justice workers must also be cognizant of the complicating presence of the "white savior" complex. That is, whites who seek to correct situations of injustice within communities of color *for* communities of color are imposing yet another form of colonization when they seek to impose their own solutions (Cole, 2012).

Perhaps, then, when considering how to manage those ethical conflicts with Nonhuman Animals which are human created, social justice workers might also be careful not to impose a colonialist approach in dictating how these ethical conflicts are resolved. Hall sees humanity's need to control and dominate as a major encumbrance to ending speciesism, but she also sees these traits as problematic for advocacy efforts. Humans should not replicate domination in their efforts to help. First and foremost, humans have a responsibility to stop oppressing. For example, humans should stop "fishing" and curtail pollution because it is harmful to free-living animals in the oceans. However, humans should be wary about dictating how those ocean dwellers manage suffering and death within their own communities. Continuing with the ocean example, humans should be hesitant to prevent dolphins from killing and eating jellyfishes. Jellyfishes have millions of years of evolutionary progress that have equipped them to deal with violence committed by dolphins. It is not within human jurisdiction to manage how jellyfish cope (or how dolphins survive). In these cases, we should not impose our "human savior" complex on them, as this would represent another act of human colonization in Nonhuman Animal communities. This is not to say humans should always err on the side of letting "nature take its course." In situations where human privilege can be enacted to assist Nonhuman Animals in a way that respects their autonomy (and does not interfere with the autonomy of others in the society or ecosystem), humans should be obliged to help.

In situations of conflict that result from human oppression, humans have an obligation to intervene as well. Areas where Nonhuman Animals have become "invasive" as a consequence of human behavior and are causing difficulties for other Nonhuman Animals, for instance, would likely require intervention. Humans should seek to protect both the vulnerable communities *and* the domesticated or "invasive" species in a manner that respects the interests of both parties as much as is reasonably possible. For example, "feral" cat colonies that are committing acts of violence on birds, mice, and chipmunks as a matter of survival are a human responsibility because this situation is one of moral conflict that is human created. In this case, humans would have an obligation to protect free-living animals hurt by human-created domesticated cats and feline homelessness. Feral cats might be targeted for trap-neuter-release programs, provided alternate food sources, or relocated to sanctuaries. In another example, largely herbivorous black bears may be driven to commit more frequent acts of violence against other free-living animals as their homes are destroyed by human institutions and their normal plant-based food sources are diminished. In this case, humans would be obligated to intervene to protect those animals hurt by this human-produced situation. Providing bears with alternate food sources and improving their habitable spaces might be appropriate human interventions. Even in a post-liberation world, the impacts of human supremacy will continue to disadvantage nonhuman communities. Therefore, humans will remain obligated to repair the autonomy of other animals by dismantling human supremacist structural conditions. Part of this obligation will also necessitate humans becoming allies and active participants in the project of species-inclusive social justice.

CONCLUSION

The moral consideration of Nonhuman Animals often demonstrates an unfortunate inconsistency between theory and practice. It is an inconsistency that recognizes Nonhuman Animals as possessing moral worth, while stopping short of demanding a cessation of their use. If it is accepted that Nonhumans are worthy of humanity's moral concern and if it is accepted that use and death constitutes a violation of telos, it cannot also be acceptable to continue the consumption of Nonhuman Animals. This argument is particularly pertinent with the rising interest in the "humane" food products and alternative food systems. Regardless of the degree of "humaneness" attained, the death of the Nonhuman Animals for human benefit still constitutes harm. Indeed, the belief that Nonhuman Animals can be used at all is indicative of human supremacy. Likewise, the belief that Nonhuman Animals can be used in a way that also respects their interests represents the false consciousness of post-speciesist ideology. As an oppressed social group, Nonhuman Animals remain vulnerable to human privilege. All human-nonhuman relationships should be understood in this context.

As a political protest, veganism challenges human privilege by positioning Nonhuman Animals as objects of moral concern who are worthy of equal consideration. Veganism recognizes the personhood of other animals. Importantly, this ethical framework encompasses more than liberation. I have identified the position of non-interference as both misapplied and illogical. A vegan ethic should not abandon liberated Nonhuman Animals, as they would continue to suffer the ill effects of several millennia of violent speciesism. Therefore, ending use is presented only as the first step in the long and complicated process of repairing the damage inflicted by a legacy of human supremacy. These reparations should take care not to replicate colonialist practices and should also respect the independence and self-determination of nonhuman communities. In a post-liberation world, humans must accept that other animals are capable agents. I have suggested that human privilege should instead be put in the service of social justice. This will entail a cessation of use and a new role for humans as allies.

REFERENCES

Adams, C. (2003). *The pornography of meat.* New York, NY: The Continuum International Publishing Group, Inc.

Bahn, P. (1984). Do not disturb? Archaeology and the rights of the dead. *Journal of Applied Philosophy, 1*(2), 213–225.

Bekoff, M., & Pierce, J. (2009). *Wild justice: The moral lives of animals.* Chicago, IL: University of Chicago Press.

Cigman, R. (1981). Death, misfortune, and species inequality. *Philosophy & Public Affairs, 10*(1), 47–64.

Cole, T. (2012, March 21). The white-savior industrial complex. *The Atlantic.* Retrieved from http://www.theatlantic.com/international/archive/2012/03/the-white-savior-industrial-complex.

Cron, J., & Pobocik, R. (2013). Intentions to continue vegetarian dietary patterns: An Application of the theory of planned behavior. *Journal of the Academy of Nutrition and Dietetics, 113*(9), A90.

Donaldson, S., & Kymlicka, W. (2011). *Zoopolis: A political theory of animal rights.* New York, NY: Oxford University Press.

Food & Agriculture Organization of the United Nations. (2013). *FAOSTAT – Production, livestock primary.* Retrieved from http://faostat.fao.org/site/569/DesktopDefault.aspx?PageID=569#ancor.

Francione, G. L. (2008). *Animals as persons: Essays on the abolition of animal exploitation.* New York, NY: Columbia University Press.

Francione, G. L. (2000). *Introduction to animal rights: Your child or the dog?* Philadelphia, PA: Temple University Press.

Francione, G. L. (1996). *Rain without thunder: The ideology of the animal rights movement.* Philadelphia, PA: Temple University Press.

Hall, L. (2010). *On their own terms: Bringing animal-rights philosophy down to earth.* Darien: Nectar Bat Press.

Haverstock, K., & Forgays, D. (2012). To eat or not to eat. A comparison of current and former animal product limiters. *Appetite, 58*(3), 1030–1036.

Highet, M. (2006). Body snatching & grave robbing: Bodies for science. *History & Anthropology, 16*(4), 415–440.

Hussar, K., & Harris, P. (2010). Children who choose not to eat meat: A study of early moral decision-making. *Social Development, 19*(3), 627–641.
Knight, A. (2011). *The costs and benefits of animal experiments.* New York, NY: Palgrave Macmillian.
Nibert, D. (2013). *Animal oppression and human violence: Domesecration, capitalism, and global conflict.* New York, NY: Columbia University Press.
Phelps, N. (2007). *The longest struggle: Animal advocacy from Pythagoras to PETA.* New York, NY: Lantern Books.
Prunty, J., & Apple, K. (2013). Painfully aware: The effects of dissonance on attitudes toward factory farming. *Anthrozoös, 26*(2), 265–278.
Rachels, J. (2008). *The basic argument for vegetarianism.* Amherst: Prometheus Books.
Regan, T. (2004). *The case for animal rights* (3rd ed.). New York, NY: Routledge.
Rollin, B. (2006). *Animal rights & human morality.* Amherst, NY: Prometheus Books.
Rudavsky, S. (2009). Q&A Peter Singer Princeton philosophy professor and author of 'The life you can save.' *Indianapolis Star*, March 9.
Scully, M. (2002). *Dominion: The power of man, the suffering of animals, and the call to mercy.* London, England: Souvenir Press Limited.
Singer, P. (1993). *Practical ethics* (2nd ed.). Cambridge, MA: Cambridge University Press.
Singer, P. & Mason, J. (2006). *The way we eat: Why our food choices matter.* Rodale.
Torres, B. (2007). *Making a killing: The political economy of animal rights.* Oakland, CA: AK Press.
Vegan Society. (n.d.) *Vegan basics – FAQs: What is a vegan?* Retrieved from http://www.vegansociety.com/hubpage.aspx?id=495&terms=vegan+basics#8).
Winograd, N., & Winograd, J. (Forthcoming). *Welcome home: An animal rights perspective on living with companion dogs & cats.*
Wrenn, C. (2013). Nonhuman animal rights, alternative food systems, and the non-profit industrial complex. *Phaenex: Journal of Existential and Phenomenological Theory and Culture, 8*(2), 209–242.
Wyckoff, J. (2014). Toward justice for animals. *Journal of Social Philosophy, 45*(4), 539–553.

NOTES

1. "Nonhuman Animal(s)" is capitalized to denote their status as a distinct social group.
2. Euphemisms, misleading terms, and speciesist terms are placed in quotations to denote their problematic nature and contested meaning.
3. "Deers" has been pluralized to denote that they are individuals. The term "deer," "fish," and "sheep," speaks to individual animals in mass terms, which is objectifying.
4. Preserved Nonhuman Animal corpses are often positioned and portrayed as vicious and aggressive, and therefore deserving of their subjugation and death. Nibert explains that stories and narratives are constructed around the dead bodies of other animals in such a way that human supremacy is normalized.
5. Veganism has been an important component of Nonhuman Animal rights efforts since the early 1800s, but it first appeared as an explicit political position or "movement" in the 1940s with the founding of The Vegan Society in the United Kingdom (Phelps, 2007).
6. Vivisection stands as one of the most contentious forms of Nonhuman Animal use, generally protected under the guise of "necessity." However, research indicates that most animal-based research is seriously flawed and persists primarily as a profitable mechanism of the pharmaceutical-medical complex. In other words, sentient test subjects are used as a matter of convenience, not necessity (Knight, 2011).
7. Nonhuman Animals are also largely regarded as moral patients, and are generally thought incapable of moral decision-making (Wyckoff, 2014). Biologists have suggested that many nonhuman species do possess morality, however (Bekoff & Pierce, 2009). I chose to omit this argument because it detracts from the all-important lowered social position of all Nonhuman Animals within human society. It is this vulnerable and oppressed position that accounts for the vast majority of unjustifiable death and suffering among sentient communities.

Chapter Five

Anthropocentrism and the Issues Facing Nonhuman Animals

Andrew Woodhall

INTRODUCTION

Within 'animal ethics', and indeed in most contemporary debates concerning nonhuman animals, 'speciesism' has become the championing phrase of activists and ethicists alike. The term, however, is more than just a by-word used by nonhuman advocates to condemn their adversaries. Rather a charge of speciesism is intended to indicate that someone–or some position–is assuming a genuinely problematic ethical belief. The term is defined (and indeed was coined) via analogy with racism and sexism, i.e. as the unjustified bias towards, and preferencing of, a particular group to the detriment of another; in this case one species over others. The intention behind the use of speciesism is that if one rejects racism and sexism as unjustifiable prejudices, and speciesism is analogous to both, then one ought to reject speciesism also.

Much ink has been spilled considering whether speciesism *is* comparable to the other two prejudices and many compelling arguments have been made both for and against this claim-Peter Singer and Mary Midgley are two notable examples. The reason for this is clear. First, if speciesism is relevantly similar to racism and sexism, and these are morally unacceptable prejudices that ought to be avoided, then if we are to be consistent, we must also avoid speciesism. Second, many of the arguments made by nonhuman advocates aim to show that upon critical examination the justifications put forward in support of our current practices involving nonhuman animals, though purported to be unbiased and objective, really involve a speciesist assumption. Thus, if speciesism ought to be avoided then many of our current practices–such as factory farming and nonhuman experimentation–must be abolished or altered. The social, political, economic, and ethical ramifications of rejecting speciesism are therefore considerable, to the extent that many have used these consequences as objections to either the analogy itself or the conclusion that speciesism must be eliminated. Whether one is for or against either, the importance of the term within debates about nonhumans is indubitable.

Increasingly however theorists have begun to think that 'speciesism' as a term inadequately represents the intended prejudice. By definition 'speciesism' simply refers to the prejudicial bias in favour of a species or group of species, and thus the term does not specify *which* species is being favoured. In theory then any species (or individual of any species) can be speciesist. For example, an extra-terrestrial species that prejudicially favours its species over humans would be speciesist. However when the term is used in the debates over nonhuman animals the intended meaning is that *humans* are, without justification, being biased in favour of the *human* species. The term, as commonly used then, is therefore not intended as its unspecified, generic form.[1] While this narrowly used version of the word is *a type* or *form* of speciesism–i.e. that which favours humans over nonhumans–it can lead to a lack of clarity[2] when used in this way. As a result, many theorists have begun to use terms such as 'human-speciesism,' *Homo Sapiens*-speciesism,' 'anthropocentric speciesism,' or 'human chauvinism' as a more accurate terms to describe the prejudice being objected to (Jamieson, 2008; Milligan, as cited in Boddice, 2011; Horta, 2010; Hayward, 1997).

In brief, then, objecting to human-speciesism (or human chauvinism, as the more often used term) is a regularly employed strategy when approaching issues facing nonhuman animals. The aim of this strategy is to identify whether a position or practice within the debate relies on this belief or on a more justifiable basis. If human chauvinism is involved, by invoking our intuitions about the moral impermissibility of racism and sexism, nonhuman advocates can then call into question the moral permissibility of the position or practice under consideration. While this is by no means the only method used within the debates, this strategy has been–and is–an often used and important means of objecting to various practices and positions. For by claiming that this bias is, most often, the underlying assumption behind problematic uses and views involving nonhumans, and that without this prejudice such would have to be rejected or altered, the lives of nonhuman animals can be significantly improved. This simple claim that we must understand, identify as a prejudice, and subsequently eradicate human chauvinism, before being able to approach the issues fairly, is therefore a good tactical move to make, and has largely been convincing.

Despite this rather positive evaluation of using speciesism/human chauvinism within the debates, I would like to argue that, while this is a positive and useful philosophical strategy, the focus on human chauvinism is flawed.

I will argue instead that it is anthropocentrism that ought to be focused on rather than human chauvinism, and that this focus not only highlights more problems that nonhumans face, and the hidden depths of the current issues, but also better illustrates the underlying bias and assumption that gives rise to the issues facing nonhuman animals. These deeper problems and biases, I shall contend, are arguably why many nonhuman advocates question the success of the current approach. Thus, if correct, focusing on anthropocentrism may not only provide a new, more robust, means to argue in support of nonhuman animals, and new insights into how we must alter as a society to be fairer and less biased, but also may provide new momentum for the movement, and a greater–and more fair–place for nonhumans within society.

ANTHROPOCENTRISM AND ANDROCENTRISM

Before proceeding it would make matters clearer if I first offered an explanation of what I mean by 'anthropocentric,' for although the term quite literally means 'human-centred' there is surprisingly little consensus within the literature as to exactly what this involves. For instance, some theorists equate anthropocentrism with human chauvinism, whereas others claim that anthropocentrism is necessary and therefore benign; i.e. we are human, therefore we see things from a human perspective, and this is inescapable (Boddice, as cited in Boddice, 2011; p. 1). Others have distinguished 'epistemological' from 'ethical' anthropocentrism (Faria & Paez, 2014; p. 87), 'meta-ethical' from 'ethical' (DeLapp, as cited in Boddice, 2011; p. 37), 'normative' from 'ontological' (Hayward, 1997; p. 50), 'strong' from 'weak' (Fox as cited in Light & Rolston, 2008; p. 257). Finally, others have taken anthropocentrism to mean 'humans as central' (Horta, 2010; p. 258), or either taking 'the human', human norms or values, i.e. a human perspective, as the *modus operandi* when approaching nonhumans and nature (Smith, 2008, p. 4) or when approaching moral theory (Donaldson & Kymlicka, 2011; p. 33).

Simply put, there are three broad meanings for anthropocentrism that can cover all of the uses within the literature: (1) *benign* (i.e. we cannot help but see things from a human-centred position as we are human), (2) *perspective* (i.e. approaching the world from a human perspective via human norms, values, experiences, etc., and (3) *valuational* (i.e. that humans are more valuable/important/central). Within the literature few mean more than one of these definitions at once when considering whether anthropocentrism is problematic. What I shall propose is that anthropocentrism should be defined as *both* the perspective *and* valuational aspects, rather than as any one meaning. This I shall argue not only is a more clear and correct definition, but also illustrates previously unseen difficulties for nonhumans, as well as linking the term–as Ecofeminism suggests–with other relevantly similar centrism's.

What I shall mean by anthropocentrism then is as follows:

1. Interpreting or regarding the world in terms of human values, experiences, or thoughts, and
2. Considering humans as the most important, significant, superior, or central entity that exists.

While either of these alone is sufficient for something to be anthropocentric it is both that I shall refer to when I use the term 'anthropocentrism,' and I shall use A(1) to refer to the former, and A(2) to refer to the latter.

Before continuing some clarifications must be made. First, it ought to be noted that this definition fits with the both the dictionary definitions[3] and all of the important uses in the literature outlined above. The definition also fits with how anthropocentrism is used by major theorists, including Deep Ecology (Donaldson & Kymlicka, 2011; p. 33 and de Jonge, as cited in Boddice, 2011). Second, I do *not* include 'benign' anthropocentrism under this definition. A(1) should be understood to mean that when approaching any subject (e.g. nonhumans, moral theory, and so on) or attempting to construct an understanding of the world and values, a human perspective, human norms or values, and/or human interpretations are adopted, just as male perspectives, norms and values, and understanding are adopted, but are not necessary, in our current patriarchal world. Third, as either A(1) or A(2) are sufficient for anthropocentrism, most have considered this to mean that the two are distinct; I however shall argue that there is a relation between the two. Finally, the definition of anthropocentrism is clearly distinct from the meaning of speciesism/human chauvinism outlined earlier. Even so, A(2) noticeably reflects the core assumption of human chauvinism–i.e. that humans are to be favoured–and is often used as an alternative expression for this assumption within the literature (Boddice, as cited in Boddice, 2011). Both this distinctiveness and similarity will be important.

While the first clarification provides support for the intuitiveness of my definition, this appeal is strengthened by considering why I do not include 'benign' anthropocentrism. I do this for two reasons. First, as the uses of anthropocentrism within the literature indicate, the intended use of the term is rarely, if ever, of the 'benign' type. Practically all of the outlined uses, and the objections against anthropocentrism within nonhuman and environmental literature, all regard either A(1) or A(2). Therefore, while 'benign' anthropocentrism is, at most, anthropocentrism *in a sense*, it is not relevant to how the term is used or what is meant by the term within the literature. Second, it is not even clear that 'benign' anthropocentrism ought to be termed anthropocentrism at all. For instance, my definition fits well with other relevantly similar centrism's, such as egocentrism, ethnocentrism, and androcentrism. These terms however all refer to either the taking or privileging of certain groups' perspectives when addressing the world or superiority claims, but are never defined in a way that is necessary and inescapable. For instance, androcentrism is defined as:

> . . . Androcentrism occurs when theories take males, men's lives, or "masculinity" to set the norm for humans or animals generally, with female differences either ignored or represented as deviant; when phenomena are viewed from the perspective of men's lives, without regard to how women see them differently; and when male activities or predicaments are represented as the primary causes or sites of important changes, without regard to the roles of females in initiating or facilitating changes or the ways the situation of females has been crucial to determining structural constraints and potentials for change...[or] in describing or defining phenomena from the perspective of men or typically male lives, without paying attention to how they would be described differently if examined from the point of view of women's lives. (Anderson, 1995; pp. 57-58)

And:

> . . . The first lens embedded in cultural discourses, social institutions, and individual psyches is the lens of *androcentrism*, or male-centeredness. This is not just the historically crude perception that men are inherently superior to women but a more treacherous underpinning of that perception: a definition of males and male experience as a neutral standard or norm, and females and female experience as a sex-specific deviation from that norm. It is thus not that man is treated as superior and woman as inferior but that man is treated as human and woman as 'other' . . . (Bem, 1993; p. 2)

Simply put then, androcentrism is when one intentionally or unintentionally views something or everything in a way that assumes the male (or a male viewpoint) as default, superior, common sense, the evaluative norm (or as how things should be seen), or with an attitude of dismissiveness towards anything non-male. This definition clearly mirrors the two elements to the anthropocentrism definition (i.e. a perspective and a valuational element).

If we recall how 'benign' anthropocentrism is defined, as 'we cannot help but see things from a human perspective as we are human', an analogous 'benign' androcentrism would be that 'men cannot help but see things from a male perspective as they are male.'[4] However, nowhere in this definition is it claimed that every male is necessarily androcentric by virtue of their being male, and thus there is no 'benign androcentrism' included within the definition of androcentrism.

Similarly, there is no 'benign' ethnocentrism or egocentrism, nor is this what is intended when either term is used. While we are necessarily and inescapably 'stuck' in our own minds, for example, it does not follow (and no use within the literature intends) that we must necessarily and inescapably interpret and see the world in *our* own way, using our norms or values. The point of arguments against egocentrism is that we are interpreting the world from *only* our perspective, and valuing *only* ourselves and our norms, *but* we can learn to see the world in a different way. As we are more necessarily stuck in our own mind than in a human mind, if a 'benign' interpretation could be made of any centrism it would seem that egocentrism would be the most necessary candidate. Yet this type of inescapability does not intuitively warrant the use of egocentrism or even 'benign egocentrism.'

In each of these centrism's there is an identical sense that we are inescapably stuck in our own mind–whether individually, racially, or sexually. However 'benign ethnocentrism' and 'benign androcentrism'–in the sense that we are necessarily only able to see and interpret the world via our biological sex or 'race,' etc.,–does not seem to reflect any intuitive part of the definition of either of these terms, nor would we likely concede that either makes sense of what we mean when we use these terms. Nor do we accept that we are necessarily stuck in interpreting the world in either way. Similarly then even if we are necessarily human this does not warrant the label anthropocentrism, nor would such a use of the term seem intuitive. As it would seem odd, and arbitrary, to claim that anthropocentrism is not analogous with these other centrisms, there seems no reason to include 'benign' anthropocentrism within its definition either.

The analogy with androcentrism also clarifies what is meant by A(1). The parallel for this part of the definition in the above outline of androcentrism would be: the taking of 'the male' as central, taking male norms or values as 'the norm' by which everything is judged by, the taking of 'the male' as the perspective from which everything is viewed, 'the male' as that from which change is judged and everything is judged from, and as the 'neutral standard or norm.' Thus A(1) has a similar perspective-based meaning where 'the human' replaces 'the male.' This results in the 'use/giving of preferences to, or relying on, human perspectives, norms and values when looking at/defining/understanding the world, morality, and so on.' Just as with androcentrism, (and ethno- and egocentrism), A(1) is thus to be interpreted as the intentional or unintentional taking of a perspective as 'neutral,' 'central,' or 'the norm,' which is *not* inescapable or inevitable and *can* be changed. A(1) therefore includes world-views and systems of belief just as the androcentric equivalent does.

The analogy also shows how A(2) relates to human chauvinism. As noted above, A(2) clearly reflects the intended intuition behind the use of speciesism/human chauvinism outlined at the beginning of this chapter; i.e. that humans are superior to or more valuable than nonhumans. In the definition of androcentrism there is also a clear conception of men being superior to women that reflects the corresponding intuition of A(2). This conception in androcentrism is clearly intended to represent the valuational aspect of sexism or male chauvinism. If so, then as A(2) is the anthropocentric analogue of this conception, and further reflects the core intuition behind human chauvinism, it seems reasonable to claim that A(2) can account for what is being objected to when human chauvinism is posited. The only difference between human chauvinism and A(2) is that the former is *defined* as being unjustified. While this may seem to make the two concepts distinct this would rely on anthropocentrism (as I have defined it) being *possible* to justify, which is at least not apparently obvious. Moreover, the valuational aspects of androcentrism (and the other centrism's) is largely not thought of as justified, and thus it does not seem implausible to conclude that A(2) may, upon examination, also be unjustifiable. Finally, human chauvinism is only posited as the unjustifiable variation of valuing humans over nonhumans, and thus even if only some instances of A(2) were unjustifiable and others not this could still account for the intuition behind human chauvinism. As a result, it does not seem presumptuous to claim that A(2) reflects what is important about the intuition behind human chauvinism.

Defining anthropocentrism via analogy with androcentrism also illustrates how A(1) and A(2) relate to each other. Before explaining how, it should be noted that within the literature when anthropocentrism is used theorists often shift between what they mean by the term, sometimes meaning 'benign,' or A(1), or A(2), or both A(1) and A(2), often within the same discussion. Equivocations within this meaning have led to theorists claiming that anthropocentrism is neither problematic nor escapable (Faria & Paez, 2014), and has also led to the confusing of A(1) and A(2) with so-called 'benign' anthropocentrism. Few theorists have in fact considered whether A(1) and A(2) share any relation, and most generally conclude that they do not. The analogy with androcentrism, however, reveals this conclusion to be at least premature, and likely false.

That A(2) involves, or at least implies, A(1) ought to be fairly obvious, for it seems difficult to conceive, without being arbitrary, how one can make the judgement that humans are superior or more valuable without also either taking a human perspective or using human norms/values to make this judgement.[5] This is borne out by the literature. For instance, claims that posit moral value to be dependent on sentience, nervous systems that are like humans and in other similar nonhumans, etc.,[6] (Fox as cited in Light & Rolston, 2008) rely on defining what is morally-relevant by: (a) looking at what humans possess, deciding that this is what makes something morally considerable, and then extending this outwards to those beings that fit (i.e. those like us), and (b) ultimately comparing nonhumans to humans when deciding their moral value (i.e. if their nervous system is like ours, or if they are sentient in the way that we are sentient, etc.). These claims also often entail that humans, due to 'more sentience,' 'higher intelligence,' 'more capacities to suffer,' etc., are thus of more moral value.[7]

The same relation can also be shown regarding the perspective and valuational aspects of androcentrism. The definitions of androcentrism offered by the *Oxford Dictionary* and *Merriam-Webster* are, respectively: (a) "Focused or centred on men", and (b) "dominated by or emphasizing masculine interests or a masculine point of view." Male chauvinism is defined as: "Male prejudice against women; the belief that men are superior in terms of ability, intelligence, etc.," Simple reflection clearly shows that the definition of male chauvinism requires the definitions of androcentrism; a claim that many feminists often make.[8] In other words, male chauvinism involves or implies androcentrism. As a result it seems reasonable to conclude that there is a relation between A(2) and A(1), where the former involves or implies the latter.

The more controversial claim is that there is a relation that goes from A(1) to A(2); however, there are reasons to believe that this is so. While this relation may not be a necessary connection, the reasons below suggest that adopting A(1) means that one is more likely to, and usually does, adopt A(2); especially if A(1) is adopted unreflectively, such as through social or cultural influence. For instance, Rob Boddice points out that "the process of acquiring these [i.e. A(1)] world perspectives is to us invisible, and we therefore operate with and within them, unaware that we overlay cosmology with ideology at every step" (Boddice, as cited in Boddice, 2011; p. 7). In other words, by interpreting or regarding the world in terms of human values, etc., we then begin to apply this interpretation *to* the world. An identical explanation is given for how androcentrism begins to be applied to the world (Bem, 1993). In the explanation of androcentrism, this interpreting of the world, or seeing the world with males as the norm, by being applied to the world, then leads to anything that differs from that norm being considered 'other,' 'deviant' or 'inferior' (Bem, 1993). Thus with androcentrism, the 'perspective' aspect of the definition often leads to the 'valuational' aspect, or in other words, to a male chauvinism. While this connection is perhaps neither necessary nor inevitable, it is a common, and plausible, feminist argument that taking 'the male' as the norm, the centre, or adopting male norms/values is likely to lead to, or at least often leads to, a devaluing of 'the female'–both in terms of norms/values and thus also as an 'other' that is not male, and as being inferior to men that satisfy those norms/values. If this is acceptable for androcentrism, and it has been strongly argued in feminist literature, then as androcentrism is analogous with anthropocentrism it seems reasonable to extrapolate that the same connection occurs with anthropocentrism, and thus that A(1) leads to A(2).

That this is a plausible conclusion is supported by observations that Val Plumwood makes for how androcentrism leads to male chauvinism, ethnocentrism to racism, and A(1) to A(2) (Plumwood, 1996). Plumwood also argues that in Western views nature is sharply discontinuous or ontologically divided from human reason, and that this perspective on what is human and what is nature "leads to a view of humans as apart from or 'outside of' nature, usually as masters or external controllers of it" (Plumwood, 1991; p. 10). Deep Ecologists argue along a similar line that it is A(1) that has led humans to treat nature instrumentally.

Further, viewing the world from a single perspective alone or predominantly is often causally connected to one then holding views of superiority, as is evidenced by ethnocentric or nationalistic thinking, and the old adage that 'broadening one's horizons' leads to different values and beliefs. That this is so for A(1) and A(2) is evidenced in how anthropocentric views always lean in favour of humans. For example, many ethical theories—including those in nonhuman ethics - take what it is to be human, or characteristics or preferences that humans possess or value, to be the basis of the value of life. Both Singer and Regan do this (Singer, as cited in Armstrong & Botzler, 2008; p. 38; Singer, 1993; pp. 106-107; Fjellstrom, 2003; p. 95; Johnson, as cited in Miller & Williams, 1983; pp. 131-132; Warren, 2000; pp. 81-82; Regan, 2004; p. xxix; Francione, 1995; p. 83; Edwards, 1993; p. 232; Bailey, 2009; pp. 130-132), yet this is clearly a case of A(1) leading to A(2). Taking humans as central, it is not surprising, when basing judgements upon this world-view, that one concludes that anything outside of this centre is less to some degree. Even if not necessary, that this occurs and may be made more likely does not seem an implausible claim.

These relations, the similarity between my definition and the other centrisms (androcentrism, ethnocentrism, and egocentrism), the ability of my definition to cover all relevant uses of the term within the literature, are all reasons why I shall thus refer to *both* A(1) and A(2), rather than one alone, when using the term 'anthropocentrism.' When referring to either alone I shall refer to therefore refer to them as A(1) and A(2).

THE ANTHROPOCENTRIC TROJAN HORSE

This new clarified definition of anthropocentrism not only seems acceptable, but also brings to light several important consequences. First, the term does not involve any reference to so-called 'benign' anthropocentrism and thus positing an argument objecting to anthropocentrism does not involve any implausible claim about attempting to reject the inescapable, as many critics argue. Second, references to human chauvinism as anthropocentrism are clearly shown as not entirely accurate, as while anthropocentrism includes the intuition behind human chauvinism, the latter does not include all of the former. If anthropocentrism is problematic for nonhuman animals, then, it is clear that human chauvinism may not reveal all the issues that nonhumans face, and thus that the strategy outlined at the beginning of this paper is inadequate. That this is so can be demonstrated by considering the problems for nonhumans that this definition of anthropocentrism reveals.

For instance, anthropocentrism[9] is arguably incompatible with, or at least suspect for, nonhuman ethics, due to its aim to fairly and unbiasedly consider, and represent, nonhumans ethically. For example, Steven F. Sapontzis points out that most nonhuman ethic theories have purported to avoid or remove anthropocentrism and thus to make way for non-anthropocentric reasoning and morality from which ethical theories that are both practical and equal for nonhumans can be posited (Sapontzis, 1987). Liberating nonhuman animals, Sapontzis writes, "would eliminate anthropocentric prejudice from morality" (Sapontzis, 1987; p. 272). Given that few have defined anthropocentrism clearly, that fewer consider A(1) and often mistake it for 'benign' anthropocentrism, that even fewer have considered any link anthropocentrism may have with other centrism's, that most nonhuman ethic theories focus on human chauvinism (and often mistake this for anthropocentrism), and that even Singer and Regan's theories can be shown to involve anthropocentrism,[10] it is unclear whether nonhuman ethics has avoided or removed anthropocentrism (or even begun to do either) as Sapontzis believes.

Yet clearly Sapontzis thinks that nonhuman ethics aims at this end. Whether it has or not, the very idea of anthropocentrism is incompatible with the aim of nonhuman ethics (and all ethics, in fact) to propose an unbiased, non-prejudice based ethic that fairly considers issues concerning nonhumans. Anthropocentrism (due to A(1)) will undoubtedly bias any investigation into nonhuman issues, even if only slightly, either in favour of humans or to the disfavour of nonhumans, just as with other centrism's. For it seems at least peculiar to aim at impartial reflection in order to devise a fair resolution to each issue while simultaneously taking *only one* specific perspective. It is inevitable that this perspective will influence any deliberations made, and thus it seems troublesome–and perhaps question-begging–to attempt to answer questions about nonhumans from only a human-centred perspective, or a perspective dominated by human-centeredness, norms and values. The analogy with androcentrism, and feminist arguments regarding androcentrism, clearly make this a concern. That this bias occurs in nonhuman ethics can be seen by considering that Singer, the 'father' of animal liberation, considers a human life more worth living than any nonhuman life–according to a judgement made in a supposedly intersubjective, neutral state–based on what he thinks makes a life more valuable, notably human capacities, regardless of the possibility that to nonhumans *their* lives–*to them*–may be more worth living (Singer, as cited in Armstrong & Botzler, 2008; p. 38; Singer, 1993; pp. 106-107; Fjellstrom, 2003; p. 95; Johnson, as cited in Miller & Williams, 1983; pp. 131-132; Warren, 2000; pp. 81-82). This biasing would not only be problematic for ethics, but is arguably worse for nonhuman ethics given its aim to *fairly* consider issues facing nonhumans *for the sake of the nonhumans themselves*, and to advocate for nonhumans in their stead in relation to human actions. This bias however can not be seen when considering human chauvinism, but is only visible when focusing on anthropocentrism. This is because the former only considers A(2) whereas anthropocentrism also includes A(1), and it is A(1) that reveals this bias.

A second problem anthropocentrism reveals is that removing human chauvinism may not solve all of the issues facing nonhuman animals. Some feminists have argued, for instance, that removing inequality–while a positive step–will not solve all of the problems that women face in a patriarchal society. Similar arguments have been given throughout history (and still are) in regard to ethnocentrism also. For example, opponents to both andro- and ethnocentrism have argued that enacting a policy of 'separate but equal' (even if it *were* equal) would still involve many incorrect beliefs that limit the group that is not part of the 'centre' and can easily lead to political, social, moral, and economic situations that hamper the 'Other' group. History is ripe with examples for members of each group. Similarly then, even if human chauvinism were somehow removed it would not follow that nonhuman animals would be free of problems due to the lingering anthropocentric bias of A(1).[11] Nonhumans could still be considered as living less valuable lives, their 'place' in the world or their nature can still be taken for granted–giving rise to how *we* think they should be treated based on these points–their preferences could still be seen as less than what any 'higher' being would prefer, or not given as much serious consideration for the well-being of their lives. This latter has often been put forward as a reason for why nonhumans can be kept in zoos and that freedom, or the capacity to engage in their natural activities, is not necessary for their 'good life' (DeGrazia, 1996).

Consideration of feminist arguments regarding androcentrism reveals an abundance of examples for how women can still face difficulties even if 'equal', and given the analogy with androcentrism it would not be difficult to find numerous other problems nonhumans could similarly face from anthropocentrism. For instance, discussions on andro-and ethnocentrism reveal that such biases include more problems for the 'Other' group(s) than simply sexism or racism. Challenging only the valuational aspects of these biases leaves unchallenged the underlying norms, views, perspectives, systems of belief, and assumptions about those 'Others.' All of these, as Marilyn Frye and others have convincingly shown, are important aspects that together form a network or 'cage' that traps and oppresses the 'Other' group. Whether individually or together, feminist arguments, for example, have shown how such norms and perspectives not only lead to problems for women (say, by how women are defined, what is natural for a woman, how women should be, what women should value, how women should be treated in relation to men, what women can and cannot do, and so on), but also lead to biases even amongst those who truly aim to be fair and reject sexism.

Similarly then, anthropocentrism (notably A(1)–via taking human perspectives, systems of belief, norms and values) may lead to at least some analogous biases that cannot be seen or revealed by simply considering human chauvinism or A(2). Similar networks or cages that form oppressions that are not challenged by focusing solely on speciesism. For example, humans and 'human-created' nonhumans (as 'domestic' nonhumans are often referred to as) may morally require protection, yet 'wild' nonhumans because of 'what they are' ought not. 'Domestic' nonhumans have a certain level of consideration for their interests and preferences requisite with what humans have deemed acceptable for them to have a 'good life', but may only express these within certain acceptable spaces and to certain degrees within human society based on what we humans consider 'their nature' requires. This of course plays a key role in 'welfare' laws. Finally, nonhuman animals have no political power, no legal recourse in-and-of-themselves, and depend entirely upon human kindness and consideration. This is despite many nonhumans–such as dogs, cats, and primates–being naturally social creatures, naturally engaging in social and moral systems, expressing preferences and dislikes, and actively initiating cooperative contact both historically and at present. Many other examples can be given–such as how nonhumans are represented as Other, defined against the human Centre, and, as in androcentrism, are 'ignored or represented as deviant' or 'nature' as opposed to human 'culture/nurture.' All of this requires looking beyond human chauvinism at the whole of anthropocentrism and the impact underlying norms and views can have on nonhuman lives.

Such anthropocentric norms and views can also be seen to be the cause of, or at least a justification for, many issues that nonhumans face, rather than human chauvinism. For instance, killing and eating nonhumans is often justified by arguing that 'that is what those animals are for', or that 'humans are the top of the food chain–it is natural,' and so on. Such reasons involve ideas of what nonhuman animals, and humans, are, what they are for, what their place is in the world, and what nature is. All of these depend not on A(2) (or at least not entirely), but on A(1)–i.e. on perspectives about the world and judgements of the world made from human ideas. Similarly, issues concerning how we should treat 'wild' and 'domestic' nonhuman animals differently, what laws should apply to which nonhuman animals and why, and whether we should intervene in nature, all involve not only human conceptions of what it is to be 'wild' or 'domestic' (both of which are usually defined in terms of its proximity to humans and human control), but also human ideas of how nature ought to be, and only take into consideration what humans think ought to be done. For instance, some theorists believe humans ought not to prevent predation and that we should leave nature and 'wild' nonhumans alone. This not only involves the idea that what is 'wild nature' is what is not human (hence A(1)), but also may in some instances only consider what humans think ought to be done rather than what the 'hunter' and 'prey' nonhumans may prefer. [12] Numerous other examples can be given [13] and thus by focusing on human chauvinism we miss other important causes for the issues facing nonhuman animals. As a result, anthropocentrism–not human chauvinism–is a much more important concept to consider when considering nonhuman animals.

A third point is that anthropocentrism may also lead to previously unnoticed problems. For instance, some moral theories begin by considering why humans are morally considerable and then argue that some nonhumans also fulfil the criteria, as some 'animal rights' positions such as Tom Regan's do. If so then it could be argued that (a) this involves including or excluding nonhumans based on their similarity with humans, and (b) such a theory (and this means of 'arguing from humans to nonhumans') will exclude some nonhumans from moral consideration based on criteria derived from humans. This of course biases the outcome of who is to be included from the outset. Both of these are clearly anthropocentric and for any nonhuman ethic these consequences ought to raise concern. This is emphasized by considering that both of these results would be (or at least ought to be) suspect if applied to sex or 'race.' For all one must do is substitute nonhumans for 'women' or a specific 'race,' and humans for 'men' or another race, and this reasoning would be clearly problematic and biased against those classes of humans. This method of reasoning, however, is only problematic when considering anthropocentrism and not human chauvinism.

Other previously unnoticed problems have already been noted above. Another example is that anthropocentrism can lead to a lack of appreciation and respect for that which nonhuman animals value themselves, yet humans do not. Such a disregard has gone so unnoticed that the recent claims of Will Kymlicka and Sue Donaldson's *Zoopolis*, i.e. the positing of a theory for nonhuman citizenship which argues that certain nonhuman animals ought to be citizens on at least a more equal footing as human citizens via arguing that society literally ought to be altered to accommodate nonhuman interests and preferences, have seemed radical. [14] This reveals that many nonhuman preferences are set aside in favour of a society more acceptable to humans. While A(2) no doubt is involved here, it seems indubitable that A(1) also plays a role. A more serious consideration of anthropocentrism within nonhuman ethics, then, may reveal many other previously unconsidered issues facing nonhuman animals.

A more troublesome problem is revealed by the relation of A(1) to A(2). As the examples above have shown, the assuming of a human perspective, and the basing of judgements (especially ethical) on humanity and human norms or values, often results in positions that favour humans and disfavour nonhumans. From what grants moral considerability to whose life is more valuable (and thus who should be protected more), anthropocentrism in the form of A(1) has undoubtedly been shown to influence nonhuman ethic theories and in several cases has led these to adopt A(2). This is clearly a problem for those wishing to reject human chauvinism. As A(1) leads to A(2), or even if it just makes it more likely–and the examples above clearly show this–then it is important for nonhuman ethics to seriously address not only A(2) but also A(1), and thus anthropocentrism as a whole.[15] As mentioned earlier, given the aim to aid nonhuman animals fairly even the possibility that this relation occurs ought to be enough for a position to take A(1) seriously.

Anthropocentrism also leads to the perpetuation of incorrect views of nonhumans and humans alike. As Anna L. Peterson has shown in *Being Animal* and Plumwood has extensively argued in *Feminism and the Mastery of Nature*, humans and nonhumans are defined in opposition to each other in ways that impact both and the environment. What it is to be human, and what human society is, is defined as 'domestic' or 'non-natural.' Humans are 'mind' or 'reason' rather than being 'body' or 'animal,' and so on. Such views have led to excluding nonhumans from reason entirely and even in contemporary debates similarities between humans and nonhumans are often downplayed or claimed as far more unlike than they often are. Differences are constantly sought to set humans aside, often to the detriment of those 'less rational, and more animal-like.' Human dependency on nature and the interdependency of life has only in the last few decades even begun to be taken seriously. Yet as Peterson points out, while the impact humans have had on domesticating nonhumans is rife throughout the literature, that humans were similarly domesticated by nonhumans is left out (Peterson, 2013). That our views about humans and nonhumans influence our theorizing regarding them is arguably beyond doubt, however even if it is just a possibility this in itself is enough to raise concern over basing theories on false views and perpetuating incorrect ideas. That anthropocentrism does this ought now to be clear.

Numerous other problems can be highlighted by defining anthropocentrism via analogy with other centrisms. For instance, as androcentrism fits the criteria of being a prejudice then so does anthropocentrism. Androcentrism is also related to the perpetuation of the patriarchy, and thus anthropocentrism is analogously related to the perpetuation of what nonhuman ethicists have begun to term the anthroparchy. There are even human-centred reasons to consider anthropocentrism problematic (de Jonge, as cited in Boddice, 2011; pp. 309-312) though I shall not address these here.

What should be apparent by now is that by clearly defining anthropocentrism, and considering it in relation to androcentrism, and other centrisms, we can not only better understand the meaning of the term but also show additional issues that face nonhumans. Furthermore, these issues can neither be seen, nor adequately addressed, by the strategy outlined at the beginning of this chapter–i.e. by focusing on speciesism/human chauvinism as the main problem facing nonhuman animals. This method of understanding anthropocentrism illustrates not only that the problematic intuition behind human chauvinism can be accounted for under A(2), but that A(1) is also a source of problems for nonhumans and for those attempting to aid them, and arguably a more severe one–especially for largely being unseen. Focusing on anthropocentrism then, rather than human chauvinism would provide a more complete and fair approach to the issues facing nonhuman animals. Just as with androcentrism, how we look at nonhuman Others, the perspectives we take and the assumptions we make, are just as important–perhaps more–than the valuational conclusions/assumptions we arrive at.

This conclusion may have one further implication. The current 'political turn' in nonhuman liberation and nonhuman studies began due to questions being asked by theorists as to why, despite the forcefulness of its arguments, nonhuman ethics has not resulted in a similar social change as other liberation movements. Despite some important changes to welfare laws, the cessation of some types of experiments on nonhumans, the increase of vegetarianism and veganism, amongst others, the amount of nonhumans killed, eaten, hunted, and experimented upon has actually increased (quite dramatically) over the past forty years. All of this despite challenges to speciesism/human chauvinism, and how difficult this prejudice is to justify.

Having defined anthropocentrism and seen how it is analogous to other entrenched centrism's like androcentrism, and seeing not only the problems that it causes for nonhumans but also how A(1) gives rise to most of these and how it leads to A(2), I would like to propose that this lack of progress in nonhuman issues may actually be the result of anthropocentrism and not addressing both A(1) and A(2), not a failure of nonhuman ethics itself. Feminist arguments have shown that real progress for women has not been made without challenging androcentrism, and that without challenging the underlying norms, values, and male perspectives as central that equality can never truly be attained for women. Anthropocentrism, then, especially in the form of A(1), may be the reason why nonhumans are more exploited than ever, as until a change of perspective is undertaken in how nonhumans are seen, human chauvinism will continue to resurface (as A(1) will still result in A(2)) and nonhumans will continue to be considered Other; the primary cause of the issues confronting them and their exploitation. Challenging the effect of A(1), i.e. A(2), will not remove its cause, and thus until anthropocentrism as a whole is tackled, no matter how much good occurs from removing some inequalities more problems will always arise. If so, then by focusing on anthropocentrism rather than speciesism/human chauvinism, the current lack of progress may also be remedied by challenging the world-view that lies behind the problems nonhumans face.

To summarize thus far then; (a) the focus on anthropocentrism offers new significant problems facing nonhumans and nonhuman ethics, (b) the focus on anthropocentrism can account for what is objectionable about human chauvinism, (c) human chauvinism is not synonymous with anthropocentrism, and (d) the strategy of addressing human chauvinism/speciesism leaves unconsidered the problems that A(1), i.e. interpreting or regarding the world in terms of human values, experiences, or thoughts, (and its relation to A(2), i.e. considering humans as the most important, significant, superior, or central entity that exists) generates. As a result, if we are to truly address the issues facing nonhuman animals, and make true progress for nonhumans, we must address the proverbial Trojan Horse of anthropocentrism that has sneaked passed our current watchfulness and threatens our defence of nonhuman animals.

RESOLUTIONS

My aim here has been to show that anthropocentrism needs to be taken seriously when considering the issues facing nonhuman animals. Although space prevents a fuller account, I would like to present some possible means for how this can be accomplished. It should be pointed out, however, that I am not claiming that all anthropocentrism can be removed, nor that it will be easy to do so. [16] While ideally this should be the aim, beginning by recognizing anthropocentrism and its importance to the issues, and then taking it seriously and attempting to reduce it as much as possible, would at least be a positive step forward and would likely aid many nonhumans, some of which may not even be currently considered.

To this end I would propose two ways in which anthropocentrism could be addressed via a modified version of the strategy outlined at the beginning of this chapter. First, we must be aware of how we conceive of what it is to be human and reconceive of this in a non-anthropocentric way. For instance, if as humans we considered ourselves actually, and really, as just another animal, with similarities and differences with numerous other beings, that shares the biotic community and is embedded in interdependent relationships that not only make us who we are but are also necessary for our existence, this shift from 'humans over nature' to 'humans as just another part of nature' would have a dramatic impact on the perspective we take towards nonhuman animals, the theories we posit, and our relations to other parts of nature. While A(2) would still be possible, genuinely changing our perspective in this (and similar) way(s) would have an significant impact on our valuational perspective. For instance, on such a view–while anthropocentrism could still exist–we could begin to consider humans as of no greater value than other animals [17] and just an equal member of nature.

While this may seem like an idyllic fantasy that could not practically occur, Kymlicka and Donaldson's proposals for practically altering human society to be less human-focused show that reducing anthropocentrism is not so far-fetched. Moreover, 'world peace,' amongst other ideas, may seem an ideal fantasy yet doing what we can to try to reach it, as best we can, is arguably not only possible, but laudable. While this suggestion is only outlined here it does provide one means for reducing anthropocentrism, and even brief as it is, it is not difficult to see that such a change would have a dramatic impact on nonhuman lives, how humans interact with nonhumans, and how human society is formed.

A second, more in-depth suggestion would be to include nonhuman animal perspectives into our deliberations, and considering them to be of equal validity and worth to our own. Again, one may object that this would be humans thinking what these perspectives are, but (i) it has already been granted that removing anthropocentrism may not be simple or done straightaway, (ii) one must recall that anthropocentrism as defined is not necessary, but an system of beliefs that humans have adopted, like androcentrism, and can like this other centrism be removed with time and diligence,[18] and (iii) nonhumans offer many ways of expressing their preferences or desires to those that pay attention–consider the examples given by ethologist Marc Bekoff, for instance. Furthermore we can err on the side of caution when considering whether nonhumans have perspectives or what their preferences may be, rather than 'not making assumptions' (however much these appeal to common experience) until 'some perspective, preference, or characteristic has been proven to be possessed.' While this would not be perfect, putting equal weight and validity onto these perspectives and including them with our own when deliberating about nonhuman issues would be far fairer than the current human-only perspectives, humans-as-priority perspectives, or human perspectives of what we think nonhumans prefer/require (and often only at minimum or so long as it does not conflict with human preferences).

For example, including nonhuman perspectives in this way would radically impact debates about predation, the expansion of human living space or interests into nonhuman living space, the treatment and structure of society given 'domestic' and 'liminal' nonhumans living within our society, whether nonhumans ought to be hunted or experimented on, 'welfare' laws and punishments, and so on. Similarly, when proposing ethical or political theories we can–as we often do with feminist and cultural arguments–look at nonhuman societies and see what norms, structures, or values they use, how these crossover with ours, and so on. Such perspectives could introduce new ideas/norms, provide understanding into the 'natures' and preferences of the nonhumans, perhaps strengthen, change, or enhance our own values, or even provide support for some of our already held beliefs (such as if moral rules are similar across different groups). All of this could help us formulate theories that are not so anthropocentric nor based solely on human values, beliefs, or norms.[19]

These suggestions would have a large impact on proposed theories of moral value, on what entities ought to be considered, what criteria ought to be used, and how we ought to interact with the resultant morally considerable nonhumans. While some may object that humans would have to be sacrificed for nonhumans, one must consider that similar objections have been made against ethnocentric, and other, prejudices. Furthermore, this is only a problem when considered from within a prejudicial or biased belief system, for this assumes–as Dale Jamieson has argued–that nonhumans should then sacrifice themselves for humans (Jamieson, 2008). This however does not seem intuitive, especially if we consider that nonhumans may not only include nonhuman animals but also extra-terrestrial beings. More importantly, morality is never so clear-cut in actual practice as we would like to imagine in the abstract, and while the sacrificing of humans for nonhumans may occur at times upon reaching the ideal this presents no impediment to reducing anthropocentrism as much as possible in the meantime, as the changes that would likely occur for now would be less dramatic.[20]

While these may be the two major means for addressing anthropocentrism, other approaches are available. For instance, by simply being aware of anthropocentrism and how it affects nonhuman issues we can simply try our best to look for it and countermand it as best we can. Even if we do not aim to eliminate it, reducing or removing what we can, when we can, when proposing theories or policy would still impact many nonhumans for the better. While some may find such small steps not to be enough my aim here is only to illustrate how anthropocentrism can be approached and why we should take it seriously.

We can also be aware that just as with androcentrism and ethnocentrism, anthropocentrism homogenizes the 'Other,' and thus we can recognize that nonhuman animals are individuals that are each unique. As such we would have to reject the traditional view that nonhumans are interchangeable or replaceable and adopt a new view that recognizes that each individual nonhuman animal has their own quirks and preferences, and their own perspective. That each nonhuman is a unique part of a number of interdependent, interrelated, and embedded groups and relationships, just as each human is. Moreover, many nonhumans (perhaps more than we know) recognize each other as individuals and often miss or mourn those individuals that go missing or die. This would clearly impact debates on meat-eating, nonhuman experimentation, hunting, and arguments such as 'the existence argument' or 'the painless killing argument.'

Relatedly, challenging anthropocentric ideas of nonhumans would also lead to a greater sensibility towards how different nonhumans express themselves. For instance, while humans display their emotions through facial expressions, other nonhumans do so via scent. Many other means of expression could exist that we cannot pick up on, and thus erring on the side of caution and challenging views that judge nonhuman capacities based on similarities in humans and human behaviours would likely benefit many nonhuman animals, in ways we may not even know.

While these suggestions are not exhaustive, nor without kinks that need to be ironed out, they do at least provide insight that is possible and practical into how we can approach and reduce anthropocentrism, and thus aid nonhumans considerably. As I have attempted to show, considering human chauvinism or speciesism is not enough when addressing issues concerning nonhuman animals. Many problems arise due to anthropocentrism, and as the problematic intuition behind human chauvinism is included within its definition, a focus on anthropocentrism would be more beneficial for nonhumans within nonhuman ethics and society at large. Moreover, addressing anthropocentrism is practically possible–from small steps, to more (arguably moral) major methods. Simply put, including nonhumans as nonhumans, and as equal beings with their own perspectives and uniqueness, and attempting to accept the similarities and differences, rather than ignoring, dismissing, or dominating them, would provide a more fair and unbiased nonhuman ethic and world. This would not only be better for nonhumans, but because nonhumans are so important a part of being human, and inextricably bound up as part of our interdependent human-nonhuman society, the result would also ultimately benefit human animals also.

REFERENCES

Anderson, E. (1995). Feminist epistemology: An interpretation and a defense. *Hypatia*, *10*(3), 50–84.

Bailey, C. (2009). A man and a dog in a lifeboat: Self-sacrifice, animals, and the limits of ethical theory. *Ethics & the Environment*, *14*(1), 129–148.

Bem, S. L. (1993). *The lenses of Gender*. New Haven, CT: Yale University Press.

Boddice, R. (2011). Introduction: The end of anthropocentrism. In R. Boddice (Ed.), *Anthropocentrism: Humans, animals, environments* (pp. 348). Leiden, The Netherlands: Brill.

de Jong, E. (2011). An alternative to anthropocentrism: Deep ecology and the metaphysical turn. In R. Boddice (Ed.), *Anthropocentrism: humans, animals, environments* (p. 348). Leiden, The Netherlands: Brill.

DeLapp, K. (2011). The view from somewhere: Anthropocentrism in metaethics. In R. Boddice (Ed.), *Anthropocentrism: Humans, animals, environments* (p. 348). Leiden: The Netherlands: Brill.

Donaldson, S., & Kymlicka, W. (2011). *Zoopolis: A political theory of animal rights*. Oxford, NY: Oxford University Press.

Edwards, R. B. (1993). Tom Regan's seafaring dog and (un)equal inherent worth. *Between the Species*, *9*(4), 231–235.

Faria, C., & Paez, E. (2014). Anthropocentrism and speciesism: Conceptual and normative issues. *Revista de Bioética y Derecho*, *32*, 82–90.

Fjellstrom, R. (2003). Is Singer's ethics speciesist? *Environmental Values*, *12*, 91–106.

Fox, W. (2008). Deep ecology: A new philosophy of our time? In A. Light, & R. Rolston III (Eds.), *Environmental Ethics: An Anthology* (p. 554). Malden, MA: Blackwell.

Francione, G. L. (1995). Comparable harm and equal inherent value: The problem of dog in the lifeboat. *Between the Species*, *11*(3), 81–89.

Hayward, T. (1997). Anthropocentrism: A misunderstood problem. *Environmental Values*, *6*(1), 49–63.

Horta, O. (2010). What is speciesism? *Environmental Ethics*, *23*(3), 243–266.

Jamieson, D. (2008). *Ethics and the environment: An introduction.* Cambridge, NY: Cambridge University Press.

Johnson, E. (1983). Life, death, and animals. In H. B. Miller, & W. H. Williams (Eds.), *Ethics and Animals* (p. 400). Clifton, NJ: Humana Press.

Milligan, T. (2011). Speciesism as a variety of anthropocentrism. In R. Boddice (Ed.), *Anthropocentrism: Humans, animals, environments* (p. 348). Leiden, The Netherlands: Brill.

Peterson, A. L. (2013). *Being animal: Beasts & boundaries in nature ethics.* New York, NY: Columbia University Press.

Plumwood, V. (1996). Androcentrism and anthrocentrism: Parallels and politics. *Ethics and the Environment*, *1*(2), 119–152.

Plumwood, V. (1991). Nature, self, and gender: Feminism, environmental philosophy, and the critique of rationalism. *Hypatia*, *6*(1), 3–27.

Regan, T. (2004). *The case for animal rights.* Berkeley, CA: University of California Press.

Singer, P. (1993). *Practical ethics* (2nd ed.). Cambridge, NY: Cambridge University Press.

Singer, P. (2008). Practical ethics. In S. J. Armstrong, & R. G. Botzler (Eds.), *The animal ethics reader* (2nd ed.). (p. 646). London, England: Routledge.

Smith, M. J. (2008). *Ecologism: Towards ecological citizenship*, Minneapolis, MN: University of Minnesota Press.

Warren, M. A. (2000). *Moral status: Obligations to persons and other living things* Oxford, NY: Oxford University Press.

NOTES

1. Numerous examples can be given. For instance, the *Oxford Dictionary* defines speciesism as "[t]he assumption of human superiority leading to the exploitation of animals". Within the literature, Paola Cavalieri, Peter Singer, Cora Diamond, James Rachels, and Richard A. Epstein, amongst others, all use the term in reference to human bias rather than generically.

2. For instance, some nonhuman advocates are as equally guilty of favouring nonhumans over humans. Furthermore, as the term is defined in the dictionary and by the most popular theorists in terms of the human, using speciesism to refer to how extra-terrestrials, etc, could be speciesist could easily lead to some conceptual confusion. Finally, while prejudicially favouring humans entails speciesism, being speciesist does not entail favouring humans, and thus it is conceptually incorrect to use the term to refer to a human bias.

3. I refer here to the *Oxford Dictionary* and *Merriam-Webster Dictionary*. The former defines one who is as anthropocentric as "[r]egarding humankind as the central or most important element of existence, especially as opposed to God or animals" and provides the following illustration for this meaning: "when we assess animal intelligence we tend to take a very anthropocentric view". This plainly fits A(1) and A(2), though less clearly expressed. The *Merriam-Webster Dictionary* is similar.

4. Even if 'being male' is largely a cultural construct this would not alter the point here, as (a) 'being human' is often considered social/cultural also, rather than biological (i.e. this is one defence humanists make against environmental ethics' arguments that attempt to claim that humans are just animals also), and (b) there is still something that is biologically male (however limited) and the 'benign' androcentrism still would not follow from this.

5. Of course, one could argue that an objective, impartial god could value humans without doing either of these. As no human satisfies this criterion, however, this does not need considering – especially as the debate that anthropocentrism is used in is between humans, and thus any human that endorses A(2) would seemingly do so via A(1). Furthermore, such a god could also do the same in regards to androcentrism and ethnocentrism, i.e. judge one sex/'race' as more valuable without seemingly taking any of their perspectives. Not only is this unpalatable

(and thus only arbitrariness can allow accepting this with anthropocentrism but not these –isms), but also we can neither prove what such a being would think nor conclude that it also didn't share the same values as humans, and thus still be as biased.

6. As many nonhuman ethic theories do; cf. Peter Singer and Tom Regan, at least.

7. Again, see Singer and Regan's admissions that they do grant hierarchies of value with humans at the top.

8. See the quote by Bem above.

9. Again, recall that by using the full term I refer to both A(1) and A(2).

10. In fact all of the major 'animal ethics' theories can be shown to involve both A(1) and A(2), but I shall not discuss this here.

11. Moreover, as I have demonstrated that there is a relation from A(1) to A(2), if A(1) were to remain then even if A(2) were somehow removed the former remaining would likely lead to the latter re-emerging.

12. While this statement seems controversial it may not be. For instance, this could be read as 'what would be in their interests for them', where an interest is defined similarly to Regan's 'having an interest' rather than 'taking an interest'. Alternatively, it could be read as it seems, and this may not be so controversial as it first appears. Many instances have been recorded of so-called 'wild' nonhumans expressing gratitude and affection, or anger/annoyance for human intervention in their lives (or for saving their lives). It does not seem so far-fetched then that in at least some predation instances nonhumans may have preferences. Our morality allows us to consider human preferences when they clash, why not nonhuman?

13. As a possible example, how we define 'pain' or the capacity to suffer or have preferences. Usually this is done via considering similarity to human nervous systems or expressions of sentience, often ignoring that nonhumans may have evolved similar capacities differently or express preference in ways that we cannot (or do not, via too-limited-a-focus) perceive.

14. Though problematic anthropocentrism remains in this theory even so.

15. On a related note, this point may be made more serious by considering that many ecofeminists argue that all forms of discrimination and oppression are necessarily linked. Thus if one of the –isms (i.e. androcentrism, ethnocentrism, egocentrism, anthropocentrism, etc) is not addressed then all of the others will remain also. This consideration has not been addressed by many 'animal ethicists', however given the points raised in this chapter, and the implications of leaving any of these problematic biases in play, this ought to be at least considered.

16. Nor do I claim that I am free of anthropocentrism either.

17. I purposely leave out environmental considerations here, for brevity's sake.

18. Androcentrism is not necessary, and as I note below combating anthropocentrism in the sense defined may draw on techniques suggested within feminist literature for dealing with the widespread androcentric perspective. This bias is possibly as entrenched in our way of thinking as anthropocentrism, and yet it seems possible to change our male-centred perspectives and society/culture via, as many feminist arguments purport, considering female perspectives, norms, values, etc, more seriously. This without concern that the threat that any such shift is doomed to be androcentric.

19. In fact, looking at how we approach and deal with androcentrism, ethnocentrism, and egocentrism could provide many insights into how we can effectively approach anthropocentrism.

20. Objecting that this is not an ideal we should seek would be problematic also, as unless a justification could be provided we then would be guilty of advocating the retention of a bias that is structurally-identical to biases we reject. Being inconsistent in this way not only undercuts normative force but calls into jeopardy any means of convincing those that do not share other moral beliefs we wish to convince them of. We then run the risk of moral imperialism or moral arbitrariness.

Chapter Six

Sea Otter Aesthetics in Popular Culture

Richard Ravalli

INTRODUCTION

A YouTube video posted in March of 2007 shows two sea otters at the Vancouver Aquarium in British Columbia. The animals are "holding hands" at the beginning of the one minute and forty one second clip (emphasized by a quick zoom on their clasped paws), which prompts responses such as "Absolutely adorable!" and "Cute!" from observers at the aquarium. At the fifty five second mark the creatures float apart, only to drift back toward each other and reconnect their paws some twenty five seconds later, followed by a chorus of "Aww." One comment from a YouTube viewer (posted on April 8, 2009) cynically captured the video's gushy sentiment: "[M]y head will explode from cuteness" (Otters holding hands, 2007).

"Otters holding hands" was viewed 1.5 million times in just two weeks after it was posted, making it YouTube's most popular animal video at the time. According to a report on the Internet phenomenon, "Aquarium officials said they hope the internet audience learns that the otters are not only cute, but are an endangered species as well" ("Vancouver sea otters," 2007). Such mixed feelings from individuals associated with sea otter conservation reveal tensions surrounding the popular perception of the animals. "Otters holding hands" is one of the more dramatic examples of public affection for sea otters, but it is far from alone. In this essay, I consider the development of aesthetic appreciation of the species *Enhydra lutris* in recent North American culture. Since the mid-20th century, biologists and conservationists have learned a great deal about the animals and considerable strides have been made toward their environmental recovery, yet they have also been subject to degrees of anthropomorphism and aesthetic indulgence from various sources that may be counterproductive to their continued needs. Hence, benefits as well as liabilities of sea otter cuteness in popular culture are considered here. For a general overview of debates regarding anthropomorphism and possibilities for transcending sharp dichotomies, (see the introduction to Daston & Mitman, 2005).

As a historian of the maritime fur trade, I am mindful of how the fascinating natural qualities of this sea mammal led to its global commodification and ultimately near extinction by the beginning of the 20th century. To be sure, furry sea otter toys and children's books replete with captivating images of the charismatic creatures are not as destructive human impacts as the widespread killing of them and the selling of their skin. Yet it may be worth considering how much modern-day fascination with and commercialization of sea otters works against efforts to assist the recovery of the fragile species. Officials at the Vancouver Aquarium no doubt appreciated the increased visitation that their celebrity sea otters likely produced. Still, their warning suggests that sharing a sea otter video online or buying a t-shirt at a Pacific Coast tourist stop can be mistaken for fulfilling an obligation to nature. It may be that these are the kinds of enthusiastic social and cultural activities that the animals inevitably generate today, similar to other appealing and photogenic species. As marine ecologist Glenn VanBlaricom (2001) observes, "There is a short list of mammals whose inexplicable appeal overwhelms our best efforts to be logical and dispassionate. ...Sea otters are surely on the list" (p. 8). In spite of this, whether sea otter cuteness can or should be complicated with more "realistic" depictions of the species is a concern that has been expressed by others. Hence I highlight ways that some have attempted to promote nuanced and less pleasing understandings of sea otters.

At the beginning of the 20th century, the sea otter was at its historical nadir. Decades of hunting in the late 1800s left the species at near extinction throughout its North Pacific range, and during the first quarter of the 20th century it was extirpated within significant portions of its coastal habitat. Progressive Era environmental reform aimed at protecting dwindling sea mammal herds ultimately led to the North Pacific Fur Seal Convention of 1911, which despite its name included an international provision for sea otters. Subsequent United States federal and state legislation provided the necessary safeguards for gradual recovery (Ravalli, 2009; Dorsey, 1998). Sea otter numbers increased significantly in Alaska by the 1930s, when the animals were studied by the naturalist Olaus Murie in the Aleutian Islands. Around the same time, a dramatic "rediscovery" took place along the Central California coast in 1938 as the existence of a sizable population was announced. The event brought renewed public attention to the sea otter and effectively inaugurated it as a celebrity species (Murie, 1940; Macdonald, 1938; Ravalli, 2009; Palumbi & Sotka, 2011).

World War II disrupted conservation efforts in the Aleutians but soon thereafter wildlife refuge manager Robert "Sea Otter" Jones became an important advocate for the animals at the islands. Jones fought against American military plans to test nuclear weapons at Amchitka Island, home to one of the largest populations of sea otters by the 1950s (Kohlhoff, 2002). While he wrote in 1951 that the sea otter "endears itself to the average human being because of its habits" (Jones, 1951, p. 378), Jones and other researchers who studied the species in these years tended to shy away from romantic natural history writing, leaving such prose to more popular authors. A 1949 article in *The Saturday Evening Post* obliged, with details about the "playful," "gregarious" creatures including dramatic descriptions of sea otter mothers and pups. The sentiments were included along with predictions of the return of hunting the Alaska population for the fur trade (Murphy, 1949). Even ostensibly dispassionate reports on sea otter recovery found it difficult to completely resist highlighting the appeal of the species. A 1958 article in *Outdoor California* (a magazine produced by the California Department of Fish and Game) titled "The Playful Sea Otter" included a photograph of a taxidermied sea otter holding a shellfish, with the caption, "Even a mounted specimen looks playful" ("The Playful Sea Otter," 1958, p. 12). It marks an early example of a sea otter photograph joined with an anthropomorphic caption. The *Saturday Evening Post* article's sole image of live Alaskan representatives was underscored by economic data: "The return on the investment for catching them once ran to 600%" (Murphy, 1949, p. 30).

Despite efforts to stop them, underground nuclear tests at Amchitka posed a major threat to sea otters yet the bombs ultimately helped to stir environmentalist activity that benefited the animals. Project Long Shot in October of 1965 was the first atomic detonation at the island, despite fears expressed in *Life Magazine* that it would "do irreparable damage to sea otters" (Kohlhoff, 2002; "Uproar over Otters," 1965). Shot Milrow in 1969 was followed by Shot Cannikin in 1971. Cannikin, the "largest underground nuclear explosion ever undertaken by the United States" (Kohlhoff, p. 110) according to historian Dean Kohlhoff, killed between 700 and 2,000 sea otters from rockfall and shockwave (also see McGrath, 2014). In response to mounting concerns, the United States Atomic Energy Commission funded some of the first successful translocations of sea otters in the late 1960s, moving the animals from Amchitka to coastal areas in Southeast Alaska, British Columbia, and Washington State, range locations where they had been eliminated. The efforts were showcased by officials in what was apparently one of the first sea otter documentaries, titled "The Warm Coat," produced in 1969. "In the sea, he has grace and style," declares the narrator, as the approximately 13 minute government film relies on what by then were becoming common tropes in describing the species for audiences. "The Warm Coat" also includes an early attempt to personalize the sea otter, showcasing the antics and experiences of an ostensibly fictionalized translocation representative named "Harvey" (Talkingsticktv, 2007). The somewhat whimsical nature of the documentary is partly explained by the needs of the AEC to generate good will among Alaskan citizens in the midst of its increasingly controversial testing activities in the Aleutian wildlife refuge.

Reaching larger audiences, programs on American television also promoted the creatures in these years. Naturalist Jacques Cousteau dedicated an episode of his *The Undersea World of Jacques Cousteau* series to the sea otter in 1971; *Mutual of Omaha's Wild Kingdom* followed suit in 1973 (Ron, 2013; Wild Kingdom, 2009). These were generally mainstream nature documentaries with little in the way of aesthetic indulgence, although Cousteau provided a brief anthropomorphic voiceover: "Otter, with your bristling silver whiskers, you look most wise to me." As Cousteau reported, the gradual expansion of sea otters along California shores was leading to increasing tensions with commercial abalone fishermen during the early 1970s. Sea otter cuteness had a role to play in this debate, as noticed by a central coast columnist who quipped that people "actually cooed" when looking at pictures of the animals in a biologist's office and who made the following admission: "[O]ne of the characters in the story is one of the most appealing and formerly one of the most abused creatures of the sea [which] makes it such an emotional issue that it is hard to get down to the facts and view the situation dispassionately" ("We All Love Sea Otters," 1970).

Enthusiastic captivation with *Enhydra* was likely more pronounced in California than it was in Alaska due in part to the relative difficulty the species has had in rebounding in the Golden State, its rarity eliciting acute cultural and social responses. The non-governmental organization Friends of the Sea Otter, founded in 1968 in the Monterey Bay area and the first organization dedicated to protecting the sea mammal, also played a role in cultivating sentimental attachment as part of its vigorous advocacy. A 1972 article in the local press dubbed sea otters "Teddy Bears of the ocean" and highlighted an watching trip organized by Friends of the Sea Otter that brought 375 people together to view the animals at close range: "Four boats made two trips each from Fishermen's Wharf and each spent about an hour among the otters while cameras captured their antics and visitors from as far away as New York and Florida 'ooh'd' and 'ah'd' in admiration" (Woolfenden, 1972, 10). A *Sports Illustrated* report on the controversies involving shellfishermen and conservationists took note of Friends of the Sea Otter's "feisty" newsletter, *The Otter Raft*, and its inclusion of sea otter testimonials "[a]long with a lot of cute otter illustrations, ads for otter books, posters and movies, [and] fund raising appeals" (Gilbert, 1976). In short, by the mid-1970s various regional and national dynamics converged to begin to bring sea otters into a wider public imagination. The species received additional United States environmental protection with the Marine Mammal Protection Act of 1972 and in 1977 it was listed as threatened under the Endangered Species Act of 1973 (Busch, 1985; For a recent history of the Endangered Species Act, see Alagona (2013), chapter 4).

Yet more than landmark victories in American environmental law, California tourism and the establishment of the Monterey Bay Aquarium advanced sea otter notoriety while popularizing the creatures as cute and endearing during the last decades of the 20th century. The aquarium grew out of associations between the family of David Packard (of Hewlett-Packard fame), university professors, and Stanford University's Hopkins Marine Station, the last of which sold the deteriorating Hovden Cannery building in Monterey to a non-profit organization established by the Packards in 1978. The opening of the facility six years later was a large celebration heralded by the declaration "The Fish Are Back!," a reference to the city's former sardine industry (Chiang, 2008, pp. 155-157). As with the aquarium's other exhibits, planners and staff met a variety of challenges in attempting to present sea otters in their "natural" state. The first sea otters scratched the acrylic panels of their tank with shellfish shards, and toys had to be introduced to prevent boredom. As historian Connie Chiang (2008) writes, "The aquarium renovated the tank in 1993, adding other fish and new rockwork covered with algae and invertebrates, in the hope of creating an exhibit more true to the otters' habitat" (p. 170).

Eventually, sea otters became a star attraction for the internationally-recognized Monterey Bay Aquarium, "[the] closest thing to a 'celebrity' species," according to Chiang (2008, p. 173). Visitors today are greeted with all manner of stuffed toys, books, and children's material in the aquarium's gift areas. Outside along Monterey's Cannery Row seaside district, tourist shops sell shirts and memorabilia depicting the animals, clear evidence of their status as cute and furry emblems of the city. Fostering the merchandising of the sea otter allows the aquarium's many upper-middle class patrons to further express green values through consumer culture. Yet the degree to which exhibit spectacle and popular consumption produces a beneficial perception of sea otters instead of blurring and trivializing their historic challenges is open to question. One may counter that the aquarium's many contributions to sea otter conservation more than offsets any cultural dilemmas related to what it does. Still, the facility's officials themselves have recognized over the years some of the inherent problems with exhibiting sea otters. An article from a 1987 issue of Monterey Bay Aquarium's newsletter discussing their sea otter rehabilitation program begins with the question, "Are sea otters too cute and lovable for their own good?", and it warns readers not to try and take home seemingly abandoned pups found the wild: "[P]eople who enjoy the antics of the otters in the aquarium may have the idea that otters in the wild would make ideal pets" (Rodriguez, 1987). Culture and

conservation are ultimately linked in complex ways that can run counter to
the environmental needs of the species.

It was an oil spill—not captivated beachcombers—that represented the
greatest man-made threat to sea otters in the late 20th century. In 1989, some
3,000 sea otters died when the *Exxon Valdez* struck a reef in Prince William
Sound in Alaska, spilling hundreds of thousands of barrels of crude oil. The
reputation that the creatures had gained by that time allowed them to be
pictured in media coverage as iconic victims of the environmental disaster.
As a columnist for the *Chicago Tribune* noted, "[I]f one image stands out in
the aftermath of America's worst oil spill, it is of these once-healthy animals
rubbing their eyes and grooming their fur in a futile attempt to rid their coats
of slimy crude oil" (as cited in Batten, 1990, p. 33). Although thousands
more seabirds died from the *Exxon Valdez* spill, the plight of sea otters and
subsequent efforts to rescue them received the most public attention. According to B. T. Batten (1990) of the U.S. Fish and Wildlife Service, "Small,
furry, childlike, and vulnerable, sea otters became compelling victims with
whom everyone could identify, and thereby made the perfect universal symbol for the injured party. Nearly a year after the spill, one national magazine
summarized this sentiment when it referred to the Federal indictment for the
oil spill as 'the case of *Otter et. al. v. Exxon*'" (p. 35). Thus the unique appeal
of the sea otter helped build beneficial sympathy for the struggling population beyond the tragic year of 1989. (For a recent study of the *Exxon Valdez*
oil spill, (see also Day, 2014).

Yet if memory of the perils faced by Alaskan sea otters faded over time,
other sources of popular attention were enlivened. General audience books
dedicated to *Enhydra* have been some of the most influential cultural artifacts relating to sea otter cuteness in recent years. Often oversized volumes
featuring stunning color photographs of the animals in the wild, they have
helped to define and promote sea otter aesthetics on a mass scale. Two of the
most notable of these popular natural histories are by Roy Nickerson, a
California journalist, and VanBlaricom. Nickerson's (1989) *Sea Otters: A
Natural History and Guide*, with photographs by Richard Bucich, is filled
mostly with close up shots of sea otter faces with captions occasionally
evocative of the expressiveness of the animals in the photos: "This resting
sea otter does not look happy at being disturbed," "I can still touch my toes"
(pp. 13, 26). VanBlaricom's (2001) *Sea Otters* includes a wider variety of
images and a more clinical approach to captioning, yet VanBlaricom cannot
resist casting his subject in a human light with narrative prose:

> One day I stood with a colleague on the public pier at the town
> of Pismo Beach, watching sea otters feed on Pismo clams. . . We
> saw a young male otter with one clam securely tucked into an
> axilla. He dove repeatedly, but could not find a second clam.

Periodically he would stop to rest, bring the clam to his mouth,
bite at the unforgiving shell and, in frustration, even pound the clam
against his chest. Again and again he would dive, and again and
again he would resolutely probe the equally stubborn clam in
hopes of breaking through. Finally, just as the sun dropped into
the western sea, the otter gave in. Resting quietly on the surface
with his gaze averted, he released his grip and allowed the clam to
slide from his chest. In the growing darkness he moved off to the
north after an embarrassed glance in our direction. (p. 26)

Numerous children's books have been devoted to sea otters. Of these, non-fiction titles regularly employ the "teddy bear" analogy in the body of the text, or, as in one example, as a chapter title. Equating the animals with stuffed toys complements many charming photographs and affirms their cuddly identity in the minds of young readers:

Certain animals inspire our curiosity and love. Sea otters are like that. Perhaps it's their teddy-bear faces" (Leon, 2005, p. 5).

To many people, sea otters look a little like floating teddy bears. But they are much bigger—sea otters can grow to be about 100 pounds" (Murray, 2001, p. 11).

[Chapter 1] Teddy Bear of the Sea" (Silverstein, 1995, p. 7).

One drawback of these romantic images is that instead of being afforded the serious attention which its environmental status demands, the sea otter and its charismatic profile can at times be regarded as a cultural and even political punchline. In 2013, Alaska State Senator Bert Stedman proposed a $100 bounty on the species to incentivize Native Alaskan hunters to help alleviate pressures on Southeastern Alaska fishermen. (Under the Marine Mammal Protection Act, only Native Alaskans are legally allowed to hunt sea otters.) As one article on the proposal reports: "They're cute and cuddly guys,' says Stedman. 'But their impact, when you just let them overpopulate, on the human side of the equation, is substantial'" (Kheiry, 2013). Elsewhere Stedman was quoted as saying: "This is serious. I try to put humor in it, because we all recognize they are cute and cuddly animals in the water. It sounds Draconian at first but when you take a look at the impact of coastal Alaska, it's a whole different outlook" (Klouda, 2013). "They're cute…but" suggests that the physical appeal of sea otters is what is most important about them, a mentality that complicates efforts to protect the animals. When I express my own interest in researching the history of the species to others, a common response (even from professional colleagues) follows: "You mean those cute things that float in the water?" As already seen, aquatic teddy bears often prove resistant to sober attention.

The point here is not that the benefits of sea otter cuteness are outweighed by these dilemmas. In a 2011 report, researchers Sadie S. Stevens, John F. Organ and Thomas L. Serfass discussed the usefulness of sea otters as a "flagship species." According to the authors, "Flagship species are defined as 'popular, charismatic species that serve as symbols and rallying points to stimulate conservation awareness and action....'" (Stevens, Organ, & Serfass, 2011). They note the value of sea otter tourism in California and point to the viral success of "Otters holding hands." No doubt a flagship candidacy for *Enhydra* is secure, and the popularity of the species has done much to raise awareness for its needs over the years. Nevertheless, future authors might benefit by acknowledging and scrutinizing the periodically counterproductive aspects of sea otter notoriety and charisma more often than is currently the case.

One way that biologists and others have attempted to mitigate the excesses of sea otter cuteness is through emphasizing the "wild" characteristics of the species. Interviewed by the *San Francisco Chronicle* in 1994, Marianne Riedman, Monterey Bay Aquarium's chief sea otter research at the time, contended: "No doubt they're cute and fun to watch, but remember, they are, after all, wild carnivorous animals" (Perlman, 1994, p. A19). Among the less appealing facts about sea otters, Riedman noted that the creatures often steal food from each other and that females are commonly wounded during mating, sometimes with lethal injuries. The animals "are immensely powerful—so strong, Riedman says, that it would take three strong men to hold one down" (Perlman, 1994, p. A20). While photos of females with mating wounds on their noses often appear in books and nature documentaries, the image of sea otters as aggressive and even sinister has found some resonance in recent Internet media. *Slate* columnist Brian Switek reported on research that analyzed sea otters in Monterey Bay attempting to mate with harbor seal pups, even after the violent encounters led to the deaths of the young seals. "At least two of the sea otters had been previously held at the Monterey Bay Aquarium as part of their rehabilitation program," writes Switek, explaining that "the trouble they experienced early in their lives might have made them more likely assailants" (Switek, 2013).

Such information, not widely known outside of marine mammal research, could perhaps work to complicate the species in the public imagination and promote more careful understandings of it. Larry Pynn of the *Vancouver Sun* reported on the "dark side" of sea otter behavior by recounting the story of Whiskers, a Vancouver Island sea otter who repeatedly attempted to entice dogs into the surf until one day he was found trying to mate with a dead dog in the water. As Pynn writes, "[C]ute and cuddly—not rapist and murderer—are mentioned in the typical bio on sea otters" (Pynn, 2014). Mirroring Riedman's corrective, Vancouver Aquarium sea mammal curator Brian Sheehan is quoted as saying: "That's one thing we have with our visitors: 'Oh, they look adorable like stuffed animals,'…But they definitely have the potential for being strong and aggressive" (Pynn, 2014). Nevertheless, as poignant as the commentary may be that "[t]he dark side of superficially cute animals is a part of their nature that reminds us that the wild does not exist for our entertainment and whimsy" (Switek, 2013), how this less sentimental appreciation for the species could take hold in a sea of fuzzy toys, emblazoned sweaters and kids' books is at least difficult to contemplate. Even the photos accompanying Pynn's online article that capture the animals engaged in instances of odd sexual behavior do not appear overtly sinister—in a couple examples, a sea otter seems to be playing with, not attempting to molest, a cormorant seabird.

The turn of the 21st century saw sea otter cuteness enter the Internet age most dramatically with 2007's "Otters holding hands." The two animals in the video, Nyac and Milo, have since passed away but have been featured in other online tributes. Nyac and Milo also inspired Canadian author Dina Del Bucchia (2013) to memorialize them in a recent poetry collection. Perhaps her irreverent literary commentary best summarizes the inherent tensions of sea otter celebrity. For Nyac, whose notoriety dates back to being an *Exxon Valdez* survivor, Del Bucchia writes:

> From slicked black, snout not even visible,
> to picture-perfect, made for advertisements, plush toys, mugs.
> Fur-print tote bags instead of torn from your flesh.
> You had the right story, a TV movie starring
> Jennifer Love Hewitt, that you overcame with
> take-a-look-at-me-now appeal. You were a girl fished
> from a well, a kidnapping survivor, a wartorn orphan,
> a slim pup reborn in oil. (p. 93)

For Milo:

Like an ailing politician, we weep for Milo, hold vigils on the Internet. I advise we make small shrines in our homes: tasteful glitter pens, foam core, fake candles, ceramic replicas looted from the gift shop (p. 95).

REFERENCES

Alagona, P. (2013). *After the grizzly: Endangered species and the politics of place in California.* Berkeley, CA: University of California Press.

Batten, B. T. (1990). Press interest in sea otters affected by the T/V *Exxon Valdez* oil spill. In K. Bayha & J. Kormendy (Eds.), In *Sea otter symposium: Proceedings of a symposium to evaluate the response effort on behalf of sea otters after the T/V* Exxon Valdez *oil spill into Prince William Sound, Anchorage, Alaska, 17–19 April 1990,* (pp. 32–40). Washington, DC: U.S. Department of the Interior, Fish and Wildlife Service, and National Fish and Wildlife Foundation.

Busch, B. C. (1985). *The war against the seals: A history of the North American seal fishery.* Kingston, OT: Mc-Gill-Queen's University Press.

Chiang, C. (2008). *Shaping the shoreline: Fisheries and tourism on the Monterey coast.* Seattle, WA: University of Washington Press.

Day, A. (2014). *Red light to starboard: Recalling the* Exxon Valdez *disaster.* Pullman, WA: Washington State University Press.

Datson, L. & Mitman, G., (Eds.) (2005). *Thinking with animals: New perspectives on anthropomorphism.* New York, NY: Columbia University Press.

Del Bucchia, D. (2013). *Coping with emotions and otters.* Vancouver, BC: Talonbooks.

Dorsey, K. (1998). *The dawn of conservation diplomacy: U.S.-Canadian wildlife protection treaties in the Progressive era.* Seattle, WA: University of Washington Press.

Gilbert, B. (1976, July 26). Dept. of otter confusion. *Sports Illustrated.* Retrieved from http://157.166.253.202/vault/article/magazine/MAG1091361/1/index.htm.

Jones, R. (1951). Present status of the sea otter in Alaska. In E. Quee (Ed.), *Transactions of the sixteenth North American wildlife conference,* (pp. 376–383). Washington, DC: Wildlife Management Institute.

Kheiry, L. (2013, April 17). Stedman talks oil tax, sea otters. *KRBD.* Retrieved from http://www.krbd.org/2013/04/17/stedman-talks-oil-tax-sea-otters.

Klouda, N. (2013, March 30). A bounty on sea otters? *Homer Tribune.* Retrieved from http://homertribune.com/2013/03/a-bounty-on-sea-otters/.

Leon, V. (2005). *A raft of sea otters: The playful life of a furry survivor.* Montrose, CA: London Town Press.

Macdonald, A. (1938). *Pacific pelts: Sea otters chose California coast.* Oakland, CA: N.p.

McGrath, S. (2014, January-February). An accidental science project reveals how crucial sea otters are to kelp forests. *Audubon Magazine.* Retrieved from http://www.audubon.org/magazine/january-february-2014/an-accidental-science-project-reveals.

Murie, O. (1940). Notes on the sea otter. *Journal of Mammalogy, 21*(2), 119–131.

Murray, P. (2001). *Sea otters.* Chanhassen, MN: The Child's World, Inc.

Otters holding hands (2007, March 19). *Otters holding hands* [Video file]. Retrieved from http://www.youtube.com/watch?v=epUk3T2Kfno.

Palumbi, S. & Sotka, C. (2011). *The death and life of Monterey bay: A story of revival.* Washington, DC: Island Press.

Perlman, D. (1994, February 4). Cuddly otter image in the tank. *San Francisco Chronicle,* A19, A20. "Otters, Sea" clippings file, Monterey Public Library California Room, Monterey, CA.

Pynn, L. (2014, April 10). Fifty shades of fur? Exposing the dark side of a sea otter's sex life (with video). *The Vancouver Sun.* Retrieved from http://www.vancouversun.com/technology/Fifty+shades+Exposing+dark+side+otter+life+with+video/9721555/story.html.

Ravalli, R. (2009). The near extinction and reemergence of the Pacific sea otter. *Pacific Northwest Quarterly, 100*(4), 181–191.

Rodriguez, M. (1987, September). Significant otters. *Monterey Bay Aquarium Newsletter,* n.p. "Otters, Sea" clippings file, Monterey Public Library California Room, Monterey, CA.

Ron (2013, August 28). *The.Undersea.World.of.Jacques.Cousteau.Collection1-The.Unsinkable.Sea.Otter,* [Video file]. Retrieved from http://www.dailymotion.com/video/x13s4rs_the-undersea-world-of-jacques-cousteau-collection1-the-unsinkable-sea-otter_shortfilms.

Silverstein, A.V., & R. (1995). *The sea otter.* Brookfield, CT: The Millbrook Press.

Stevens, S., Organ, J. F., & Serfass, T. L. (2011). Otters as flagships: Social and cultural considerations. *Proceedings of Xth International Otter Colloquium, IUCN Otter Specialist Group Bulletin 28*(A), 150–161. Retrieved from http://iucnosg.org/Bulletin/Volume28A/Stevens_et_al_2011.html#Fig1.

Switek, B. (2013, October 28). Sea otters are jerks. So are dolphins, penguins, and other adorable animals. *Slate.* Retrieved from http://www.slate.com/blogs/wild_things/2013/10/28/sea_otter_dolphin_and_penguin_behavior_your_favorite_animals_are_jerks.html.

Talkingsticktv (2007, October 13). *Declassified U.S. Nuclear Test Film #37* [Video file]. Retrieved from http://www.youtube.com/watch?v=0jbz_zD00hk.

"The Playful Sea Otter." (1958, August). *Outdoor California,* 12–14.

"Uproar over Otters." (1965, October 15). *Life,* 151–152.

"Vancouver sea otters a hit on YouTube." (2007, April 3). *CBC News*. Retrieved from http://www.cbc.ca/news/canada/british-columbia/vancouver-sea-otters-a-hit-on-youtube-1.688725.

"We All Love Sea Otters." (1970, April 1). *Independent Coast Observer*, 1, 4. Retrieved from http://ico.stparchive.com/Archive/ICO/ICO04011970p01.php.

Wild Kingdom (2009, June 2). *World of the Sea Otter* [Video file]. Retrieved from http://www.youtube.com/watch?v=lECZuIAiJVI.

Woolfenden, J. (1972, October 21). The darlings of tourists. *Herald Weekend Magazine*, 2–3; 12. "Otters, Sea" clippings file, Monterey Public Library California Room, Monterey, CA.

Chapter Seven

Media Representations of Animals in Urban Canada

Linda Kalof, Cameron Thomas Whitley, Jessica Bell

INTRODUCTION

The cultural meanings of animals are linked to the historically-specific norms and values of the society in which they are constructed, and popular culture images of animals are particularly reflective of cultural messages and historical shifts in social and political structures (Arluke & Bogdan, 2010; Kalof, 2007; Kalof & Amthor, 2010; Dunaway, 2008). Our chapter explores the visual and narrative representations of animals in urban Canada over the 20th century in *National Geographic*, one of the most widely read magazines in the world based primarily on its photographic illustrations. Among the myriad sources of popular culture representations, photography is unique in its cultural significance, global influence and the role it plays in the recall and memorization of specific events (Gaskell, 1991; Sontag, 2003). Further, animal photography is especially notable in that it is embedded in and contributes to contemporary social discourses on animals, people and the natural world (Dunaway, 2008; Kalof & Fitzgerald, 2003; Kalof & Amthor, 2010; Whitley & Kalof, 2014; Kalof, 2015). Cultural representations of animals are also connected to the *social meanings* of a physical space (Jerolmack, 2013), and representations of urbanity and nature impact the perceived legitimacy and inclusion of certain animals in urban areas. The scholarship on urban animals has flourished in the last three decades, addressing a variety of topics from problem animals (those considered out of place in urban landscapes) to "biophilic cities" (where animals and plants are enthusiastically encouraged) to the negotiation of wildness based in part on media representations (Atkins, 2012, p. 6). But while animals in urban areas have been the subject of a wide range of scholarship, to our knowledge there is no scholarship on the visual and narrative representations of animals in urban Canada. This lack of research is surprising. Canada has experienced a rapid increase in urbanization since the late 1860s, and given the ethical, cultural and ecological impacts of increases in urban populations of humans and other animals, a study of the visual and narrative representations of animals in that country is long overdue. Our research fills that void. We ask, how do media representations in *National Geographic* magazine reflect the cultural meanings of animals in urban Canada?

BACKGROUND

What do we know about animals in urban Canada?

Our review of the literature found that most of the research on animals in urban Canada that included a human-animal dimension came primarily from wildlife and natural resource management and urban ecology or ethology. Much of that work was either management-oriented or problem-oriented with a focus on mitigating or eliminating the negative economic and health repercussions of animals who live in urban areas. For example, studies on disease and disease prevention in animal populations in urban Canada typically focused on disease prevalence, spread and/or prevention (Broadfoot, Rosatte, & O'Leary, 2001; Catalano, Lejeune, Liccioli, Verocai, Gesy, Jenkins, Kutz, Fuentealba, Duignan, & Massolo, 2012: Jardine, Lindsay, Nicholson, Ojkic, & Prescott, 2011; Lu, Ryu, Hill, Schoen, Ashbolt, Edge, & Domingo, 2011; Schubert, Rosatte, MacInnes, & Nudds, Ward 2002). This line of research primarily addressed urban animals who walk a thin line between wild and domestic and are common in dense urban centers, including raccoons, skunk, gulls, and pigeons. These studies had diverse research agendas such as the development of spatial models in urban areas to predict deer vehicle collisions (Found & Boyce, 2011) and examining the health impacts a fire at a PCB plant has had on bird populations (Phaneuf, Des-Granges, Plante, & Rodrigue, 1995). In Found and Boyce (2011), deer were framed as a threat to human safety, in Rosatte (1998) the threat was raccoons, and in Phaneuf et al. (1995), humans were framed as a threat to wildlife. Other studies contain insight into the complexity of human-animal relationships and their reciprocal safety threats. A good example is Mos, Jack, Cullon, Montour, Alleyne, and Ross (2004) who investigated the Sencoten First Nation's eating habits to identify the degree to which it contains persistent organic pollutants (POPs) that would threaten human health. The Sencoten people continue to survive largely on a traditional subsistence diet that includes large amounts of fish and sea life, which are likely to carry high concentrations of POPs and heavy metals.

An important line of research in urban ecology and ethology focused on the encroachment of urban development on animal habitat and its influence on animal behavior. In the literature on urban ethology in Canada, birds were the primary focus animal (Campbell, 2009; Lancaster & Rees, 1979; Morand-Ferron, Lalande, & Giraldeau, 2009; Tremblay & Clair, 2011). Other species represented in the urban ethology literature were fish (Gillis, Rapp, Hasler, Wachelka, & Cooke, 2010; O'Connell & Gibson, 1989), invertebrates (Whiting & Clifford, 1983), small mammals (Racey & Euler, 1982) and cougars (Thornton & Quinn, 2009). These studies work from the premise that expanding human development diminishes and/or degrades animal habitat, and from this basic understanding scholars develop research questions centered on the degree to which the degraded habitat influences the behavior and wellbeing of animal life. On the whole, studies of urban ecology find that some species flourish with increased human presence and the food, opportunities for shelter and alerted environment humans bring to the landscape, while other species struggle to adapt with negative consequences. For example Lancaster and Rees (1979, p. 2358) investigated how increasing levels of urbanity and available natural habitat in Canada influenced the presence, diversity, and density of bird populations; they found that "cavity-nesting, ground-feeding graminivorous or omnivorous bird species" flourished in highly urban settings while birds outside of this category failed to thrive.

Urban wildlife ecology generally accepts that cultural factors influence the viability of urban animal populations as much as ecological factors. Gilbert (1982) focused on general perceptions of wildlife in a study of how the amount of natural habitat in one's neighborhood influenced knowledge and perceptions of wildlife. However, most urban ecological research investigated human perceptions of large carnivores, including brown/grizzly bears, black bears, cougars and wolves (Campbell, 2013; Campbell & Lancaster, 2010; Kellert, Black, Rush, & Bath, 1996). These studies begin from two premises: first, large carnivores are distinct from other animals, in part because of their social construction as dangerous predators in euro-American culture, and second, people are increasingly likely to have interactions with these animals because of urbanization and human encroachment on animal habitats. Although research had found that survey respondents and interviewees generally have favorable opinions towards large carnivores (Campbell, 2013; Campbell & Lancaster, 2010; Gilbert, 1982), the articles typically included recommendations for local communities to increase education and prevention efforts to mitigate potential human-animal conflicts. For example, Beier's (1991) research addressed the claim that cougar attacks on humans are increasing and as a result local communities need to respond in ways that limit this threat. Noting that there was no reliable historical record of cougar attacks, and thus no real basis to argue the attacks were increasing, the author detailed every reported case of a cougar attack in the United States and

Canada over the previous 100 years. He documented that cougar attacks are in fact on the rise, but human encroachment on cougar habitat has likely precipitated the increase, with many occurring in urban or semi-urban areas. The author noted that attacks on Vancouver Island had increased as human populations increased and the decline of prey species for the cougar.

Some research investigated companion animals in Canada. Perrin (2009) documented findings from a nationally-representative survey on Canadians' opinions and behaviors regarding companion animals, including such diverse topics as the reasons for pet ownership, how respondents handle age-related health concerns in their animals, and whether respondents have had their companion animals micro-chipped. Interestingly, the primary purpose of the survey was to provide information for businesses that provide goods and services for companion animals. The study originated when businesses throughout the country expressed a need to better understand Canadian perspectives and behaviors so that they could tailor their business models to meet local needs concerning companion animals. Labrecque and Walsh (2011) conducted intensive interviews with women in homeless shelters in six Canadian cities to understand the role and importance of animal caretaking in the women's lives. Many women expressed the devastating loss of having to relinquish their animals when they became homeless and discussed how much easier it would have been if there were shelters that allowed pets. The authors encouraged cities to develop programs that would allow the homeless to keep their animals when they seek assistance, since pets can be a barrier to individuals pursuing the help they need. Further, in a study of women in Canadian shelters for abused women, Fitzgerald (2007) found that companion animals are uniquely situated to provide social support to some abused women and can even serve a protective function against suicide. She concluded that to adequately address the needs of abused Canadian women, the important roles companion animals can play in their lives must be taken seriously. The recent increase in the number of shelters that allow companion animals (albeit still alarmingly low)[1] is indicative of the important role the cultural meanings of animals play in social life.

Finally, in a study most relevant to our research, Alexander and Quinn (2011) examined coyote-pet and coyote-human interactions as reported in Canadian newspapers published between 1995 and 2010. They found incongruence between the perceived threat of coyotes and the actual number of coyote attacks and argued that since many urban residents viewed the coyote as unnatural or out of place in cities, even benign sightings of coyotes in urban areas became risky "incidents." The finding that amplification of perceived risk can occur when an animal is viewed as "out of place," is closely connected to the cultural meanings of animals in urban areas, the subject of our next section.

CULTURAL MEANINGS OF ANIMALS IN URBAN AREAS

The cultural meanings of urban animals are fluid and can fluctuate across time, space, and cultures. For example, the cultural meaning of urban pigeons has drastically changed over the 20th century; once viewed as valuable sources of food, fertilizer, and recreation, pigeons are now widely despised as pests (Jerolmack, 2008). Issues of place and boundaries are also integral to the cultural representations of animals in urban areas. The construction of place influences which animals are seen as legitimate and which are seen as illegitimate. Ideological constructions of the city as a "human place" and the wilderness as an "animal place" de-legitimize and stigmatize wild animals who live in urban areas (Donaldson & Kymlicka, 2011). In addition, many urban areas have been defined historically as cultural centres that must exclude all traces of the country from their midst (Wolch, 1998). Urban geographers have examined how this conceptualization of urbanity has led to the exclusion of both livestock and wildlife from urban centers (Wolch, 1998; Philo, 1998; Atkins, 2012). These exclusionary practices were, and continue to be, closely linked to ideas about purification and sanitation (Atkins, 2012; Jerolmack, 2008). Notions of sanitation often include moral overtones. For example, in Victorian England, the exclusion of slaughterhouses and meat markets from cities was seen as essential to both physical and moral sanitation (Wolch, 2002; Philo, 1998).

Some wildlife species such as rats and coyotes have the ability to live off anthropogenic food sources and adapt to life shared with humans in cities. This "liminality" positions them at the urban-nature boundary and contributes to ambiguity in how they are viewed and treated (Nolan, Jones, McDougal, McFarlin, & Ward, 2006; Griffiths, Poulter, & Sibley, 2000; Jerolmack, 2013; Ritvo, 2007). The negative representations of some urban animals emerge from their status as boundary crossers. They may be viewed as out of place and can evoke anxiety, disgust, and fear about disorder, impurity, and the merger of culture and nature (Griffiths et al., 2000). Themes of disorder and pollution are prevalent in the cultural meanings of wildlife in urban areas, suggesting that these species threaten social ideals about "orderliness." Much of the documentation on the cultural meanings of animals has come from studies of the representation of animals in narrative and visual media, which is the subject of the next section.

MEDIA REPRESENTATIONS OF ANIMALS IN URBAN AREAS

Several scholars have examined how the print media contributes to social representations of animals, particularly regarding problem animals in urban areas. For example, Jerolmack's (2008) study of pigeons as problem animals was based on a content analysis of *New York Times* narratives on pigeons over a 155 year period. In a study of the photographs and narratives in *National Geographic*, Kalof and Amthor (2010) documented the magazine's contribution to the cultural knowledge of animals as noxious, alien, foreign and invasive. In their study of coyote events in urban areas mentioned earlier, Alexander and Quinn (2011) examined the digital archives of Canadian newspapers published between 1995 and 2010. Their finding that amplification of perceived risk can occur when an animal is viewed as "out of place" was supported by content analyses of cougar-related coverage appearing in the *Los Angeles Times* (Wolch, Gullo, & Lassiter, 1997). They documented how attitudes toward cougars shifted between 1985 and 1995 as reflected in the tenor of coverage, specific attitudes expressed, and the terminology used to describe cougars in the news. They concluded that the analysis of public discourse around wildlife management issues is a useful method of tracking broad shifts in public attitudes toward wildlife.

Atkins (2012, pp. 2-3) has argued that the discourse on animals in urban areas usually places them into one of four thematic areas: 1) useful animals, for traction or meat; 2) those who can be enjoyed, such as wild garden song birds; 3) those who are desirable, for example companion animals; and 4) species who have transgressed, such as rats, cockroaches and pigeons, and are considered "vermin" because they are "out of place" in the city. We use Atkins' thematic structure to examine the visual and narrative representations of animals in urban Canada. Based on 70 years of *National Geographic* magazine, we ask, what are the primary thematic representations of animals in urban Canada and how do they reflect the social meanings of animals in that country?

METHOD

Our methodology was a qualitative analysis of the photographs, narratives and captions from all feature articles (n = 21) that addressed animals in urban Canada published in *National Geographic* over the 20th century.[2] Relevant articles were identified through a complex search function of *National Geographic*'s complete archives using search terms including 1) urban areas in Canada (British Columbia, Alberta, Toronto, Ontario, Montreal, Calgary, Edmonton, Quebec, and Nova Scotia); 2) relevant terms (such as "wildlife" and "animal"); and 3) specific animal species (such as beaver, moose, caribou, and fox). We examined the animals pictured in the photographs of the articles and the accompanying narratives (photograph captions and text of the articles). There were 64 photographs of one or more animals in urban Canada published in the 21 articles; the first article appeared in 1930.

RESULTS

Three broad themes reflecting the social meanings of animals in urban Canada emerged from the data: 1) useful animals, primarily for traction or food, 2) aesthetic animals, or species who are enjoyed for their beauty or rarity, and 3) animals out of place in urban areas.[3]

USEFUL ANIMALS IN URBAN CANADA

Traction Animals

Representations of animals used for transport were dominant during the first few decades in *National Geographic*. The first article in our sample, "Old World Charm in Modern Quebec" (April 1930)[4] used images of urban Canada to paint a picture of traditional appeal in a modern context. Animals were featured in five images that accompanied the text of the article; each photograph depicted working animals: horses bound to buggies, dogs pulling sleds, and oxen towing farm equipment. It is interesting that while the text addressed the natural beauty, history and regality of urban life, those characteristics of urbanity were illustrated with photographs of animals. Similarly, in an article on "Old France in Modern Canada" (February 1935), a boy was pictured with a dog pulling a mail cart; the caption was a self-advertisement that highlighted the wide distribution of *National Geographic* through various modes of transportation:

> Both dog and master are determined that the mail shall go through: Each month several copies of the *National Geographic Magazine* go into this region near Lake St. John, Quebec. Nearly every mode of transportation takes The Geographic to its destination–from canoes, camel caravans, and dogsleds to fast liners, trains, and airplanes. (February 1935, p. 193)

In the 1940s, there was a change in how transportation as a form of work for animals was depicted. An article, "Exploring Ottawa" (November 1947), published an image of the Royal Canadian Police mounted on horseback with a caption noting that there was a time when riding horseback was standard, but this practice had since been replaced by other means of transportation:

> Not all Royal Canadian Mounted Police are dismounted; a few still ride. Time was when all Mounties had to know horseflesh. Nowadays they use motorboats, cars, motorcycles, planes. In the Far North, where a handful keeps order, they must handle dogs. Behind this fur-coated, fur-capped squad patrolling Parliament Hill in Ottawa rises the Parliament Building's Peace Tower. (November 1947, p. 571)

The functional role of animal transport in urban environments was replaced in the late 1950s with a nod to simplicity and old world charm. An image of horses pulling a tourist wagon was published in "British Columbia: Life Begins at 100" (August 1958): "Rubber-shod horses draw rubber-tired Tallyho, one of Victoria's open-air sightseeing coaches. The wagon team pauses for water beside one of the city's many flower-decked lampposts. Turreted Empress Hotel overlooks the inner harbor" (August 1958, p. 186).

A similar photograph was published in "Canada, My Country" (December 1961), "Sightseers' tallyho passes an art show and a flower-decked lamppost, one of 300 that brighten Victoria, capital of British Columbia. Red Hudson's Bay blankets shield riders against sea breezes" (December 1961, pp. 770-771).

And again a few years later ("Servant of Good Neighbors: Niagara Falls" April 1963): "Fringe-topped carriage rolls through Queen Victoria Park. Riders peer at American and Luna Falls" (April 1963).

Also in the 1960s, the depiction of traction animals of the early years was replaced with photographs of horse-drawn sleighs whose captions described the horse and sleigh transport with aesthetic appeal, but functional in ice and snow: "Study sleigh suffers no skids or stalls in Quebec icy upper town. France transplanted, the old section preserves Gallic charm with small hotels, intimate restaurants, and a chimneypot skyline. Horse-drawn taxi is known as a cariole" (December 1961, p. 807). "Dashing through the snow in one-horse and one-pony sleighs, mother and daughter defy the drifts of Ile d'Orléans" ("The St. Lawrence River, Key to Canada" May 1967, p. 660).

The rapid expansion of urban space means that areas once considered remote and rural are now bordered by suburban communities, and this transition was observed in the representation of animals in urban Canada. For instance in the narrative of a 1984 article, "Calgary: Canada's Not-so-wild West" (March 1984) was illustrated with an image of a group of people leading their horses through a suburban area:

> Saturday morning saunter takes Helene and Camile Savard and friends through a new subdivision. The Savards rent a nearby farm to stable their horses. Whether the land will soon sprout condominiums may hinge on the ability of Calgary's oil-dependent economy to avoid a prolonged stall and pick up where it left off. (March 1984, p. 402)

Common in the discourse of the article on the not-so-wild Calgary was a discussion of urbanization and its impact on animals. With a focus on the changing landscape from the Wild West to an urbanized community, the article was sprinkled with images of city life. Most notable among those images was a photograph of horses galloping across an open field with high-rises and skyscrapers of Calgary towering in the background, with a caption that read: "Unbridled sprits still range in Calgary, whose towering skyline reflects its dizzying transformation from cow town to prairie metropolis" (March 1984, pp. 378-379).

FUR BEARING ANIMALS

Raising animals for their fur was a consistent theme in the sample, particularly in the 1930s and 40s. For example, in the article "Ontario, Next Door" (August 1932), it was noted that fur farms "compensate for the retreat of free wild animals ... Canada operates many thousands" (August 1932, p. 165). In one illustration, a man held a fox wrapped around his neck, the animal's front and hind paws bound by the man's hands. The fox's eyes looked straight into the camera. While it is impossible to determine if the fox was alive, the caption informs us of his fate:

> Fox, lynx, beaver, mink, fisher, raccoon, skunk, marten, and muskrat all grow in captivity on Ontario fur farms. More fur of both wild and tame animals is marketed from Ontario than from any other province of Canada. Muskrat leads in all trapped pelts. By law, only Indians may trap otter and beaver. (August 1932, p. 155)

Some images conveyed messages that were different from the article text. For example, in the February 1935 article, a young girl was pictured on a wood fence with her companion, a silver fox. The picture depicted a relationship between the girl and the fox, but the text discussed a prevailing economically salient industry:

> when trappers caught these animals in warm weather, they kept them alive until fall, when the fur was prime. Since that time, fox farming has become an important industry, particularly in the Provinces of Ontario and Quebec and on Prince Edward Island. (February 1935, p. 189)

The discourse of fur farming was shrouded in ethical claims of good lives for the commoditized animal. For example, in "Men, Moose and Mink of Northwest Angle" (August 1947), the text claimed that: "ranch-raised mink live pampered lives in individual cages until their pelts are ready for a fur coat" (August 1947, p. 280).

Two photographs illustrated the article, one of two men standing amid fifty or more one-foot-by-one-foot wooden crates, each the home for a mink. The second picture shows a man holding two mink, both described in the text for their value as future garments:

> Shorty Joyce keeps a wary eye on two valuable mink. The mutation at left is a Royal Kohinoor, or black cross, whose pelt is esteemed for scarves. The other

is a silver blue, or platinum mink. Both types bring higher prices than the dark-brown pelts of standard mink. (August 1947, p. 283)

The next article on Canadian furs was published in 1961 in an article on a Montreal fashion show where women modeled mink jackets: "Magic of mink in a model's jacket stirs interest at a Montreal fur fashion show. Furriers prize Canadian pelts for luster and thickness, the gift of cold winters" (December 1961, p. 800).

By 1970 the cultural acceptance of raising animals for their fur had shifted, and the transformation was obvious in the next photograph published on furs. In "Canada's Heartland, the Prairie Provinces" (October 1970) a photograph of women modeling fake fur in Edmonton had the following caption: "Fake fur of Du Orlonm costing a fraction of the real thing, attract buyers at Hudson's Bay Company store in Edmonton. Still the largest fur dealer in the world, the company finds these coats popular among economy and conservation-minded customers" (October 1970, p. 456).

Conservation was also the topic of the representation of one of the most important fur bearing animals in Canada, the beaver:

> Conservation efforts have also revived the beaver, the amphibious rodent whose fur brought the white man into the north. He's a hardy beast with an ancestry going back to the age of mammoths–but then he was almost eight feet long and weighed 400 pounds. (October 1970, p. 482)

While fur was the dominant animal commodity mentioned in the articles, animals valued as livestock and food sources were occasionally pictured, such as the display of butchered animals in a window in Vancouver's China-town ("Canada's Window on the Pacific: The British Columbia Coast" March 1972), and a livestock show in Toronto:

> Prize-winning horses parade at a Toronto livestock show. Riders and horses from Germany, Austria, Sweden, Ireland, the United States, and elsewhere give the Royal Agricultural Winter Fair an international character. The amphitheater of the Royal Coliseum, with its buildings for cattle, sheep, and swine, covers 20 acres. (August 1932, p. 147)

Visuals and narratives of cattle drives north of Calgary illustrated the nostalgic narrative of traditional ways of raising food animals. In the October 1970 article, the caption read:

> Golden fingers of afternoon sunlight transfigure an Alberta scene that might have been lifted from the pages of a Western novel–an old-fashioned cattle drive. Rancher Bob Cosgrave and his crew round up the steers each autumn on 13,000 acres of land near Drumheller and drive them 45 miles to the 3,000 –acre family farm near Rosebud. There they are fattened and trucked to mar-

ket. Cosgrave nostalgically preserves the traditional drive because it affords a congenial get-together for his family and their neighbors. (October 1970, p. 483)

The problem of declining bird species traditionally hunted for food was also part of the narratives in the articles. In the article on the prairie provinces (October 1970) scientists examined pheasants and partridges who had died from eating poisoned seed:

> Victims of lethal grain, ring-necked pheasants and Hungarian partridges died from eating seed treated with mercury fungicide. Scientists in Edmonton check the amount of mercury in the tissue. Levels far above the limit for human consumption forced Alberta to close its 1969 hunting season on the birds. Officials have called for stricter control over use and disposal of mercury-treated grain. (October 1970, p. 477)

ANIMALS IN SPORT AND ENTERTAINMENT

Animals in urban Canada were frequently represented as useful in human sport and entertainment. An example of the value placed on sport animals was well illustrated in a photograph of a group of medical professionals at the University of Saskatchewan working to heal a Thoroughbred race horse who had a bone chip in his knee (October 1970).

However, Canadian animal sports focused primarily on dog-sled racing and rodeos. Dog-team racing was highlighted in multiple illustrations in the early article on Ottawa (August 1932):

> Race fans view the International Dog Derby at Ottawa. From Maine to Alaska mushers are lured by this exciting race. In one derby, when a dog fell and was hurt, its driver put it on his sled and finished the race with his team short one animal. The race is run in laps, over three days. In 1930 the 100-mile course was run in eight hours, 13 minutes, and 23 seconds. (August 1932, p. 150)

Canadian fondness for sled dogs, along with the unique characteristics of Canadian law that favored labouring animals, was also discussed in a narrative published in October 1970:

> A team of sled dogs had swerved into a front yard and killed a little girl's pet dachshund. Sergeant Beaudette declared the team innocent, since the law, which still favors working dogs, decrees that pets much be kept leashed. I talked to the sled dogs' owner, Mrs. Jane Sherman, an English immigrant who races her team as a hobby. She admitted their reputation for viciousness, but added, "The small dog most likely attacked the team. Little dogs have a suicidal tendency." Yet she preferred her team to snowmobiles, which have replaced dogs throughout much of the north. (October 1970, p. 450)

While early sport related narratives included a depiction of a hunt club ("A new sport starts in Ontario–the Toronto Hunt Club at Lady Eaton Farm") (August 1932, p. 144), rodeos, stampedes and chuck wagon races appeared to be the most popular animal sport activity in Canada. For instance, in December 1961, a man was photographed riding a bucking bronco as part of a celebration of Indian Days in Banff, Alberta. In October 1970, a photograph busy with galloping horses pulling chuck wagons in a race in the Calgary Stampede had this caption:

> Chuck wagons clatter in a figure eight around infield barrels, then pound down the track as drivers vie for $44,000 in prize money… It's all part of the ten-day Calgary Stampede, "when it's Saturday every night … and Canada's number-one cow town relives its boisterous past." (October 1970, p. 448-449) (see Image 1).

Calgary's famous chuck wagon race was depicted again in the article on Calgary (March 1984), with the substantial increase in prize money over the last 14 years, indicative of the popularity of the sport:

> Hell-bent for victory, drivers jockey for position as they thunder around the bend in a chuck-wagon race held during the Stampede. The competition origi-

Image 1. Chuck wagon race, published October 1970, p. 448-449 (copyright National Geographic Society).

nated, according to one legend, when the last crew to reach town was stuck with buying drinks. Entrants now vie for nearly $200,000 in prize money. (March 1984, pp. 398-399)

AESTHETIC ANIMALS IN URBAN CANADA

The animals appreciated for their beauty or rarity in the visuals and narratives of the articles were primarily free roaming wildlife species. There were only two photographs in the sample that illustrated the appeal of gazing upon animals who were not free roaming: a Beluga whale photographed in a marine exhibit at Vancouver Aquarium (April 1992) and a ceremonial goat pictured in "New St Lawrence Seaway Opens Great Lakes to the World" (March 1959). With these few exceptions, the vast majority of the images were of wild animals fondly observed resting, foraging or just passing through urban areas. For example, in August 1932, attracting wild animals to areas where they can be seen and enjoyed by people was celebrated in the caption for a photograph of wild geese in a sanctuary near Kingsville:

> Wild geese resting and feeding in an Ontario private sanctuary. Years ago, Jack Miner, an amateur naturalist, placed a few decoy geese on a small pond formed by an old brickyard excavation near Kingsville. For the first four years, no passing wild geese halted to visit the decoys; then 11 came. The following spring the 11 returned with 32 more; these migrated, returning the next season with about 250. Now, after 28 years, the ceaseless flights of wild geese calling at the sanctuary can no longer be counted. (August 1932)

In another passage, the allure of watching a variety of wild species in urban contexts was clearly conveyed:

> You should have (seen) a moose (who) wandered in near our Rivermead Golf Club; then off into the bush along the Ottawa River. And last year many early risers saw deer in the streets of Aylmer, near Ottawa; and one actually grazing in the grounds of the Aylmer convent. This year bears go so hungry, even near the busy city of Hull, just across the river in Quebec that farmers had to get up nights and go shooting, to save their pigs and sheep. (August 1932, pp. 155, 157)

Wild animals were not always represented as the observed, sometimes they were the observer. For example, in one interesting photograph from September 1966, there was a mutual gaze between human and animal: "Picture window works two ways: Apartment dweller in Banff admires a buck mule deer, which returns her stare. When snow becomes too deep at higher elevations, deer often move down into town and panhandle through the streets" (September 1966, pp. 370-371).

In March 1972, wild animals were depicted as an aesthetically pleasing amenity of a public park in Vancouver. The photograph featured swans and ducks swimming in a large body of water graced with a large working water fountain in the middle of the lake:

> Under winter's robe, Stanley Park offers a lonely haven to swans and ducks on Lost Lagoon. In summer as many as 20,000 people come each day. Only a 15-minute walk from Vancouver's heart, the park greets visitors with an aquarium and zoo, picnic grounds, beaches, swimming pools, a miniature railway, and playing fields. (March 1972, p. 344)

In a striking photograph published in August 1973 ("The Great Lakes: Is it Too Late?"), an image of a woman feeding geese was superimposed against the Toronto cityscape, providing a romanticized depiction of urban life, "Urban idyll" (August 1973) (see Image 2).

Linked to the theme that animals in urban areas provide enjoyment for humans, the need to conserve Canadian wildlife was always mentioned in connection with the problem of increasing urbanization. For example, a short

Image 2. Urban Idyll, woman feeding geese with Toronto cityscape in the background, published August 1973, p. 178-179 (copyright National Geographic Society).

article on one of the world's most endangered mammals, the Vancouver Island marmot, lamented the problem of urban development for perpetuating the decline of the species ("Perilous Future of Rare Marmots" June 2000). As part of conservation efforts, 27 (of only 62) individuals were taken to captive-breeding programs at the Calgary and Toronto zoos. The fascination with seeing almost-extinct species roaming near urban areas was also mentioned in the article:

> Just before reaching Edmonton, Alberta, we saw another creature saved from extinction by conservationists, the plains bison. Fifty million of them grazed the North American plans in the 1840's. Within 40 years only a few hundred survived in both Canada and the United States. (October 1970, p. 480)

But at the same time, the danger posed by wild species to humans who live close by was illustrated in another narrative in the article:

> One (wild buffalo) bull at Elk Island won a victory over a man a few years ago with a flip of his head. He tossed an automobile upside down into a ditch with its four tourist passengers inside. The owner sought damages from the park, but left quickly when warned he could be held liable if the animal had suffered an injury ... Tourists needn't fear–the bison haven't bothered a car or a visitor since. But (there is worry) ... about tourists who think a bison standing still is tame and can be petted. Don't try! (October 1970, p. 480)

In the same article, the background narrative for a photograph of five whooping cranes illustrated the excitement Canadians had for the preservation of some wild species:

> (Dennis invited me) ... to a prebreakfast search for some migrating whooping cranes reported to be nearby. Within an hour of leaving my hotel, Dennis spotted nearly one-eleventh of the world's wild population: four adults and one brown-and-white immature bird feeding in a wheat-stubble field. In hushed excitement, aware of our rare privilege, we photographed the elegant white birds–like ghosts returned from extinction. Intensive conservation efforts have raised their numbers from a total of 15 in 1941 to the present 56 wild and 23 captive birds. (October 1970)

On the other hand, it was interesting to find evidence that animal conservation in Canada was perceived to be in conflict with the sustenance of the indigenous Indian population. Buried in the narrative of the article on the prairie provinces, "(A) young Indian commented bitterly, "Canada shows more interest in preserving its whooping cranes than its Indians" (October 1970, p. 473).

In the article, "Dream On, Vancouver" (October 1978), there was an interesting image of Canada geese crossing a road single file in front of a lineup of cars, the animals were described not as pests or problems disrupting traffic, but rather as appealing wildlife: "Honkers meet honkers. Early morning rush-hour traffic awaits a file of Canada geese in Vancouver, where the brisk pace of life defers to the enjoyment of nature." (October 1978, pp. 490-491).

The link between urbanization and some wildlife species was acknowledged from early 1930 to the late 1980s:

> Certain species, like the catbird, seem to follow human settlements ... We learn more about bird migratory habits as Canadian towns multiply northward ... I have seen warblers that were not supposed to come to Canada ... I have also discovered here a few rare instances of water birds known previously only along the Atlantic coast ... Migrating swans, resting on Niagara River, are sometimes swept over the falls to their death, not realizing the danger till it is too late. Many hundreds were so drowned in the spring of 1932. (August 1932, p. 165)

The danger of urbanization to wildlife was illustrated in one compelling narrativein "The Great Lakes Troubled Waters" (July 1987). A brace of Pekin ducks was photographed waddling across a dreary, scorched landscape near a steel plant:

> Shock troops for science, Pekin ducks forage near a steel plant at Windermere Basin–a waterfowl wintering site on western Lake Ontario. The Canadian Wildlife Service uses the ducks to test pollution effects. After six weeks most ducks had high levels of lead and PCBs–and most died. (July 1987, p. 24)

It is important to note that the ducks were allowed the freedom to roam in their wintering site, a landscape now contaminated by industrial pollution. Their presence was used as a scientific experiment, with their health sacrificed as an indicator of human-induced environmental problems caused by technological advancement.

ANIMALS OUT OF PLACE IN URBAN CANADA

While there were few references to animals out of place in the articles on urban Canada, those few were compelling examples of how problem animals were perceived. In a compelling article on "Henry Hudson's Changing Bay" (March 1982), the wildlife abundant close to the town of Churchill, Manitoba,[5] was highlighted, but the focus was on the local polar bears who:

> rule Cape Churchill in October and November when they migrate onto the frozen bay to stalk ringed seals. From 1,200 to 2,000 bears roam the western

bay; in the late 1960s biologists discovered one of the world's largest polar bear denning sites about 40 miles southeast of Churchill. (March 1982, p. 392)

But these polar bears are clearly depicted as problem animals for the town. In an image of a bear up on his hind legs peering into a bus had this caption: "Unbearably savory aroma of frying bacon lures a brazen (bear) panhandler... Tourists book Churchill's four hotels months in advance for the Polar Bear Alert during October and November" (March 1982, pp. 394-395).

Another striking image showed a soot-covered, not-so-white polar bear rummaging in a fiery garbage dump with the number 13 spray-painted on his side. The caption explained the context of the photograph:

> Waiting for the bay to freeze, bears invade the town and scavenge its nearby dump. Biologists use dye to identify chronically aggressive bears; three to five repeat offenders must be destroyed every year. Lucky Number 13, a subadult male, avoided the dump last season. A compromise solution will provide holding pens until free-up for as many as 16 problem bears. Meanwhile, "A safe polar bear is a distant polar bear" remains Churchill's commonsense slogan. (March 1982, p. 395)

The town of Churchill was the subject of two additional articles in *National Geographic*, almost 60 years apart. In "Birds of Timberline and Tundra" (September 1946), the town was highlighted as a haven for the observation of wild bird species, and in February 2004 a short front matter blurb on the polar bears did not mention the bears as problems but only as local wildlife who are safe to observe by tourists riding in customized, big-wheeled tundra buses, "You can watch bears from the vehicles for hours, and bears often come close to watch you."

In another example of animals out of place, three black bears were photographed taking their breakfast at a table fully set and waiting for the human diners ("Canadian Rockies: Lords of Beckoning Land" September 1966): "Who wants porridge when a full-course breakfast awaits the taking? Three black bears, ambling onto the lawn of the Jasper Park Lodge, spied the laden table and helped themselves. An alert college-student maid snapped the once-in-a-lifetime picture" (September 1966).

While the bears were depicted as not belonging at the breakfast table, the narrative gave the incident a humorous tone, representing the bears as wildlife who were opportunistic in obtaining food and praising the smart young woman who photographed a rare and special wildlife viewing event.

CONCLUSION

Our study documents three broad thematic areas in the depiction of animals in urban Canada in *National Geographic* magazine. The first theme was "useful animals" as sources of labour (pulling sleds and tourist trolleys), recreation (rodeos and racing events), and commodities (fur bearing and food animals). The second theme was "aesthetic animals" (wild species enjoyed for their beauty or rarity), and the third theme was "animals out of place" (wildlife who are disruptive in urban areas).

The image of traction animals changed over the 70 year period, from the traditional depiction of animals at work in the 1930s (dogs pulling mail carts, oxen towing farm equipment) to the "old world charm" of horses pulling tourist trolleys and small sleighs in the 50s and 60s. In 1984, and illustrative of the rapid increase in urbanization, horses were photographed galloping wild and free in a field with an urban skyline in the background. The 1930s and 40s also had numerous images of fur production (foxes draped over human shoulders or sitting placidly next to a child, photographs of furs being modeled in fashion shows), and the early discourse on the activity of fur farming claimed that fur bearing animals live pampered lives until their pelts are ready. Food animals did not have much of a presence in the articles, only a few in the 1970s: cattle drives and the problem of accidentally poisoned pheasants and partridges. Animals in sport and entertainment were frequently pictured, particularly dog-sled racing and chuck wagon races. Dog-sled racing was popular in the early years through 1970; chuck wagon racing in the 1970s and 1980s.

Animals out-of-place in urban Canada were bears: black bears helping themselves to breakfast at a table set for humans diners and the polar bears of Churchill, Manitoba, who were (and still are) problems for the town. During the fall, polar bears are marooned on land waiting for the bay to freeze over, and they roam the town and the garbage dumps looking for food. The polar bear representations depicted the bears' wildness while ensuring they exist in a contained context. The co-construction of space shared by humans and wildlife becomes an intricate balance in aesthetics and domination, where humans assume animals are free to explore and thrive, but where management strategies and physical barriers confine and restrict species' movements. While images that depict the connection between wildlife and the urban environment often attempt to "tame" the wild, referencing human qualities in a particular animal or species, the Churchill bears were exemplary of "liminal" animals, or wild species who take advantage of human food and/or shelter. While some liminal animals are represented as pollution incarnate, as disgusting, valueless or "trash" (Nagy & Johnson, 2013), the Churchill bears were pictured as bothersome only in that they were scavengers, who, as argued by Corman (2011), physically and socially disrupt the place of garbage in society by reconfiguring it as food and drawing attention to human wastefulness. Unfortunately, this relatively positive social discourse on the Churchill bears may be shifting. There was an incident in November 2013 between a polar bear and two humans in Churchill that ended with the humans hospitalized and two bears dead having been "dispatched" by conservation officers.[6] In human-carnivore conflicts, the animal almost always ends up dead, killed as a cautionary measure to control problem predators.

The themes of animals in urban Canada depicted as useful, aesthetically pleasing or out of place documented in our work have a striking resemblance to the argument recently posed by Ingram (2013) that Canada's conservative response to animal welfare since the 19th century reflects the country's upper and middle-class dependence "on animals as resources, sources of labour, and objects of sport" (p. 221). We found substantial evidence of a focus on using animals for economic gain, particularly the raising of animals for fur and food and using horses and dogs in sport and entertainment activities that offer large cash prizes. However, the representation of the fur industry in Canada changed over the time period under study, indicating that the traditional conceptions of the treatment of commodity animals were being challenged. By the 1970s the cultural acceptance of raising animals for their fur had shifted to a more welfare-oriented perspective. However, we found no evidence of a shift in the public discourse on using animals in sport or for labour; indeed, in the discussion of the Canadian fondness for sled dogs during the 1970s, we found mention of the Canadian law that favored laboring animals over domestic animal companions, supporting Ingram's (2013) claim that the country still depends on animals as resources, particularly as objects of labour and sport.

The one consistent and overwhelming theme throughout the sample was the enjoyment humans derived from watching wild animals. Aesthetic animals were represented as lovely-to-behold wildlife–swans and ducks floating in an urban lake, moose sighted at a golf club, wild geese, whooping cranes, deer, bison and beaver–all of whom were depicted in photographs and narratives as species valued for their aesthetic appeal. This theme was observed throughout the sample, from the early 1930s to the end of the century. In these stories, the co-existence of humans and wildlife is beautiful, desirable and enhances our urban experience, as noted by the caption for the image: "honkers (cars) meet honkers (geese), where the brisk pace of life defers to the enjoyment of nature." In some urban contexts the aesthetically-pleasing animals observed in our sample would be considered pests or problems, such as the geese and deer, but in urban Canada, these species are appreciated.

It would be interesting to conduct a content analysis of the representation of animals in urban areas of other western countries to compare the results with those found here for urban Canada. As Wolch (2002, 733) has argued, "the moral compass of human-animal relations in the city is shifting and, like so many other aspects of city life, is subject to constant renegotiation." If the cultural meanings of animals are linked to the historically-specific norms and values of the society in which they occur, then there might be less emphasis on animals as resource in the US and England, for example, given their traditions of a deeper engagement with the animal welfare movement than has been the case in Canada (Ingram, 2013). Such a comparative analysis would be of great value in a deeper understanding of how popular culture images of animals reflect cultural messages and historical shifts in the social discourse on animals, as has been found for our study of animals in urban Canada.

ACKNOWLEDGMENTS

This research was funded by a grant from the National Science Foundation (Award SES-1247824).

REFERENCES

Alexander, S. M., & Quinn, M. S. (2011). Coyote (canis latrans) interactions with humans and pets reported in the Canadian print media (1995–2010). *Human Dimensions of Wildlife, 16*, 345–359.

Arluke, A., & Bogdan, R. (2010). *Beauty and the beast: Human-animal relations as revealed in real photo postcards, 1905–1935*. Syracuse, NY: Syracuse University Press.

Atkins, P. (Ed.). (2012). *Animal cities: Beastly urban histories*. Burlington, VT: Ashgate Publishing Group.

Beier, P. (1991). Cougar attacks on humans in the United States and Canada. *Wildlife Society Bulletin, 19*, 403–412.

Bocking, S. (2005). The nature of cities: Perspectives in Canadian urban environmental history. *Urban History Review, 34*, 3–8.

Broadfoot, J. D., Rosatte, R. C., & O'Leary, D. T. (2001). Raccoon and skunk population models for urban disease control planning in Ontario, Canada. *Ecological Applications, 11*(1), 295–303.

Campbell, M. O. (2009). The impact of habitat characteristics on bird presence and the implications for wildlife management in the environs of Ottawa, Canada. *Urban Forestry & Urban Greening, 8*(2), 87–95.

Campbell, M., & Lancaster. B. (2010). Public attitudes toward black bears (ursus americanus) and cougars (puma concolor) on Vancouver Island. *Society and Animals, 18*(1), 40–57.

Campbell, M. O. (2013). The relevance of age and gender for public attitudes to brown bears (ursus arctos), black bears (ursus americanus), and cougars (puma concolor) in Kamloops, British Columbia. *Society and Animals, 21*, 341–359.

Catalano, S., Lejeune, M., Liccioli, S., Verocai, G. G., Gesy, K. M., Jenkins, E. J., Kutz, S. J., Fuentealba, C., Duignan, P. J., & Massolo, A. (2012). Echinococcus multilocularis in urban coyotes, Alberta, Canada. *Emerging Infectious Diseases, 18*(10), 1625–1628.

Corman, L. (2011). Getting their hands dirty: Raccoons, freegans, and urban 'trash'. *Journal for Critical Animal Studies, IX*, 28–61.

Donaldson, S., & Kymlicka, W. (2011). *Zoopolis: A political theory of animal rights*. New York, NY: Oxford University Press.

Dunaway, F. (2008). *Natural visions: The power of images in American environmental reform*. Chicago, IL: University of Chicago Press.

Fitzgerald, A. J. (2007). They gave me a reason to live: the protective effects of companion animals on the suicidality of abused women. *Humanity and Society, 31*, 355–378.

Found, R., & Boyce, M. S. (2011). Predicting deer–vehicle collisions in an urban area. *Journal of Environmental Management, 92*(10), 2486–2493.

Gaskell, I. (1991). History of images. In P. Burke (Ed.), *New perspectives on historical writing* (pp. 168–192). Cambridge, England: Polity Press.

Gilbert, F. F. (1982). Public attitudes toward urban wildlife: A pilot study in Guelph, Ontario. *Wildlife Society Bulletin, 10*(3), 245–253.

Gillis, N. C., Rapp, T., Hasler, C., Wachelka, H., & Cooke, S. J. (2010). Spatial ecology of adult muskellunge (esox masquinongy) in the urban Ottawa reach of the historic Rideau Canal, Canada. *Aquatic Living Resources, 23*(2), 225–230.

Griffiths, H., Poulter, I., & Sibley, D. (2000). Feral cats in the city. In C. Philo, & C. Wilbert (Eds.), *Animal spaces, beastly places: New geographies of human-animal relations* (pp. 59–72). New York, NY: Routledge.

Ingram, D. (2013). Beastly measures: Animal welfare, civil society, and state policy in Victorian Canada. *Journal of Canadian Studies, 47*, 221–252.

Jardine, C., Lindsay, L. R., Nicholson, V. M., Ojkic, D., & Prescott, J. F. (2011). Longitudinal study on the seroprevalence of avian influenza, leptospirosis, and tularemia in an urban population of raccoons (procyon lotor) in Ontario, Canada. *Vector-Borne and Zoonotic Diseases, 11*(1), 37–42.

Jerolmack, C. (2008). How pigeons became rats: The cultural-spatial logic of problem animals. *Social Problems, 55*, 72–94.

Jerolmack, C. (2013). *The global pigeon*. Chicago, IL: University of Chicago Press.

Kalof, L., & Fitzgerald, A. (2003). Reading the trophy: Exploring the display of dead animals in hunting magazines. *Visual Studies, 18*, 112–122.

Kalof, L. (2007). *Looking at animals in human history*. London, England: Reaktion.

Kalof, L., & Amthor, R. F. (2010). Cultural representations of problem animals in *National Geographic*. *Etudes Rurales, 185*, 165–180.

Kalof, L. (2015). The shifting iconography of wolves over the 20th century. In P. Masium, & J. Sprenger (Eds.), *A fairy tale in question: Historical interactions between humans and wolves*. Isle of Harris, Scotland: White Horse Press.

Kellert, S. R., Black, M., Rush, C. R., & Bath, A. J. (1996). Human culture and large carnivore conservation in North America. *Conservation Biology, 10*(4), 977–990.

Labrecque, J., & Walsh, C. A. (2011). Homeless women's voices on incorporating companion animals into shelter services. *Anthrozoos, 24*(1), 79–95.

Lancaster, R. K., & Rees, W. E. (1979). Bird communities and the structure of urban habitats. *Canadian Journal of Zoology, 57*(12), 2358–2368.

Lu, J., Ryu, H., Hill, S., Schoen, M., Ashbolt, N., Edge, T. A., & Domingo, J. S. (2011). Distribution and potential significance of a gull fecal marker in urban coastal and riverine areas of southern Ontario, Canada. *Water Research, 45*(13), 3960–3968.

Morand-Ferron, J., Lalande, E., & Giraldeau, L. (2009). Large-scale input matching by urban feral pigeons (columba livia). *Ethology, 115*(7), 707–712.

Mos, L., Jack, J., Cullon, D., Montour, L., Alleyne, C., & Ross, P. S. (2004). The importance of marine foods to a near-urban first nation community in coastal British Columbia, Canada: Toward a risk-benefit assessment. *Journal of Toxicology and Environmental Health, Part A, 67*(8–10), 791–808.

Nagy, K., & Johnson, P. D. (Eds.). (2013). *Trash animals: How we live with nature's filthy, feral, invasive and unwanted species*. Minneapolis, MN: University of Minnesota Press.

Nolan, J. M., Jones, K. E. McDougal, K. W., McFarlin, M. J., & Ward, M. K. (2006). The lovable, the loathsome and the liminal: Emotionality in ethnozoological cognition. *Journal of Ethnobiology, 26*, 126–138.

O'Connell, M. F., & Gibson, R. J. (1989). The maturation of anadromous female Atlantic salmon, salmo salar l., stocked in a small pond in urban St John's, Newfoundland, Canada. *Journal of Fish Biology, 34*(6), 937–946.

Perrin, T. (2009). The business of urban animals survey: The facts and statistics on companion animals in Canada. *The Canadian Veterinary Journal, 50*(1), 48–52.

Phaneuf, D., DesGranges, J. L., Plante, N., & Rodrigue, J. (1995). Contamination of local wildlife following a fire at a polychlorinated biphenyls warehouse in St. Basile le Grand, Quebec, Canada. *Archives of Environmental Contamination and Toxicology, 28*(2), 145–153.

Philo, C. (1998). Animals, geography and the city: Notes on inclusions and exclusions. In J. Wolch, & J. Emel (Eds.), *Animal geographies: Place, politics and identity in the nature-culture borderlands* (pp. 51–71). New York, NY: Verso.

Racey, G. D., & Euler, D. L. (1982). Small mammal and habitat response to shoreline cottage development in central Ontario. *Canadian Journal of Zoology, 60*(5), 865–880.

Ritvo, H. (2007). Animal planet. In L. Kalof, & A. Fitzgerald (Eds.), *The animals reader: The essential classic and contemporary writings* (pp. 29–140). Oxford, UK: Berg.

Rosatte, R. C. (2000). Management of raccoons (procyon lotor) in Ontario, Canada: Do human intervention and disease have significant impact on raccoon populations? *Mammalia, 64*(4), 369–390.

Schubert, C. A., Rosatte, R. C., MacInnes, C. D., & Nudds, T. D. (1998). Rabies control: An adaptive management approach. *The Journal of Wildlife Management, 62*(2), 622–629.

Sontag, S. (2003). *Regarding the pain of others.* New York, NY: Picador.

Thornton, C., & Quinn, M. S. (2009). Coexisting with cougars: Public perceptions, attitudes, and awareness of cougars on the urban-rural fringe of Calgary, Alberta, Canada. *Human-Wildlife Conflicts, 3*, 282–295.

Tremblay, M. A., & St. Clair, C. C. (2011). Permeability of a heterogeneous urban landscape to the movements of forest songbirds. *Journal of Applied Ecology, 48*(3), 679–688.

Whiting, E. R., & Clifford, H. F. (1983). Invertebrates and urban runoff in a small northern stream, Edmonton, Alberta, Canada. *Hydrobiologia, 102*(1), 73–80.

Whitley, C. T., & Kalof, L. (2014). Animal imagery in the discourse of climate change. *International Journal of Sociology, 44*, 10–33.

Wolch, J. (1998). Zoopolis. In J. Wolch, & J. Emel (Eds.), *Animal geographies: Place, politics and identity in the nature-culture borderlands* (pp. 119–138). New York, NY: Verso.

Wolch, J. R., Gullo, A., & Lassiter, U. (1997). Changing attitudes toward California cougars. *Society & Animals, 5*, 96–116.

Wolch, J. (2002). Anima urbis. *Progress in Human Geography, 26*, 721–742.

NOTES

1. See   http://www.psmag.com/navigation/health-and-behavior/protect-battered-women-protect-pets-67241/

2. The entire contents of the magazine from 1888 to 2011 are available electronically on CDs. It is possible we missed some relevant articles, but the National Geographic archive of full issues on CD is only searchable using their standard search function.

3. There was one image placed in a Miscellaneous category because it did not fit one of the major themes: an ice sculpture of a polar bear in Quebec City (May 1967).

4. We give the full name of the article and the month and year of publication at the first mention. To avoid repetition, after the first mention we cite only the publication month and year.

5. Churchill, Manitoba, is the smallest urban area in our sample, with approximately 813 residents in 2011. We include Churchill because of its reputation as "polar bear capital of the world" and because a similarly small town (Cobalt, in northern Ontario, with 1,133 residents in 2011) was included in Bocking's (2005) review of Canadian urban environmental history.

6. http://www.cbc.ca/news/canada/manitoba/man-woman-attacked-by-polar-bear-in-churchill-1.2325208

Chapter Eight

Rationalizing Natural Horsemanship

Bridging the Interspecies (and Subcultural) Divide through the Language of Equus[1]

Shawn McEntee

INTRODUCTION

Human capacity for language and the accompanying ability to symbol, afforded by the size and function of the human prefrontal cortex, has long been seen as the defining difference between human and non-human animal species. Research increasingly supports that this is a distinction of scale rather than kind, however, by revealing the existence of complex communication systems and cultures in a number of non-human species. As the species with the far greater capacity for reason, it is incumbent upon humans to bridge the species divide and find ways to ensure the survival of others who share our living space. Learning to cross the species divide may well also provide strategies for dealing with deep social conflicts manifest in our increasingly complex society.

Human progress writ large has inexorably specialized and rationalized all human-animal relationships, as it has human social relationships with a wide range of other social phenomena. Demographic shifts, industrialization, urbanization, and other structural social changes marking human progress into the contemporary world have increased social distance between many large herd animal species (among others) and majorities of human populations at the same time that they have lessened social distance between humans and their companion animals. Over the past 100 years, human interaction with horses has changed dramatically; from transportation and labor to largely

127

recreational, horses today qualify in many ways as pets, and yet due to their nature cannot achieve companion animal status.[2]

The argot and practice of Natural Horsemanship, including Equus, is an increasingly rationalized mode of communication between horse and human; like other sub-cultural world-views, it is self-reinforcing. Like all forms of code-switching and associated language skills, Natural Horsemanship/Equus provides practitioners with deepened capacities to understand the other. This human capacity to understand the other has always been fundamental: the essence of human creativity and key to species survival through adaptation to all manner of variations in environment. No less so today; human capacities to understand and empathize with the other, however defined, are crucial to finding solutions to myriad social problems our path to a better life has created.

INDUSTRIALIZATION AND THE SOCIAL RESTRUCTURING OF HORSE-HUMAN RELATIONSHIPS

Specialization and formalization of the social role of the horse accompanying the industrial revolution set the stage for a rationalized interspecies communication known today as Natural Horsemanship. Demographics of human-horse populations over the period of industrialization mark this shift. According to Kilby (2007) numbers of horses in the United States has been rising since the 1960s which marked the lowest population of horses in the U.S. in the modern era, a steadily declining number since its high in 1915. The Model T Ford, introduced in 1908, went into mass production between 1910 and 1915; Spielmaker and Lacy (2006) triggering a dramatic shift in the social role of horses in the U.S. and Europe. Shifts in both human and horse populations between 1915 and 1960 were rapid and accompanied dramatic restructuring of lived experiences. By 1960, the U.S. was arguably fully industrialized and on the cusp of moving into a "post-industrial" societal organization (e.g., Spielmaker & Lacy, 2006; Wyatt & Hecker, 2006). Arguably the peak year of the horse in the U.S. was 1915 Kilby (2007); when the population of horses was the greatest recorded up to that time at 26.5 million Kilby (2007); the human population of 100.5 (U.S. Census Bureau, 2000) was less than 4 times larger. The lowest population of horses was recording 1960 at approximately 3.05 million Kilby (2007); the growth in the human population over the same time period to 180.7 million in 1960 (U.S. Census Bureau, 2012, Table 2) shifted the ratio from more than 1 horse for 4 people in 1915 to just less than 1 horse for 60 people by 1960.

The accompanying loss of farms and changes in farm production processes, as well as the shift to more urbanized population centers included sweeping changes in the structure of the economy and transportation patterns that constituted industrialization (e.g., Spielmaker & Lacy, 2006; Wyatt & Hecker, 2006). The lived experiences of those who came of age prior to 1915 differ dramatically from those who came of age after 1960 or more recently in that only a small minority of the latter group are likely to have primary socialization experiences that included horses.

After industrialization, understanding of the nature of large herd animals in general and horses in particular was no longer a broad cultural phenomenon; those for whom interaction with horses was part of daily life had become a small subculture by 1960. Land, some shelter, and extra food for grazers whose ability to graze is limited by their work has always been necessary to keep horses healthy which means that relative affluence has always been characteristic of the social groups who keep horses (Lawrence, 1988; Stowe, 2012). In the late 1800s in the U.S., some of those affluent enough to do so, chose to maintain horses despite the structural strain accompanying industrialization that pushed horses out of their roles as economic assets. Despite the precipitous decline in horse populations in the U.S. beginning in 1915, evidence suggests that the symbolic value of horses has both broadened and deepened. Transitioning of the horse from an instrumental role in the economy to its affective role today is attributable to the social construction of a global network of formal organizations that rationalized human-horse relationships through specialization.

SPECIALIZATION OF THE ROLE OF THE HORSE

The specialization, diversification, and formalization of horse–human relationships reflected in the Appendix's brief overview of meso-level social organization(s) demonstrates the collective agency of horse-people to maintain meaningful relationships with animals they love in a challenging social structural context. In the period between early 20th Century and Mid-Century, and particularly the inter war years and post-World War II years, use of horses for recreational purposes broadened and deepened at the same time that it involved an increasingly smaller proportion of the U.S. population. As is clear from the Appendix, horses were sufficiently valued in the late 1800s that several organizations extant today, formed in support of horse-human interaction. What is now the United States Equestrian Federation (USEF) and the Federation Equestre Internationale (FEI, called the International Equestrian Federation in the U.S.) formed in the early 20th century; more specialized others formed by 1950. Much of the specialization in horse-human relationships today is evidenced in organizations formed since 1960 which are increasingly consolidated in the international organization of the FEI; the restructuring that resulted in today's USEF, and the transformation of the United States Equestrian Team (USET) into a foundation supporting it.

As noted broadly in sociological literature, affluence is associated with agency to structure and maintain formal organizations supporting individual and group interests; education, financial resources, time, and in the case of horses, land, all contribute to the social capital horse people used, and continue to use, in maintaining relationships with their horses and the organizational infrastructure supporting human-horse activities. The affluence required to maintain horses at the beginning of industrialization is characteristic of the social class of today's horse-owners as well (Stowe, 2012). The rise of horse populations since the 1960s is evidence of the successful formalization of horse-human relationships throughout early industrialization; it also accompanies expanded global affluence in the Post World War II era.

ON A PERSONAL (AND SOCIOLOGICAL) NOTE: PERSONAL EXPERIENCE

I represent a minority in the horse-world today. As a sociologist whose introspection about my role in a complex social world served as a catalyst for my Ph.D., I have put my academic skills to use in casual observation of the horse-subculture I grew up in. More recently, I've put those skills to use studying relationships between horse people and natural horsemanship enthusiasts, a borderline counter culture within which I am deeply embedded. I do most of my own training and worked as a horse trainer/barn laborer for a couple of years between undergrad and grad-school but my business is not horses. Unlike many in the horse world I inhabit, I had the advantage of being socialized directly by horses; I was nine years old when my mother talked my father into buying the family horse. My grandparents were not farmers and I grew up in suburbia, but for half my pre-college life, we were at the barn daily - every afternoon after school, for Saturday morning lessons and Sunday afternoon rides. The man who provided a great deal of my primary socialization with horses, Mr. Carter, was part of the subculture that kept horses as part of their daily lives. Mr. Carter owned and ran the farm where we kept our horse for the first 8 years. It never occurred to him that we should not know all the ins and outs of our horses' daily care, including feeding, medical needs, and horse, barn, and equipment maintenance. Mr. Carter, in his 70s in the 1960s, as were my grandparents with whom I also spent a great deal of time as a child, came of age at a time when horses permeated daily life. My grandmother used to drive her pony to school, a fact which was juxtaposed with my grandfather's deep fear of horses resulting from interaction with his own childhood pony that he swore was mean. As a result, a great deal of my primary socialization involved horses, both directly and indirectly; most of my primary agents of socialization were either horses or people who had themselves come of age in a horse-permeated world. In short, my observation is this: there is a marked difference (anecdotal though it might be) between the horse people I know who acquired their horses as adults and those like me whose primary socialization included daily interaction with large herd and prey animals, namely horses, and that difference is apparent as a horse-sense that makes interaction with horses less fraught than for those who join the horse world as adults.

DIFFERENCES BETWEEN HORSE PEOPLE AND NATURAL HORSEMANSHIP ENTHUSIASTS

In the horse world, it is common to hear about accidents that result in permanent injury even to life-long horse people. Christopher Reeves' accident is an extreme example but not unusual; broken limbs, concussions, and other lesser aches and pains from daily interaction with horses is normal. I sprained an ankle badly as a child; was bitten hard enough, and in the right place, that my arm would go numb if I bumped the spot for at least 6 months after the bite; one of my childhood friends got a concussion from falling off; my sister has chronic back pain associated with riding as a child; I once took my mother to the emergency room to get stitches after being kicked by a horse. I've had a concussion, broken ribs, and torn ligaments in my knee, all from the same fall off my current horse, and I manage lower back pain and a torn rotator cuff with therapeutic activities and OTC pain relievers in order to maintain my riding activities - as do MOST of the people I know who ride! Although I suspect most of these kinds of chronic injury and pain issues exist in all subgroups who are extreme athletes in one way or another, as in other similar subcultures, they set us apart from broader society and serve as a boundary markers between real horse-people and non-horse people.

HORSE PEOPLE ARE PEOPLE SOCIALIZED BY HORSES–LIVING WITH PAIN

Grandin and Jones (2005) make the argument that humans and horses, like humans and dogs, have co-evolved; essentially, it is natural for domestic horses to participate in human communities just as it is for dogs to do so.[3] Equine physiological differences from humans are related to brain function and horse behavior; as herd and prey animals, equine habitus is markedly different from generally agreed upon human habitus. Grandin and Jones (2005) refer to humans as generalists and to animals (and autistic people) as specifics; humans are likely to see the whole picture while horses are likely to focus on details. Larger and more developed pre-frontal lobes in human brains allow humans to see connections, relationships, and to generalize from situation to situation–in other words, our brains are the basis of our adaptabil-

ity. In contrast, the weaker and smaller cortexes of animals mean that information taken in through the senses does not get processed–it stays at the raw
data level. In prey animals in general and in horses specifically, their sensitivity to their surroundings and ability to translate raw data into action (acting
on instinct), means that humans are very likely to miss the thing that sets
horses on edge and propels them away from dangerous situations. And this is
the essence of the species biological divide. Humans have to *think* about
what might be dangerous for horses; horses don't–they simply know. Flight,
rather than fight, is the much more likely behavior in the face of (potential)
danger, and flight is likely to happen before humans have the chance to
notice and react in time to go with or get out of the way. Knowing this
subconsciously, or from a sociological perspective, having internalized this
knowledge, is generally what is meant by the term horse sense.

As do all extreme athletes and military personnel for example, horse-
people wear our injuries and our bruises with a certain amount of pride; they
allow us to boast about our exploits, share our experiences, and tell war
stories. Most of us are quick to point out that it was not (directly at least), the
horse's fault; often some other human who lacks horse sense (and more often
ourselves) play the role of proximate cause. Even with fairly good (most of
the time) horse sense, in the past year, I've been knocked down by the same
horse (not mine) twice; once into a mud-puddle in 45 degree weather (after
which I rode because I was wearing polar fleece) and a couple of months ago,
onto hard ground (we'd had no rain for a couple of weeks). My current horse
once kicked a friend of mine leaving a hoof-print shaped bruise that ultimately discolored her leg from knee to hip and took months (literally) to fade
entirely–which everyone agrees, her included, resulted from a lack of horse-
sense. A 60-ish woman broke her hand the weekend before a horse-show I
was co-managing recently and rode in the show; she and I joked about the
fact that a friend of hers had reported that she would not be riding because of
the accident. My older horse kicked at a veterinarian who had just injected
his hocks which I realized when I heard the metallic sound of my horse's
shoe as it hit the vet's wedding ring; he looked at his hand, shook it, glanced
at my (horrified) face and neither of us said a word.

Boundary maintenance between horse-people and non-horse people is
about recognizing how human behavior can set horses off and acknowledges
that when our awareness or sensitivity to the animals we choose to spend our
lives with is off or insufficient, getting hurt is simply to be expected. If our
horse-sense is low (for whatever reason), we deserve what we get. Horse
sense is a form of cognitive dissonance that allows horse people to manage
our daily interactions with animals we love who outweigh us by factors
approaching 10 and who see the world very differently than we do! For those
of us whose primary socialization included significant involvement of horses
as agents of our socialization, this acceptance of human error and the inevita-

bility of getting hurt through lack of awareness results from an internalized understanding of horse culture; the willingness to accept risk associated with human fallibility in reading horses is part of our core identities and our sense of self. We are horse people in all senses of the term.

In contrast, new generations of horse-owners are reflective of and represent changes in social relationships between humans and horses; they are much more likely to regard all domestic animals - including horses - as pets and companion animals rather than livestock and laborers (Birke & Brandt, 2009; Brandt, 2004; Fox, 2000; Stowe, 2012). Since the 1960s, the group of pleasure horse owners has expanded to include many who achieved adulthood in the absence of any regular interaction with large herd animals and have only idealized notions of how to (safely) interact with horses. As a group, they resist deeply entrenched practices of horse wrangling and breaking that reflect a subculture with roots in the use of horses for labor and transportation. The transition to achieving horse-person status can be rough for this new generation of horse owners. Their affluence, combined with their need, has driven the formalization and institutionalization of Natural horsemanship, which increasingly represents a highly rationalized[4] mode of horse-human interaction.

INTRODUCTION TO THE LANGUAGE OF EQUUS

Natural Horsemanship teaches humans to recognize and accurately interpret horse behavior; it also gives us the skills to respond effectively to horse behavior so that we can become good leaders (and partners) for our horses. Roberts (1997) rightly calls it the language of Equus because it is a contextualized and holistic understanding; it is deeply nuanced and conveys a LOT of meaning through interaction–in this case, interaction across a species divide (Savvides, 2012; Smart, 2011). I agree with Roberts' labeling of Equus a language; the label indicates that Equus is more than a highly sophisticated system of signals and signs although it is definitely that. Equus qualifies as a language because it requires at least some symbolic interpretation, developed through interaction, on the part of BOTH humans and horses (see Birke, 2007; Birke & Brandt, 2009).

All of natural horsemanship is built on the idea that communication between horses and humans must follow a model of communication patterns horses use with each other. Most emphasize that humans must take on a leadership role in relation to their horse although, for me at least, the specifics of this role is one of the biggest dividing lines within Natural Horsemanship subcultures. Dorrance and Desmond (1999), Dorrance and Porter (1987), Irwin (2000), Kohanov (2001; 2003), Parelli (1993), Rashid (2000), Resnick (2005), and Roberts (1997) all describe the human leadership role as assertive but essentially cooperative and respectful. Rashid (2000) uses the phrase passive leadership to describe how horses who avoid conflict with others provide a safe space for horses lower in the herd hierarchy. Resnick (2005) makes a distinction between leaders and dominant horses by pointing out that respected leaders in the horse world are those who avoid conflict and lead by example. Lyons, Anderson, and Miller (1999) include elements of domination in their definitions of leadership (in fact, Miller (1999) who was in his late 60s when he wrote it actually claims leadership and domination is the same thing). Maybe it's because I'm a girl and we still live in a sexist and patriarchal world that I am so sensitive to this, but to me, there is a very big difference between a partnership (which I want with my horse) and a relationship of dominance in which the majority of the power is held by one member all the time (see Birke & Brandt, 2009; Brandt, 2004; Whipper, 2000).

Ethology is increasing our understanding of large herd animal behavior through high quality observation and biological study of horses, both domestic and feral, and other large prey animal species including cattle, buffalo, bison, elk, caribou, even deer as well as others. Much of this research informs the teaching of Natural Horsemanship because it deepens our understanding of animal natures identifying both biological and social bases for behavior patterns observed across a range of herd and prey species. Ethology is rationalized and systematic observation of animal behavior; it represents a formal and rationalized pattern of behavior that documents knowledge and understandings of herd, and horse, behavior that was likely internalized by many whose entire lives were lived through daily interaction with horses. Much of what underlies the principles of Natural Horsemanship today as the nature of horses is likely to have been culturally understood, if not explicitly articulated, in broad culture prior to industrialization for example (Brainard, 2000; Dorrance & Desmond, 1999; Dorrance & Porter, 1987). The more recent and growing body of research, coupled with the rationalization and formalization of the role of the horse in today's society and driven by the affluence of those who actually keep horses as well as by horses' symbolic association with the good life, sets the stage for the rationalization of Equus and reflects the cultural diffusion of increasingly short social distances between humans and some animal (species).

CULTURAL KNOWLEDGE LOST, NOW REGAINED THROUGH SCIENCE: UNDERSTANDING HORSES AND OTHER LARGE PREY/HERD ANIMALS

While capacity for language defined as symbolic systems of communication, has long been seen as the distinction between human and non-human animal species, a growing body of research increasingly supports the existence of complex communication systems in a number of non-human species. These systems, while still largely signals and signs, are deeply complex and facilitate a high degree of social learning. Increasing evidence suggests that many of these systems include at least some symbolic understanding. Whale songs, talking beluga whales, dolphins, elephants, parrots, and, of course, chimpanzees and apes, all indicate language facility and symbolic communication–some intraspecies and some interspecies involving humans. These systems are associated primarily with high functioning, top of the food chain, and deeply social species whose cooperation is a primary survival strategy and particularly associated with species who are not fundamentally predators but instead, much more likely to be prey.

In general the term Natural Horsemanship is used to refer to handling of horses that is based on principles of non-violence because the handler takes into account characteristics of equines as a species (and often, as individuals) (see Birke & Brandt, 2009; Brandt, 2004); the result (ideally) is training practices that are resistance-free and produce calm, cooperative horses who are comfortable with (familiar) humans and safe in a broad range of situations (Miller & Lamb, 2005; Rashid, 2000; Roberts, 1997; Schaffer, 2001). It includes the general principle that humans learning to interact with horses on a regular basis become members of those horses' herds. Natural Horsemanship also acknowledges that the value to horses of humans as fellow herd members may well be negligible (Irwin, 1998; Rashid, 2000; Resnick, 2005). Horses turned out in fields with sufficient clean water and grass require almost no human intervention to survive. Even horses who are stalled for as much as 23 hours a day (solitary confinement!) need humans for very little–water, food, and the occasional stall cleaning. AND for the vast majority of horses, even those with owners who care deeply about them and do a great job of naturalizing a domestic horse's life, genuine interaction with humans is likely only a small proportion of their days, typically no more than 2 or 3 hours out of 24. Which is not to say that what humans do for and around their horses to structure their daily existences is not of vital importance; it's just likely that the horse has no cognitive appreciation of the indirect human-driven structuring of their lives.

I understand the arguments about ownership of animals. I understand that I have power in the human world to do things, to and for my horse that she cannot do to or for me; those things have only to do with human-to-human relationships involving money, decisions about what she eats, where she lives, where she goes, etc. Unlike relationships with dogs and most other companion animals, I am, like all riders must, 'giving over' the responsibility for locomotion to a horse every time I climb on her back (see Birke & Brandt, 2009; Lawrence, 1988; & Whipper, 2000). That structural relationship means that she has some responsibilities and I have others; our different responsibilities are equitable although clearly not equal. In other words, we have a partnership based on a division of labor relying upon the specific expertise and engagement of each of us. The communication between us ensures our safety and comfort. Since I am also concerned that she remain healthy and happy, I do my best to read her accurately and respond appropriately–in all our interactions. That, it seems to me, corresponds quite well with what broader culture understands as partnership (Steiner, et al., 2002; Whipper, 2000).

While there are clear differences among practitioners of natural horsemanship, as a group, they stand in stark contrast to traditional methods of horse training that relegate horses to machinery, and reflect a deep chasm between horses and humans in which humans have (and deserve) all the power, and horses are designed (or made) to comply with human desires. I think it is far harder to sort out the distinctions in practice than it is to capture and reflect the ideal types of each. My sense of it is that it is similar to child abuse and harassment: it's easy to spot the extreme cases, but much harder to decide when particular behaviors are abusive and when they are not precisely because the context in which those behaviors occur is crucial to the consequences of their use. From a sociological perspective however, my theory would be that those who do not fit in the camp of natural horsemanship would also basically claim that there is no such thing as interspecies communication largely because they regard other species as so different from humans that 1) non-human animals don't communicate even among themselves (it's all signs and signals); 2) certainly non-human animals don't communicate with humans.

In contrast, Natural Horsemanship assumes that horses have minds, that they learn a great deal through social interaction (whether that involves only other horses or includes humans), and that they are similar enough to humans that we can understand their perspectives on the world. Natural Horsemanship is grounded in the idea–and experience–that interspecies communication is not only possible (e.g., Savvides, 2012; Smart, 2011), but that humans can LEARN to communicate effectively with another species by studying and understanding how members of that species communicate with each other (Irwin, 1998; Rashid, 2000; Roberts, 1997). In other words, the concept of language being applied in Natural Horsemanship to achieve interspecies communication, while heavily reliant upon signs and signals, is symbolic because it requires interpretation by both the human and the non-human animals involved. Further, Natural Horsemanship is based on the belief that demonstrating respect for horses as unique individuals is the pathway to interspecies cooperation and true communication by creating a safe social space for both horse and human. This belief is premised on the claim that horses' basic nature is cooperative and social and therefore, humans can and should build trust into their relationships with horses through social interaction that is mutually rewarding.

All people who spend time with horses understand the basics of the language of Equus although fluency and sensitivity ranges greatly from one individual to the next. Horses, on the other hand, are indeed fluent in Equus although isolation from other horses seems to influence equine fluency also (Grandin & Jones, 2005; Irwin, 1998; Kohanov, 2001; 2003; Rashid, 2000; Resnick, 2005). Equus, or something very similar to it, is a language that is universal in the prey animals' world. Roberts successfully used it to encourage wild deer to hang out with him; Grandin and Jones (2005) point out that cows and pigs have this level of body awareness and sensitivity to others. There are unique aspects or variations for different species, but the heightened senses of horses (over humans) means the subtlest changes in position, or the tiniest flick of a finger, can set a horse on high alert.

The onus is on humans then, to learn Equus and to develop a sensitivity to our surroundings and a body awareness that approximates that of our horses so that not only do we appropriately interpret their body movements but also we have sufficient control over (and awareness of) our own. We have to get fluent enough to know what we are saying to our horses when we are around them whether on the ground or on their backs. For our own safety, we have to be sensitive enough to figure out whether the whizzed out horse between our legs is whizzed out because of something WE did or because of something the horse knows that we haven't yet become aware of–and be fluent enough to do the safe thing for both ourselves and the horse in that moment.

EQUUS IS A LANGUAGE

I'm arguing that Equus is a language; in other words, I'm arguing that Equus has symbolic components above and beyond an admittedly complex system of signals and signs. Clearly, for humans, Equus has a parallel with American Sign Language; the question is whether horses also symbol as part of their communication with humans. I'm arguing that interspecies communication requires symbolling capacities on the part of the non-human as well as the human which starts with horse abilities to see Equus when displayed by non-equine bodies. Further evidence is the number of disabled individuals who successfully communicate with their horses using Equus; these horses are interpreting individual human behavior and that *means* that they are thinking about what they are seeing and feeling, not simply reacting to it.

Human bodies are not exactly like horse bodies, and, for most domestic horses, exposure to unaware humans has desensitized them to a lot of human body language. Because human bodies are different from horse bodies, both horses and humans have to learn how to translate Equus into a set of movements that is possible for humans and bears sufficient resemblance to horse body language to be understandable to horses. I suppose it's like learning a new dialect for horses while for humans, it's more like learning a whole new language. Horses socialized by traditional horse people have learned to ignore all but the most obvious human body language because the humans, who are unconscious of displaying it, never follow it up. Equus has no conscious meaning to the human, and therefore, when displayed by humans, it has no meaning for the horse. So, when humans start learning to use Equus, they often have to re-sensitize the horse to their own (human) body language.

Horses are very sophisticated interpreters of human body language, to the point that, in some contexts, it seems they are more knowledgeable about human intent and will than humans themselves are (see Irwin & Weber, 2005; Kohanov, 2001, 2003; and McCormick & McCormick, 1997). Horses are capable of reading the minutiae of body language, changes in position, breathing, energy, etc. that are so slight that we are not even aware of them. If you have not heard about Hans, the horse whose owner believed he could count, his story provides a very good example of this (see, for example, Wikipedia on the Clever Hans effect). As it turns out, Hans couldn't count, but he knew when he'd arrived at the correct answer because his owner's breathing changed; Hans would stop pawing or striking his hoof on the ground as soon as he was aware of this change. As long as Hans' owner was in Hans' physical presence and knew the answer to the question himself, Hans never yielded a wrong answer. When they removed Hans' owner, and "strangers" asked questions, or when Hans' owner didn't know the answers to the questions, Hans couldn't count to the correct answer because the subtle body language *that Hans' owner was unaware of* didn't happen. Hans' owner had truly believed his horse could count. Frankly, I marvel at Hans' sensitivity to his owner; how long might it take you to notice that you should stop doing something when someone 5 feet from you holds their breath for a moment, or lifts their head a fraction of an inch? This level of sensitivity is not unusual for horses; it's just that most humans can't be (or simply are not) sufficiently consistent in their behavior to establish a pattern horses can recognize and respond to.

MENTAL FOCUS AND ENERGY– A FORM OF INDIRECT PRESSURE

Human perceptions of the irrationality of animals are eliminated when we understand their nature. Horses are tuned in to human energy levels and intent for much the same reasons and in much the same way they are aware of what other members of the herd are doing. Eyes on the sides of your head provide a vastly different perspective on the world than largely stereoscopic vision from eyes in the front of your face. Horses' eyes function like street lamps on two sides of a building that meet at an acute angle; humans' eyes function like car headlights. Horses' eyes function like car headlights only when horses have lifted their heads, poked their noses out and are looking at something pretty far away–that posture signals the horse is doing a danger assessment. To horses, humans (and other predators such as dogs) always look focused on whatever they are facing because of the car headlight field of vision. When humans genuinely focus their vision by staring at something, for example, it becomes laser-like for the horse. Since humans look like they are on high alert to horses all the time, with very little effort (and a lot of unconscious behavior) humans are applying indirect pressure to each horse we look at every time we look at them. Looking directly at dominant dogs or frightened dogs can be dangerous for the human; looking directly at horses is perceived as quite dangerous for the horse by the horse. Humans have to learn to have what Parelli (1993) calls soft eyes meaning that we let ourselves be aware of our peripheral vision and see as much of the horizon as possible (Dorrance & Porter, 1987; Rashid, 2000). We do this when we drive, for example. While we are watching where we are going, we also must be aware of potential dangers from all around us. We use mirrors but our peripheral vision is hugely important since we cannot be turning our heads all the time.

In the case of horses, their herd and prey animal nature makes them highly attuned, and responsive, not just to human physical behavior but also to our emotional states. Horses read humans very easily. One obvious example, is that humans are likely to walk straight toward a horse, staring at them the whole way, when they want to catch them; not only does the horse know the human's intent (it would be patently obvious even to another human), but it is scary for the horse–so, often they leave, sometimes at high speed! McCormick and McCormick (1997) and others (e.g., Irwin, 2000; Kohanov, 2001, 2003; Parelli, 1993) discuss horses' abilities to reflect human emotional states. Horses are used in psychotherapy programs because they, unlike dogs, do what is called mirroring. A dog who recognizes that a person they care about is upset will often go sit nearer the person, either within reach or up against the person which is what makes them so comforting for trauma victims (e.g., Arluke & Sanders, 1996; Serpell, 1996) quite literally, a dog's support of an emotionally distraught human empowers the human to cope with their emotions and hence the trauma. Horses, because they are prey animals and humans are (basically) predators, are far more likely to exhibit the same emotions the person handling them is experiencing (e.g., Irwin 2000; McCormick & McCormick, 1997)–for horses, human emotional states are directly linked to their safety (Dorrance & Desmond, 1999; Parelli, 1993).

Frightened, angry, or calm and confident horses are often a direct reflection of emotional states of humans handling them. This is what Chris Irwin (2000) means when he says "horses don't lie;" it is what Temple Grandin (Grandin and Jones 2005) points out when she tells the story of the Man without Language; it's also what Pat Parelli (1993) and others understand when they point out that hiding a halter behind your back and sneaking up on a horse is never going to work. Since horses read our intent, we cannot act calm; we have to genuinely BE calm. Our heart rates have to slow; our muscles have to relax; we must be in the moment, be centered, be present and yet be aware of our surroundings, including our horses, all at the same time.

As Grandin and Jones (2005) point out, spoken and written language seems to be critical to our capacities to process information, but also, apparently, what gives us the ability to lie, sometimes even to ourselves. Many humans who have suffered emotional trauma learn to manage their impressions to give off one emotion or mental state while actually feeling something entirely different. Humans are socialized to hide their emotions, especially those that make them vulnerable in the presence of others; individuals in oppressed groups (e.g., women, minorities, and of course, the abused) are more likely to learn to hide their emotions (as men are socialized to hide their fear as well as their nurturing tendencies in many social contexts). They may get so good at it that they hide their emotions even from themselves which is called emotional incongruence by psychotherapists. By contrast, horses display their emotions–doing so may well save not just your own life, but also the lives of everyone else in your group. Horses' limbic systems function by directly connecting their emotional states with their body posture: a head-high horse is a horse on high alert; a head down horse is a calm (or drugged) horse. Again, this is instinctive and part of the biological functioning of horses. Even in cases where trained human therapists cannot grasp the underlying emotional state in human-only therapy sessions, horses will reflect–or mirror–that, ignoring the managed impression given off because, as prey animals, knowing what the predator you are facing really feels is a lifesaving bit of knowledge. This mirroring capability allows (Equus fluent) human therapists to see what the horse "sees" and over time, help the human match their impression given off with an impression given. Since horses accurately identify the true emotional state of humans, Equus-literate therapists can use horses to see their patients' emotional states and over time help the patient to cope with their own feelings more effectively (Irwin, 2000; Irwin & Weber, 2005; McCormick & McCormick, 1997). The horse becomes the mirror for the patient; accurately interpreted equine behaviors (provided by a knowledgeable therapist) show the human what s/he is really feeling and therapists can help their patients learn how to process and deal with their emotional states (see Irwin & Weber's story about Stella, (2005) as well as McCormick & McCormick, 1997).

My friends and I have often discussed how perceptive our horses are about our emotional states. My mare, for example, is tuned into me enough now that I am learning from her how little thinking I have to do about something in order for her to respond to it. She does it so easily and so quickly that my initial reaction was to correct her. But she did it again, and again, and I became more aware that I was actually having that thought before she did anything; she was responding to thoughts not fully articulated. She is right though; I am thinking about asking her to stop, or trot, or disengage, or in less valuable instances for me, letting her have a good roll in the sand *before* I've removed the saddle from her back!

In a much less conscious way, my older horse taught me to leave the office at the office. I acquired him as a grad student and due to his history (misunderstood is the most polite way of putting it), as far as he was concerned, my irritation or annoyance portended a very bad day for him. In short, he made me aware of what I was doing (and hence, aware of the connection between my emotional state and my behavior), that was making him nervous. As soon as I focused on his issues (which made mine go out of my head), he calmed down. Over a period of time I made the connection and learned to leave all my emotional baggage in the car (or preferably out the window somewhere on the drive to the barn); that way we both had a pleasant time. Even though I didn't get into natural horsemanship per se until years after that, my relationship with him contributed greatly to my perspective today.

Similarly, in the midst of rebuilding my house after it burned (as a single person, I was making all the decisions and sometimes on a schedule that wasn't quite working for me), I would get to the barn and walk out to the field to get Countess, my current horse. More than once, she turned to face me directly, dropped her head so that it was directly in front of her chest and a couple of times was either at the fence-line or backed up to it putting herself as far away from me as she could get. I would stop, breathe in, do an all-over body check for tightness, and then, as I breathed out releasing the tension and ridding myself of the emotional tensions from feeling pressured into making too many decisions that were too expensive too quickly, she'd start walking toward me. She was rather obviously telling me that my high emotions were simply not safe for her and, "thank you very much, but I will stay over here until you get that taken care of." These days, if I walk out to the field and she doesn't choose to separate herself from the other horses in the field and come to me (I have to make sure the space around me is clear of the other horses), I pretty much know I screwed up the previous day, or it is spring and the grass is simply too good to leave. If I want her to voluntarily leave her horse herd and come to me, I have to be more fun and more interesting than her equine companions–and provide peppermints! As with human relationships, I have to offer her something she wants and does not get in other relationships for her to choose me. And since play is third on her list of priorities, and doesn't exist without safety and comfort assured (see Kohanov, 2001, 2003; Parelli, 1993) if she's not coming to me, I've bored her, made her uncomfortable, or worse yet, scared her. And I don't want to do that.

As social constructionists (and philosophers) would say, since most of human reality is in our heads, my horse can't overtly help me deal with my problems; but–like my human friends who hold me accountable to reality by helping me to socially construct a shared understanding of the world–she causes me to examine my attitudes and adjust my misinterpretations. If I'm slow in recognizing that I am misreading her, that's on me and she tolerates it quite well–just as our human partners are willing to tolerate our idiosyncrasies and individualism. She is my looking-glass self and as such, empowers me to manage my lived experience in a rewarding, productive, and profoundly social way (see Arluke & Sanders, 1996; Serpell, 1996; and Shepard, 1996).

CONCLUSION

To the extent that we become sufficiently versed in accurately interpreting our horses' behavior, not only can we learn Equus but we are also likely to learn a lot about ourselves by letting our horses socialize us. They will socialize us into displaying our authentic selves which is the shortest social distance between ourselves and others possible. If we let them, horses will socialize us into being more self-aware, and more responsible for the consequences of our actions, than we thought possible. Our horses already know the language of Equus and, if we let them, can serve as great teachers. All we have to do is learn to read what they are telling us and use that to shape the use of our own bodies and deal with our own emotions. As a guide for interacting with humans, particularly in teaching and in conflict resolution, Equus and Natural Horsemanship offers a pretty good set of strategies:

A shortened and slightly modified list of the principles of natural horsemanship include the following:

1. Observe, remember, and compare.
2. Make the wrong things difficult and the right things easy.
3. Let your idea become the [other's/] horse's idea.
4. Be as gentle as possible and as firm as necessary.
5. Feel what the [other/] horse is feeling, and operate from where the [other] horse is.
6. The [other/] horse has a need for self-preservation in mind, body, and spirit.

7. The [other's feelings are/] horse is never wrong (Miller & Lamb 2005, p. 28)
8. Instead of a hard tightness, try to find a soft firmness.
9. If you are going to teach [other's/] a horse something and have a good relationship, you don't make [them/] him learn it–you let [them/] him learn it.
10. THINK.
11. Notice the smallest change and the slightest try, and reward him (Miller & Lamb, 2005, p. 33).

Today we are witnessing the dysfunction of increasing social distance among politicians and other decision-makers manifest as "talking past one another" rather than finding common ground. Environmental sociology is making the argument that our modern world alienates us from the natural world. Schools are using gardens to connect children to food, the natural world, and teach math as well as biology, photosynthesis and the joy of watching things grow. We are also learning a great deal about non-human animals even as the modern world reshapes human-relationships with them by increasing our social distance from some and lessening our social distance from others. We know that language and culture, including subcultures, are inseparable; the language we use to communicate about the world reflects the world we inhabit and the world we inhabit shapes the language we use to describe it (the Sapir-Whorf or linguistic relativity hypothesis). Political correctness is based on the idea that if we become sensitive to the power dynamics reflected in language–and alter our language to eliminate gender and race-based power differentials, we can–over time–socially construct more equitable power distributions across genders and a multiplicity of racial groups.

On the one hand, the notion is self-evident; on the other, it reflects the complexity of social life, social construction, and interdependence of "real" and "ideal" in the multifaceted social interaction that constitute individuals' lived experiences. As a global sociologist who teaches the sociology of conflict and non-violence, women and development, and, of course, introduction to sociology, all with the intent to encourage students to develop sociological imaginations, I recognize that I am teaching language (and culture). I am teaching the argot of sociology so that the tools sociologists use, including scientific method and self-reflexivity, become accessible, then usable, and then (hope beyond hope), internalized.

The argot of natural horsemanship reflects a substantially different worldview of human-horse relationships than argot associated with standard equine training methods. Natural Horsemanship reflects a clear division of labor but one in which power is balanced between the partners (horse and human); natural horsemanship argot reflects an empowerment (particularly) of the horse to be a horse but also to grow into the role of good partner in the space that humans provide by accurately reading and appropriately responding to horse behavior. Natural horsemanship reflects a developmental process in which horses' understanding of human expectations is improved over time, where clarity of impression given off by humans is key to achieving desires and where nuance is sought, observed, and responded to by both horse and human. In short, learning the language of natural horsemanship is a deeply self-reflexive process for humans; knowing what to look for from the horse and learning how to interpret that behavior accurately is a crucial element of the human role in the partnership. This is learning the language of Equus that humans must do; it requires good observational skills, a knowledge base of 'the nature of horses' and the taking on of responsibility for individual action and the impact it may (or may not) have on others (specifically the horse). And these are the skills, it seems to me, that are needed far more broadly and deeply in society today to resolve deep conflicts that are stifling social change toward more sustainable social organization; learning the communication skills associated with Equus is one possible way to build a future that will not only allow humans and other species we cherish to survive, but also to flourish.

REFERENCES

Ainslee, T. & Ledbetter, B. (1980). *The body language of horses: Revealing the nature of equine needs, wishes and emotions and how horses communicate them.* New York, NY: William Morrow & Company.

Arluke, A. & Sanders. C. S. (1996). *Regarding animals*: *Animals, culture and society.* Philadelphia, PA: Temple University Press.

Birke, L. (2008). Talking about horses: Control and freedom in the world of "natural horsemanship." *Society & Animals 16*, 107–126.

Birke, L. & Brandt, K. (2009). Mutual corporeality: Gender and human/horse relationships. *Women's Studies International Forum 32*, 189–197.

Brainard, J. (2000). *If I were to train a horse.* Dallas, TX: PrintComm, Inc.

Brandt, K. (2004). A language of their own: An interactionist approach to human-horse communication. *Society & Animals: 12*, 299–316.

Bryant, C. D. (1979). The zoological connection: Animal-related human behavior. *Social Forces 58*, 399–421.

Budiansky, S. (1997). *The Nature of horses: Exploring equine evolution, intelligence, and behavior.* New York: NY: The Free Press.

Dorrance, B. & Desmond, L. (1999). *True horsemanship through feel.* Guilford, CT: The Lyons Press.

Dorrance, T. & Porter, M. H. (1987). *True unity: Willing communication between horse and human.* Clovis, CA: Word Dancer Press.

Evans, N. (1995). *The horse whisperer.* New York, NY: Delacorte Press.

Fox, A. (Ed.). (2000). *Of women and horses: A GaWaNi pony boy book. Essays by various horsewomen.* Irvine, CA: Bowtie Press.

Goodall, J. & Bekoff, M. (2002). *The ten trusts: What we must do to care for the animals we love.* New York: NY: Harper One.

Grandin, T. & Jones, C. (2005). *Animals in translation: Using the mysteries of autism to decode animal behavior.* Orlando, FL: Harcourt, Inc.

Irwin, C. with Weber, B. (2005). *Dancing with your dark horse: How horse sense helps us find balance, strength and wisdom.* New York, NY: Harlowe & Company.

Irwin, C. (1998). *Horses don't lie: What horses teach us about our natural capacity for awareness, confidence, courage, and trust.* New York, NY: Harlowe & Company.

Hess, E. (2008). *Nim chimpsky: The chimp who would be human.* New York, NY: Bantam Books.

Kilby, E. R. (2007). The demographics of the U.S. equine population. In A. N. Rowan & D. J. Salem (Eds.), *State of the Animals IV* (pp. 175–205). Washington, DC: The Humane Society of the United States.

Kohanov, L. (2003). *Riding between the worlds: Expanding our potential through the way of the horse.* Novato, CA: New World Library.

Kohanov, L. (2001). *The tao of equus: A woman's journey of healing and transformation through the way of the horse.* Novato, CA: New World Library.

Lawrence, E. A. (1988). Horses in society. *Anthrozoos, 1*, 223–231.

Lawrence, E. A. (1991). Animals in war: History and implications. *Anthrozoos, 4*, 145–153.

Loch, S. (December 2000). Tune into the horse's language. *Dressage Today.* 77–85.

McCormick, A. von Rust, & McCormick, M. D. (1997). *Horse sense and the human heart: What horses can teach us about trust, bonding, creativity and spirituality.* Deerfield Beach, FL: Health Communications, Inc.

McGuane, T. (1999). *Some horses: Essays.* Vintage; Reprint Edition. New York, NY: Random House.

McShane, C. (2001). Gelded age Boston. *The New England Quarterly, 74*, 274–302.

Midgley, M. (1983). *Animals and why they matter.* Athens, GA: The University of Georgia Press.

Miller, R. M. (1999). *Understanding the ancient secrets of the horse's mind.* Neenah, WI: The Russell Meerdink Company, Ltd.

Miller, R. M. & Lamb, R. (2005). *The revolution in horsemanship and what it means to mankind.* Guilford, CT: The Lyons Press.

Mullin, M. H. (1999). Mirrors and windows: sociocultural studies of human-animal relationships. *Annual Review of Anthropology, 28*, 201–224.

Price, S. D. (Ed.) (2001). *The greatest horse stories ever told: Thirty unforgettable horse tales.* Guilford, CT: The Lyons Press.

Rashid, M. (2000). *Horses never lie: The heart of passive leadership.* Boulder, CO: Johnson Books.

Resnick, C. (2005). *Naked liberty: Memoirs of my childhood. Guided by passion, educated by wild horses. The language of movement, communication and leadership through the ways of horses.* Los Olivos, CA: Amigo Publications, Inc.

Roberts, M. (1997). *The man who listens to horses. The story of the real-life horse whisperer.* New York, NY: Random House.

Savoie, J. (1992). *That winning feeling! Program your mind for peak performance.* North Pomfret, VT: Trafalgar Square Publishing.

Savvides, N. (2012). Communication as a solution to conflict: Fundamental similarities in divergent methods of horse training. *Society & Animals, 20*, 75–90.

Schaffer, M. (2001). *Right from the start: Create a sane, soft, well-balanced horse.* North Pomfret, VT: Trafalgar Square Publishing.

Serpell, J. (1996 [1986]). *In the company of animals: A study of human-animal relationships.* Cambridge, GB: Cambridge University Press.

Shepard, P. (1996). *The others: How animals made us human.* Washington, DC: Island Press.

Smart, C. (2011). Ways of knowing: Crossing species boundaries. *Methodological Innovations Online 6*, 27–38.

Spielmaker, D. & Lacy, M. (2006). *Growing nation: The story of American agriculture (1600–2004)* (Multimedia CD). USDA & Utah State University.

Stowe, C. J. (2012). Results from 2012 AHP equine industry survey. American Horse Publications.

Steiner, B., Lorraine, M. & Cooke, S. (August, 2002). I would not change one second. *Practical Horseman*, 28–35.

Thomas, F. M. L. (1976). Nineteenth-century horse sense. *The Economic History Review, 29*, 60- 81.

U.S. Census Bureau. 2012. Statistical Abstract of the United States. Table 2. Population: 1960 to 2009. http://www.census.gov/compendia/statab/2012/tables/12s0002.pdf.

U.S. Census Bureau, 2000. Historical National Population Estimates: July 1, 1900 to July 1, 1999. Population Division. https://www.census.gov/population/estimates/nation/popclock-est.txt.

Wipper, A. (2000). The partnership: The horse-rider relationship in eventing. *Symbolic Interaction 23*, 47–72.

Wyatt, I. D. & Hecker, D. E. (2006). Occupational changes during the 20th century. *Monthly Labor Review, 129*, 35–57.

Xenophon. Translated by Morgan, M. H. (2001 [1962]). *The art of horsemanship*. London, England: J. A. Allen & Company, Ltd.

Zettl, W. (1998). *Dressage in harmony: From basic to grand prix*. Boonsboro, NC: Half Halt Press.

Zettl, W. & Baumert, B. (April, 2001). Perfect timing for harmony. *Dressage Today,* 70–80.

NOTES

1. Equus is the genus that refers to equine species including horses, donkeys, and zebras.

2. Miniaturized horses are being transported in station wagons and spending time in peoples' homes as well as being trained as service animals.

3. Clearly, these relationships are often detrimental to individuals as well as whole groups of animals but, one could argue, animal-human interaction today is a reflection of larger oppressive social structures that create only a small elite and prioritize material things over the non-material in all instances.

4. The rationalization of human horse interaction apparent most obviously in Natural Horsemanship and represents a trend toward ensuring safety of participants apparent in broader culture as well. Throughout the horse world a concern of many is lack of understanding and appropriate training and safe handling of horses (Kilby, 2007, Stowe, 2012). The social need for a more widespread and rationalized interaction between humans and horses is about protecting both humans and horses. One characteristic of social change, particularly since the end of World War II, has been increasing regulation designed to protect the public; seatbelt laws and increasing restrictions on where and when people can smoke are two obvious examples. More recent issues, such as brain concussions associated with football, are preceded by many years of required helmet use in equine public events. Most states have legal disclaimers asserting the danger inherent in horse-human interaction to absolve them from liability; such disclaimers are prominently displayed at public horse-venues. Trainers and farm owners increasingly carry more specific and heavier insurance to protect their assets from legal claims (e.g., Stowe, 2012); activities that we engaged in as children with our horses would today be considered neglect, if not irresponsible, if sanctioned by present-day trainers/barn owners.

Chapter Nine

"Something to See Here"

Looking at Road-killing and Road-killed Animals

Stephen Vrla

"Something to See Here":
Looking at Road-Killing and the Road-Killed
Mr. Summers: "The animals need help. Other men kill them. I bury them. I bury rabbits, rats, mice, birds, frogs, hedgehogs, even snails."
Bobby: "But where do you find so many things to bury?"
Mr. Summers: "Where do you think? On the roads, boy, the bloody roads!"
—Chris Auty and Jeremy Thomas, *All the Little Animals*

Farther on in western Nebraska I pick up the small bodies of mice and birds. While I wait to retrieve these creatures I do not meet the eyes of passing drivers. Whoever they are, I feel anger toward them, in spite of the sparrow and the gull I myself have killed.
—Barry Lopez, *Apologia*

INTRODUCTION

In the film *All the Little Animals,* a mentally handicapped man, Bobby, runs away from home to the countryside, where he meets an older man, Mr. Summers, who walks along roads burying the dead animals he sees (Auty & Thomas, 1999). In the book *Apologia*, Lopez (1988) describes a trip from Oregon to Indiana during which he stops his car to carry the dead animals he sees off the road. On the surface, Summers and Lopez are very similar to each other: they both view animals as intrinsically valuable members of humans' moral community, empathize with the animals they carry from the road and bury in the ground, and feel anger toward the drivers who killed these animals. Deeper down, however, Summers and Lopez's differences

147

become apparent. Summers, on the one hand, is a recluse who has left the society that built the roads he walks along: he refuses to drive, lives in a cabin in the woods, and avoids most other people. Lopez, on the other hand, has remained in that society: he chooses to drive to Indiana to visit a friend. In short, Summers has absolved himself of the animals' deaths, whereas Lopez must accepts his complicity in them.

Summers and Lopez reflect the complex, contradictory nature of humans' killing of other animals. The Animal Studies Group (ASG) (2006) character-ized animal killing as both "ubiquitous and omnipresent" and "largely invis-ible" (p. 3). Although many people will never intentionally kill an animal, they participate in animal killing on a daily basis through the food they eat, the clothes they wear, and the lifestyles they live. Still, they are largely unaware of their participation in this killing because of the extent to which it is a structural component of their society. In (2006) the ASG argued that animal killing's seemingly contradictory combination of ubiquity and invis-ibility is in fact a complex, reciprocal relationship: its ubiquity is only pos-sible because of its invisibility, and its invisibility is only possible because of its ubiquity.

In his essay on cultural responses to the bovine spongiform encephalopa-thy epidemic in Great Britain in the 1990s, for instance, McKay (2006) contended that the media's representation of cows as commodities—that is, it's making them invisible—made the government's preemptive killing of 7,990,012 cows more publicly acceptable. Similarly, Burt (2006) suggested that the ubiquity of modern slaughter has led animal welfare advocates to focus on the practices through which cows, pigs, and other animals are slaughtered instead of the killing itself. Norment (2010) further described animal killing's ubiquitous, invisible nature in the context of biological field research: because the practice of killing birds and other animals to use as specimens is so ubiquitous, field biologists have made it invisible by calling it "euthanizing," "collecting," "taking," and "sacrificing" (p. 143), which has allowed them to continue the killing.

Road-killing, the killing of an animal by a human driving a vehicle, is another example of animal killing's ubiquitous, invisible nature. Although its history undoubtedly parallels the history of vehicles, most accounts of road-killing date from the invention of the automobile onward (Forman et al., 2003, p. 115). As the number of automobiles, speed at which they travel, and miles of road capable of supporting them have increased, so too has the number of animals their drivers kill. In 1938, Simmons estimated that American drivers killed 16,800 vertebrates every day (pp. 39–40). Ominous-ly, he also predicted that "above sixty miles per hour, if you happen to be one of the comparatively few who persistently travel at that speed, you can figure on scoring a kill every ten miles or less on most of the improved roads" (Simmons, 1938, p. 13). Certainly, his prediction has proven to be an exaggeration. Still, sixty years after he made it, when comparatively few drivers did not travel at sixty miles per hour at least some of the time, Forman and Alexander (1998) published a review of the ecological effects of roads in which they estimated that drivers killed one million vertebrates every day (p. 213). In sixty years, in other words, the number of vertebrates drivers killed had increased by a factor of sixty.

Many people have road-killed animals, and many more see road-killed animals on a regular basis. In *Flattened Fauna: A Field Guide to Common Animals of Roads, Streets, and Highways*, Knutson (1987) described road-killed animals as:

> a part of the common experience of all Americans, from the family on a drive in the country to the daily commuter travelling the same route 250 days each year, or from the bike rider on the quiet park road to the professional truck driver who spends hundreds of hours per month on major highways. (p. 2)

DeStefano (2010) "counted forty to fifty crushed snakes" on a drive through Everglades National Park and experienced a highway "littered with all manner of interesting, but dead, reptiles" in Organ Pipe Cactus National Monument (p. 105). Even the few people who do not see road-killed animals on a regular basis have likely seen representations of them in popular culture. Peterson (n.d.) has published five road-killing-themed cookbooks—the first of which has been in print for decades and sold hundreds of thousands of copies—as well as a road-killing-themed coloring and activity book. Moreover, a Google search for "roadkill"—the popular term for both road-killed animals and road-killing—returns millions of links to road-killing-themed books, movies, restaurants, toys, board games, cook-offs, computer software, television shows, and dozens of other types of cultural artifact.

Although road-killed animals and road-killing are clearly ubiquitous, they are also invisible: the relationship through which the ubiquity of modern slaughter has made the killing of food animals invisible also operates on road-killing. In *Flattened Fauna*, which includes distorted silhouettes of road-killed snakes, toads, turtles, and other animals to help readers identify their disfigured bodies, Knutson (1987) stated that road fauna, his term for road-killed animals, "when live, exists ("live" [*sic*] is too strong a word) in a habitat that is almost unique to the twentieth century" (p. 3). His striking, if unclear, explanation that road-killed animals do not fully live before they are killed suggests that he may not think of road-killing as killing. The humorous tone of Peterson's (n.d.) cookbooks, including his use of the term "shopping" for the process of gathering the bodies of road-killed animals and of titles like "Pavement Possum," "Windshield Wabbit," and "Hushed Puppies," implies that he has a similarly unconcerned attitude towards road-killing. The comparable tones of other road-killing-themed artifacts further indicate that people often think of road-killed animals as objects to study and the source of jokes, but not as once-living beings, and that they tend to consider road-killing interesting and funny, but not disconcerting.

ASG (2006) argued that despite its ubiquity and because of its invisibility, animal killing and the ideas surrounding it have "yet to receive the systematic attention they deserve" (p. 5). They further contend that:

> despite the stupefying magnitude of the killing in a global and historical sense, we must not avoid the need for an analysis of this defining aspect of human behavior. Such an analysis could, it is hoped, point toward a future where this killing becomes unnecessary. (The Animal Studies Group [ASG], 2006, p. 8)

Road-killing and the ideas surrounding it have not gotten the systematic attention they deserve, either. Although natural scientists have sporadically researched road-killing throughout the past century, social scientists only began studying it this decade. Furthermore, empirical, social scientific research on road-killing is virtually nonexistent. In this study, I begin to fill this research gap with the hope that by better understanding road-killing, we might be able to minimize it.

PREVIOUS RESEARCH

Since Barbour wrote an article on bird deaths along Nebraska railroads in 1895, natural scientists have published numerous studies on road-killing. Many of these studies date from the late twentieth and early twenty-first centuries, when ecologists became increasingly concerned about road-killing's effects on populations of endangered, threatened, and endemic species. In their literature reviews on road ecology, for instance, Trombulak and Frissell (2000), Forman et al. (2003), Coffin (2007), and Litvaitis and Tash (2008) referenced dozens of road-killing studies published worldwide over the past two decades. The creation of the Road Ecology Center (REC) at the University of California, Davis, in 2003 offers further evidence of natural scientists' recent, growing interest in road-killing, as does the REC's subsequent implementation of the California Roadkill Observation System (CROS) and a similar system in Maine (Shilling, Waetjen, & Quinn, 2010). Notably, most road-killing studies have implied that despite efforts to modify animal and driver behavior, a substantial amount of road-killing is inevitable (Litvaitis & Tash, 2008).

More recently, social scientists have begun theorizing road-killing. In 2004, Michael published one of the first social scientific studies on road-killing because he considered road-killed animals to be "a rather neglected and, on the face of it, minor category of animal" (p. 278). In the following years, several other social scientists have also published on road-killing (Lulka, 2008; Smith, 2009; Soron, 2011; Koelle, 2012; Desmond, 2013). These studies have made substantial theoretical contributions to the social scientific literature on road-killing, which has begun to develop into three focal areas: road-killing as a macroscopic connection between nature and society, a microscopic relationship between animals and people, and a form of structural and cultural violence. However, empirical, social scientific studies of road-killing are still sparse.

ROAD-KILLING AS A MACROSCOPIC CONNECTION

Some social scientists have focused on road-killing as a macroscopic connection between nature and society. Michael (2004) framed it as a pseudo-intersection between natural and societal transportation systems, or "animobilities" and "automobilities" (p. 282). At these intersections, he argued, the movements of animals and humans are both beneficially parallel and fatally perpendicular, as when an animal travels alongside a road before he or she is killed trying to cross it. Because of its simultaneous parallelism and perpendicularity, the connection between animobilities and automobilities is best described by the artistic technique of "frottage," the rubbing and transfer of matter and form across surfaces (Michael, 2004, p. 292). To Michael's framework, Lulka (2008) added the concept of hybridity. Road-killing, he asserted, highlights the fact that nature and society are no longer separate, if they ever were. Rather, so much matter and form has transferred between them that they are now indistinguishable. Like potholes on the surface of the nature-society divide, in other words, the crushed bodies of road-killed animals show people that their lives are persistently linked with those of animals

ROAD-KILLING AS A MICROSCOPIC RELATIONSHIP

Other social scientists have looked at road-killing as a microscopic relationship between animals and people. When people encounter road-killed animals, Michael (2004) argued, they have an emotional reaction to which they must respond. Their responses help them construct aspects of their identities. For example, some people might respond to the raw emotion they feel upon seeing a road-killed squirrel by understanding that squirrel as a source of humor, whereas others might respond by understanding it as that evening's dinner, and still others by understanding it as the victim of a tragedy. Through their responses, these people construct their relationships to the squirrel, all squirrels, and all of nature. Lulka (2008) also considered road-killing from the perspective of people encountering road-killed animals, or the "have-not-always-been-roadkill" (p. 39). In road-killed animals, he asserted, people see bodies and beings that, like them, are both flowing and persistent. Bothered by their identification with the animals and their inability to help them, these people experience a mixture of sadness, anger, and frustration.

Smith (2009) built upon Michael's and Lulka's arguments by developing an ethical, emotional phenomenology of people's encounters with road-killed animals. When people see road-killed animals, he argued, they experience not only sadness, anger, and frustration but also the impulse to ignore the animals. Obeying this impulse and thus "failing to express feeling for the pain and loss of Others, however different…[is] a recipe for disaster" (Smith, 2009, p. 33). To avert this disaster, people have the ethical responsibility to acknowledge their emotional reactions to road-killed animals and thereby empathize with the animals. Koelle (2012) similarly considered the ethical, emotional relationship between people and road-killed animals from the perspective of wildlife biologists, transportation planners, environmental activists, and government officials attempting to mitigate roads' negative effects on animals. By constructing overpasses, underpasses, and other structures for wild animals; tracking the animals' movement through the structures; and publicizing the results of their efforts, she asserted, these people positively relate to the animals they are trying to protect. Furthermore, in trying to protect them, the people "bring a world into being: one in which small mammals stuck in cattle guard wells may be considered in future road construction plans" (Koelle, 2012, p. 662). In this way, they actively construct their relationships with the animals.

ROAD-KILLING AS STRUCTURAL VIOLENCE

Still other social scientists have approached road-killing from a critical perspective, describing it as a form of structural violence, violence that is not committed by an actor but is rather a component of a group, organization, institution, or society (Galtung, 1969). Soron (2011), for instance, argued that automobiles and roads have "become so deeply integrated into the life of advanced capitalism as to seem like an innate fact of life" (p. 67). As a result, he continued, their negative effects have also become deeply integrated into social life. Road-killing in particular has become so deeply integrated into Americans' lives that it seems "as naturalized a part of contemporary landscapes as roads and automobile traffic themselves" (Soron, 2011, p. 58). American culture, Soron (2011) added, has responded to this naturalization of road-killing by commodifying it in forms as various as candy and guitar pedals. In this way, it has enabled Americans to "both bear witness to and dissolve responsibility for one of the most apparent consequences of our collective attachment to another commodity: the automobile" (Soron, 2011, p. 56). Moreover, it has constructed a violent, structural relationship between road-killed animals and people that can only be healed through "a wholesale political challenge to automobile dependency, the auto-industrial complex, and—more broadly—the socially, psychically, and environmentally corrosive logic of commodification itself" (Soron, 2011, p. 69).

Desmond (2013) also took a critical approach to road-killing, but she asserted that people can heal their relationship with road-killed animals through a less dramatic change than the one for which Soron called. Indeed, "the status of road-killed animals, and of human relations to those animals, is [already] undergoing a shift away from being considered unavoidable, 'accidental' killing and toward a recognition of animal subjectivity," and social scientists "may be able to hasten this shift and through [their] analyses point the way toward a less deadly and less unacknowledged highway toll" (Desmond, 2013, p. 46). Through looking at roadside memorials for and gallery photographs of road-killed animals, she added, people may come to see the animals in a new way and develop "greater emotional cognizance of animal carnage on highways" (Desmond, 2013, p. 56). In conclusion, she called for further ethnographic research into people's attitudes toward road-killing and road-killed animals. To her call, I would add other forms of empirical, social scientific research.

In this paper, I responded to this call for further research by examining American adults' exposure to road-killed animals and their attitudes toward road-killing. Specifically, I designed a survey that measures respondents' exposure to road-killed wild and companion animals, their sensitivity to individual road-killed wild and companion animals, and their concern about the number of road-killed wild and companion animals in their community. Then, I implemented the survey to a convenience sample of American adults. Finally, I used multiple regression analysis to determine the effect of respondents' exposure to road-killed wild and companion animals on their sensitivity to individual road-killed wild and companion animals and concern about the number of road-killed wild and companion animals in their community.

HYPOTHESES

H1. American adults' exposure to road-killed wild/companion animals negatively affects their sensitivity to individual road-killed wild/companion animals, controlling for their concern about the number of road-killed wild/companion animals in their community and the following extraneous variables: their attitude toward animals, human-directed empathy, and value orientations, as well as age/cohort, gender, race, education, income, religion, and political ideology.

H2. American adults' exposure to road-killed wild/companion animals positively affects their concern about the number of road-killed wild/companion animals in their community, controlling for their sensitivity to individual road-killed wild/companion animals and the above extraneous variables.

H3. The effects of American adults' exposure to road-killed animals on their sensitivity to individual road-killed animals and concern about the number of road-killed animals in their community are weaker for wild animals than for companion animals, controlling for all other variables.

METHODS

Survey Design

To test my hypotheses, I designed a survey that measures respondents' exposure to road-killed wild/companion animals (Exposure), sensitivity to individual road-killed wild/companion animals (Sensitivity), and concern about the number of road-killed wild/companion animals in their community (Concern). The survey also measures respondents' attitude toward animals, human-directed empathy, value orientations, age/cohort, gender, race, education, income, religion, and political ideology.

To measure Exposure, I asked respondents how frequently they had noticed dead wild/companion animals on or by the side of the road in the previous year. Response choices ranged from "Never" to "Once a day." "I don't see dead wild/domestic animals on or by the side of the road" was also a choice. To measure Sensitivity, I asked respondents how bothered they were when they saw dead wild/domestic animals on or by the side of the road. Response choices ranged from "Not at all bothered" to "Extremely bothered" on a five-point, Likert-like scale. To measure Concern, I asked respondents if they thought the number of road-killed wild/domestic animals in their community was a problem. Response choices ranged from "Not at all a problem" to "A very serious problem" on a five-point, Likert-like scale.

To measure respondents' attitudes toward animals, I used a five-item subscale of Herzog, Betchart, and Pittman's (1991) 20-item Animal Attitudes Scale (AAS). Response choices were on a 5-point, Likert-like scale, and higher values indicated greater concern for animals. To measure respondents' human-directed empathy, I used a 4-item subscale of Loewen, Lyle, and Nachshen's (2009) 8-item EQ-8. The EQ-8 is itself a subscale of Baron-Cohen and Wheelwright's (2004) 40-item Empathy Quotient (EQ). Response choices were on a five-point, Likert-like scale, and higher values indicated more empathy. To measure respondents' value orientations, I used Stern, Dietz, and Guagnano's (1998) Brief Inventory of Values (BIV), a 15-item subscale of Schwartz's (1992) 56-item Schwartz Values Inventory (SVI). The BIV measures biospheric, altruistic, traditional, egoistic, and openness to change value orientations. Response choices for each orientation were on 7-

point, Likert-like scales, and higher values indicated stronger endorsement of the orientation. In addition to these items, I included standard demographic items. The survey items are available from the author upon request.

SURVEY IMPLEMENTATION

I implemented the survey to a convenience sample of American adults using Amazon Mechanical Turk (MTurk), a website that enables researchers to inexpensively recruit a convenience sample of respondents. According to Buhrmester, Kwang, and Gosling (2011), samples recruited through MTurk are somewhat more diverse than other online samples and considerably more diverse than undergraduate samples.

I analyzed the sample data using Stata 13 (StataCorp, 2013). I recruited an initial sample population of 438 American adult respondents. I dropped 2 respondents because they did not correctly enter a code embedded in the survey upon completing it, which indicated that they had not read the items thoroughly and had therefore may not have provided reliable responses. I dropped 83 other respondents because they did not provide responses to one or more of the items. I recoded gender, race, and religion into binary variables, with values of 1 indicating female, white, and Christian. I recoded age/cohort into three separate dummy variables for ages 18 to 29, 30 to 39, and 40 to 67, with values of 1 indicating 18 to 29 for the first variable, 30 to 39 for the second, and 40 to 67 for the third. I performed alpha reliability scalings on the AAS and EQ-8 subscales. The AAS subscale had an alpha value of 0.675, and the EQ-8 subscale had an alpha value of 0.725. Dropping any of the subscales' items did not increase these values. The subscales' alpha values indicated that they were reliably measuring the same variables.

As shown in Table 9.1, the final sample population numbered 355 respondents. The average respondent was 30 years old, had 15 years of education, had an income of $48,000, and was slightly liberal. Forty-two percent of respondents were female, 81% were white, and 27% were Christian. The average respondent scored moderate to high on the AAS and EQ-8 subscales, and the most strongly endorsed value orientation was altruistic, followed by traditional, openness to change, biospheric, and egoistic. Compared to the 2010 General Social Survey (GSS) sample population, which is a representative sample of the U.S. population, the MTurk sample was younger, more male, and more Christian (Smith, Marsden, Hout, & Kim, 2010). Otherwise, it was demographically comparable to the U.S. population.

Table 9.1.   Demographic Comparison of MTurk Sample to 2010 GSS Sample

Variable	MTurk Sample				2010 GSS Sample			
	Mean	Std. Dev.	Min.	Max.	Mean	Std. Dev.	Min.	Max.
Age (in years)	31	9.925	18	67	49	16.674	18	89
Female (%)	42	0.494	0	1	55	0.497	0	1
White (%)	81	0.396	0	1	78	0.416	0	1
Education (in years)	15	1.584	12	18	14	2.966	0	20
Income (in $1000s)	48	34.855	12.5	200	57	42.446	1	150
Christian (%)	27	0.446	0	1	89	0.315	0	1
Liberalism	5.0	1.501	1	7	3.9	1.449	1	7
Animal Attitude	3.2	0.733	1	5	-	-	-	-
Empathy	3.6	0.794	1	5	-	-	-	-
Traditional V.O.	5.3	1.182	1	7	-	-	-	-
Openness V.O.	5.2	1.251	1	7	-	-	-	-
Altruistic V.O.	5.4	1.312	1	7	-	-	-	-
Biospheric V.O.	5.0	1.459	1	7	-	-	-	-
Egoistic V.O.	4.0	1.292	1	7	-	-	-	-
	n=355				n=4263			

RESULTS

Summary Statistics

In the final sample population, the average respondent saw 102 road-killed wild animals per year, was slightly to moderately bothered by seeing individual road-killed wild animals, and thought the number of road-killed wild animals in his community was a slight problem. The average respondent saw approximately 3 times fewer road-killed companion animals per year, was more bothered by seeing road-killed companion animals, and thought the number of road-killed companion animals in his community was less of a problem. Values ranged from the scales' minima to their maxima, and standard deviations were high for all 6 road-killing variables. These results indicate that the sample population had a considerable amount of variation.

Bivariate Regressions

Before performing multiple regression analyses of the survey data, I performed bivariate regression analyses of Sensitivity on Exposure and Concern on Exposure for the road-killing of wild and companion animals. At an *a priori* significance level of 0.05, Exposure did not have a statistically significant effect on Sensitivity for wild animals, but it did have a significant, negative effect on Sensitivity for companion animals. Exposure had significant, positive effects on Concern for both wild and companion animals. The effects of Exposure on Sensitivity and Concern were weaker for wild animals than for companion animals. Exposure explained approximately 1.8% of variance in Sensitivity for companion animals, 10.2% of variance in Concern for wild animals, and 6.4% of variance in Concern for companion animals.

Multiple Regressions

As shown in Table 9.2, I performed multiple regressions of Sensitivity on Exposure—controlling for Concern, attitude toward animals, human-directed empathy, value orientations, age/cohort, gender, race, education, income, religion, and political ideology—for the road-killing of wild and companion animals. At an *a priori* significance level of 0.05, Exposure had a statistically significant, negative effect on Sensitivity for wild animals. When Concern and the extraneous variables were controlled for, in other words, the Exposure's effect on Sensitivity became significant. Exposure also had a significant, negative effect on Sensitivity for companion animals. These results support H1. Exposure's effect on Sensitivity was weaker for wild animals than for companion animals, which supports H3. Concern, attitude toward animals, traditional value orientation, and female had significant, positive effects on Sensitivity for wild animals; and Concern, attitude toward animals, and female had significant, positive effects on Sensitivity for companion animals. Exposure and the extraneous variables explained approximately 38.3% of variance in Sensitivity for wild animals and 19.9% of variance in Sensitivity for companion animals. The highest variance inflation factor (VIF) for these regressions was 2.47, which indicates that multicollinearity did not negatively affect them.

Table 9.2.   Multiple Regressions of Sensitivity on Exposure

Variable	Wild Animals		Companion Animals	
	b coefficient	t value	b coefficient	t value
Exposure	-0.001**	-1.990	-0.003***	-3.170
Concern	0.381***	7.110	0.218***	3.680
Animal Attitude	0.438***	5.420	0.355***	3.640
Empathy	-0.004	-0.060	0.067	0.850
Traditional V.O.	0.166***	2.860	0.109	1.540
Openness V.O.	-0.018	-0.340	-0.015	-0.023
Altruistic V.O.	-0.052	-0.920	-0.083	-1.200
Biospheric V.O.	0.065	1.310	-0.066	-1.080
Egoistic V.O.	-0.029	-0.690	-0.052	-1.000
Age/Cohort (18-29)	-	-	-	-
Age/Cohort (30-39)	-0.040	-0.330	-0.288*	-1.920
Age/Cohort (40-67)	0.248*	1.750	-0.296*	-1.720
Gender (Female)	0.464***	4.410	0.589***	4.580
Race (White)	0.015	0.120	0.047	0.320
Education	-0.038	-1.220	0.068*	1.810
Income	0.001	0.520	0.003*	1.940
Religion (Christian)	0.084	0.700	0.166	1.130
Political Ideology	0.062	1.580	0.007	0.140
Intercept	-0.204	.0.340	0.025	0.030
	Adj. R^2=0.383***; $F_{(17,337)}$=13.910		Adj. R^2=0.199***; $F_{(17,337)}$=6.160	
	*** $p<0.01$, ** $p<0.05$, * $p<0.1$			
	n=355			

As shown in Table 9.3, I also performed multiple regressions of Concern on Exposure—controlling for attitude toward animals, human-directed empathy, value orientations, age/cohort, gender, race, education, income, religion, and political ideology—for the road-killing of wild and companion animals. At an *a priori* significance level of 0.05, Exposure had statistically significant, positive effects on Concern for both wild and companion animals. These results support H2. Exposure's effect on Concern was weaker for wild animals than for companion animals, which supports H3. Attitude toward animals had significant, positive effects on Concern for both wild and companion animals, and being 40-67 years old compared to 18-29 years old had a significant, negative effect on Concern for wild animals. Exposure and the extraneous variables explained approximately 26.8% of variance in Concern for wild animals and 13.8% of variance in Concern for companion animals. The highest variance inflation factor (VIF) for these regressions was 2.47, which indicates that multicollinearity did not negatively affect them.

DISCUSSION

In summary, the results of the multiple regressions support H1, H2, and H3. Respondents who had seen more road-killed wild and companion animals in the previous year tended to be less sensitive to individual road-killed wild and companion animals, controlling for all other variables. Respondents who had seen more road-killed wild and companion animals in the previous year tended to be more concerned about the number of road-killed wild and companion animals in their community, controlling for all other variables. The effects of respondents' exposure to road-killed animals on their sensitivity to individual road-killed animals and concern about the number of road-killed animals in their community were weaker for wild animals than for companion animals.

Specifically, for every road-killed wild animal respondents had seen in the previous year, they tended to score 0.001 out of 5 points lower on the item measuring their sensitivity to road-killed wild animals. For every road-killed companion animal respondents had seen, they tended to score 0.003 out of 5 points lower on the item measuring their sensitivity to road-killed companion animals. Although these numbers may seem insubstantial, one can infer from them that an American adult who saw a road-killed wild animal every day would score 0.365 out of 5 points lower on the item measuring his sensitivity to these animals than if he had not seen any road-killed wild animals. Similarly, an American adult who saw a road-killed companion animal every day would score 1.095 points lower on the item measuring her sensitivity to these animals than if she had not seen any road-killed companion animals. Cumulatively, therefore, the effects of people's exposure to

Table 9.3.   Multiple Regressions of Concern on Exposure

	Wild Animals		Companion Animals	
Variable	b coefficient	t value	b coefficient	t value
Exposure	0.003***	6.520	0.005***	5.830
Sensitivity	0.343***	7.110	0.177***	3.680
Animal Attitude	0.170**	2.140	0.242***	2.720
Empathy	-0.016	-0.260	-0.057	-0.800
Traditional V.O.	-0.084	-1.510	-0.072	-1.130
Openness V.O.	0.007	0.140	0.006	0.100
Altruistic V.O.	0.052	0.970	0.088	1.410
Biospheric V.O.	-0.025	-0.530	0.007	0.130
Egoistic V.O.	0.009	0.210	0.056	1.200
Age/Cohort (18-29)	-	-	-	-
Age/Cohort (30-39)	-0.007	-0.060	0.020	0.140
Age/Cohort (40-67)	-0.327**	-2.450	0.013	0.080
Gender (Female)	-0.066	-0.640	-0.012	-0.100
Race (White)	-0.129	-1.100	-0.117	-0.870
Education	0.037	1.260	-0.025	-0.730
Income	-0.001	-0.430	-0.003*	-1.820
Religion (Christian)	0.103	0.910	0.129	0.970
Political Ideology	-0.047	-1.250	-0.012	-0.270
Intercept	0.481	0.850	0.964	1.460

Adj. R^2=0.268***; $F_{(17,337)}$=8.620   Adj. R^2=0.138***; $F_{(17,337)}$=4.330

*** $p<0.01$, ** $p<0.05$, * $p<0.1$

n=355

road-killed animals on their sensitivity to them are substantial, which suggests that seeing road-killed animals desensitizes people to them.

For every road-killed wild animal respondents had seen in the previous year, they tended to score 0.003 out of 5 points higher on the item measuring their concern about the number of road-killed wild animals in their community. For every road-killed companion animal respondents had seen, they tended to score 0.005 out of 5 points higher on the item measuring their concern about the number of road-killed companion animals in their community. Again, these numbers may seem insubstantial, but one can infer from them that an American adult who saw a road-killed wild animal every day would score 1.095 out of 5 points higher on the item measuring his concern about the number of road-killed wild animals in his community than if he had not seen any road-killed wild animals. Likewise, an American adult who saw a road-killed companion animal every day would score 1.825 out of 5 points higher on the item measuring his concern about the number of road-killed companion animals than if he had not seen any road-killed companion animals. Thus, the cumulative effects of people's exposure to road-killed animals on their concern about road-killing are also substantial. Unlike exposure's effects on sensitivity, though, its effects on concern suggest that seeing road-killed animals increases people's concern about road-killing as a systemic issue.

The negative effect of respondents' exposure to road-killed animals on their sensitivity to individual road-killed animals was 200% stronger for companion animals than for wild animals, and the positive effect of respondents' exposure to road-killed animals on their concern about road-killing in their community was 67% stronger for companion animals than for wild animals. From these figures, one can infer that an American adult who saw a road-killed domestic animal every day would score 200% lower on the item measuring his sensitivity to road-killed companion animals than an otherwise comparable person who saw a road-killed wild animal every day would score on the item measuring his sensitivity to road-killed wild animals. Moreover, an American adult who saw a road-killed companion animal every day would score 67% higher on the item measuring her concern about the number of road-killed companion animals in his community than an otherwise comparable person who saw a road-killed wild animal every day would score on the item measuring her concern about the number of road-killed wild animals in his community. Clearly, the differences in exposure's effects on sensitivity and concern between companion and wild animals are substantial.

CONCLUSION

In conclusion, the bivariate and multiple regressions suggest that seeing road-killed wild or companion animals desensitizes people to them while also increases people's concern about road-killing as a systemic issue. At first glance, these findings may seem obvious: of course people who regularly see violence become less sensitive to its victims, regardless of whether it still concerns them on a more structural level. Moreover, desensitization to violence has a strong presence in the psychological literature (American Psychological Association [APA], 2013), and it also has a presence in the animal studies literature (Vollum, Buffington-Vollum, & Longmire, 2004; Kalof & Taylor, 2007; Fitzgerald, Kalof, & Dietz, 2009; Jules-Macquet, 2014).

Obvious though they may be, the findings suggest that road-killing has substantial, negative consequences for the people who see and participate in it. According to the American Psychological Association (APA) (2013), "research has found that exposure to media violence can desensitize people to violence in the real world." In particular, "exposure to violent video games is a causal risk factor for increased aggressive behavior, aggressive cognition, and aggressive affect and for decreased empathy and prosocial behavior" (Anderson et al., 2010, p. 151). Although these studies do not specifically address animal-directed violence, other research has. Jules-Macquet's (2014) review of the literature on the link between animal cruelty and human abuse showed that "a strong connection exists between animal mistreatment and human violence" (p. 27). For example, rural counties with higher numbers of slaughterhouse workers tend to have higher violent crime rates, which supports the "Sinclair hypothesis" that "the propensity for violent crime is increased by work that involves the routine slaughter of other animals" (Fitzgerald et al., 2009, p. 159). The violence of seeing and participating in road-killing is not identical to the violence in television shows like *The Walking Dead* or video games like *Grand Theft Auto*, nor is it the same as the violence of working in a slaughterhouse. Nonetheless, road-killing is similar to media violence in its graphic, omnipresent nature and to slaughterhouse violence in that many people must experience it on a regular basis. Therefore, the suggestion that road-killing's psychological effects are comparable to the effects of other, more heavily researched forms of violence is quite reasonable.

Road-killing also has considerable, adverse consequences for animals, including—but not limited to—the road-killed animals themselves. In their study of dogfighting, Kalof and Taylor (2007) observed that high school students who had witnessed a dog fight "believed that there was nothing wrong with dog fighting, indicating that they were highly desensitized to the violence" (p. 324). Vollum et al. (2004) offered a theoretical explanation of and empirical evidence for this relationship between exposure to animal-directed violence and desensitization to that violence. Drawing upon Bandura's (1999) theory of moral disengagement, which states that humans can disengage their moral senses in order to conduct immoral acts, Vollum et al. (2004) demonstrated that people who have "dominionistic," "property," or "dehumanization" (p. 226) attitudes toward animals are less likely to have punitive attitudes toward animal-directed violence. These attitudes correspond to Bandura's (1999) "moral justification," "dehumanization of victims," and "euphemistic labeling" (p. 193) mechanisms of moral disengagement. Notably, all three of these mechanisms appear to be active in people's attitudes toward road-killed animals: moral justification, in Koelle's (2012) argument that mitigating all road-killing is infeasible; dehumanization of victims, in Knutson's (1987) assertion that road-killed animals have never actually lived; and euphemistic labeling, in people's use of the term "road-kill," which completely removes the animal from the killing.

An understanding of how and why people become desensitized to and morally disengage from road-killing requires further theoretical and empirical research, as do understandings of how exposure to road-killed animals desensitizes people to them; why the desensitizing effect of exposure is stronger for road-killed companion animals than for road-killed wild animals; and what the consequences of this desensitization are for people, animals, and the environment. By better understanding people's desensitization to and moral disengagement from road-killing, we may be better prepared to counter their negative effects, and perhaps the negative effects of road-killing itself.

Of course, we do not need to wait for this research to take action on behalf of road-killed animals. We may not be able to make the radical changes to our automobile-dependent lifestyles for which Soron (2011) called, but we can make more moderate adjustments to our responses to road-killing and road-killed animals. The memorials to and photographs of road-killed animals to which Desmond (2013) referred may be one such change. Such a response would reframe our exposure to road-killed animals, which may decrease our desensitization to and moral disengagement from them. More sensitized to the suffering of road-killed animals, we might be more likely to change our driving behaviors and support the construction of measures to mitigate road-killing. Put differently, we may not be able to live like Summers, but living like Lopez might be enough.

REFERENCES

American Psychological Association. (2013). *Violence in the media—Psychologists study TV and video game violence for potential harmful effects.* Retrieved from http://www.apa.org/research/action/protect.aspx.

Anderson, C. A., Ihori, N., Bushman, B. J., Rothstein, H. R., Shibuya, A., Swing, E. L., Saleem, M. (2010). Violent video game effects on aggression, empathy, and prosocial behavior in Eastern and Western countries: A meta-analytic review. *Psychological Bulletin, 126(2)*, 151–173.

The Animal Studies Group. (Ed.). (2006). *Killing animals*. Urbana, IL: University of Illinois Press.

Auty, C. (Producer), & Thomas, J. (Director). (1999). *All the little animals* [Motion picture]. United Kingdom: Recorded Picture Company.

Bandura, A. (1999). Moral disengagement in the perpetration of inhumanities. *Personality and Social Psychology Review, 3*, 193–209.

Barbour, E. H. (1895). Bird fatality along Nebraska railroads. *The Auk, 12*(2), 187.

Baron-Cohen, S., & Wheelwright, S. (2004). The empathy quotient: An investigation of adults with Asperger Syndrome or high functioning autism, and normal sex differences. *Journal of Autism and Developmental Disorders, 34*(2), 163–175.

Buhrmester, M., Kwang, T., & Gosling, S. D. (2011). Amazon's mechanical turk: A new source of inexpensive, yet high-quality, data? *Perspectives on Psychological Science, 6*(3), 3–5.

Burt, J. (2006). Conflicts around slaughter in modernity. In the animal studies group (Eds.). *Killing animals* (pp. 120–144). Urbana, IL: University of Illinois Press.

Coffin, A. W. (2007). From roadkill to road ecology: A review of the ecological effects of roads. *Journal of Transport Geography, 15*(5), 396–406.

Desmond, J. (2014). Requiem for roadkill: Death and denial on America's roads. In H. Kopnina & E. Shoreman-Ouimet (Eds.), *Environmental anthropology: Future directions* (pp. 46–58). New York, NY: Routledge.

DeStefano, S. (2010). *Coyote at the kitchen door: Living with wildlife in suburbia*. Cambridge, MA: Harvard University Press.

Fitzgerald, A., Kalof, L., & Dietz, T. (2009). Slaughterhouses and increased crime rates: An empirical analysis of the spillover from "The Jungle" into the surrounding community. *Organization & Environment, 22*(2), 158–184.

Forman, R. T. T., & Alexander, L. E. (1998). Roads and their major ecological effects. *Annual Review of Ecology and Systematics, 29*, 207–231.

Forman, R. T. T., Sperling, D., Bissonette, J. A., Clevenger, A. P., Cutshall, C. D., Dale, V. H., . . . Winter, T. C. (2003). *Road ecology: Science and solutions*. Washington, DC: Island Press.

Galtung, J. (1969). Violence, peace, and peace research. *Journal of Peace Research, 6*(3), 167–191.

Herzog, H. A., Betchart, N. S., & Pittman, R. B. (1991). Gender, sex role orientation, and attitudes toward animals. *Anthrozoös, 4*(3), 184–191.

Jules-Macquet, R. (2014). Link between animal cruelty and human abuse: A review of the literature. *De Rebus, 542*, 26–28.

Kalof, L., & Taylor, C. (2007). The discourse of dog fighting. *Humanity & Society, 31*, 319–333.

Knutson, R. M. (1987). *Flattened fauna: A field guide to common animals of roads, streets, and highways*. Berkeley, CA: Ten Speed Press.

Koelle, A. (2012). Intimate bureaucracies: Roadkill, policy, and fieldwork on the shoulder. *Hypatia, 27*(3), 651–669.

Litvaitis, J. A., & Tash, J. P. (2008). An approach toward understanding wildlife-vehicle collisions. *Environmental Management, 42*(4), 688–697.

Loewen, P. J., Lyle, G., & Nachshen, J. S. (2009). *An eight-item form of the Empathy Quotient (EQ) and an application to charitable giving*. Retrieved from http://www.crcee.umontreal.ca/pdf/Eight%20Question%20ES_final.pdf.

Lopez, B. (1998). *Apologia*. Athens, GA: University of Georgia Press.

Lulka, D. (2008). The intimate hybridity of roadkill: A Beckettian view of dismay and persistence. *Emotion, Space, and Society, 1*, 38–47.

McKay, R. (2006). BSE, hysteria, and the representation of animal death: Deborah Levy's *Diary of a steak*. In The Animal Studies Group (Ed.), *Killing animals* (pp. 145–169). Urbana, IL: University of Illinois Press.

Michael, M. (2004). Roadkill: Between humans, nonhuman animals, and technologies. *Society & Animals, 12*(4), 277–298.

Norment, C. (2010). Killing things. *ISLE: Interdisciplinary Studies in Literature and Environment, 17*(1), 133–148.

Peterson, B. (n.d.). *Buck's library of public service guidebooks*. Retrieved from http://www.buckpeterson.com/bookstore.html.

Schwartz, S. H. (1992). Universals in the content and structure of values: Theoretical advances and empirical tests in 20 countries. *Advances in Experimental Social Psychology, 25*, 1–65.

Shilling, F., Waetjen, D., & Quinn, J. (2010). *California Roadkill Observation System performance report*. Retrieved from http://roadecology.ucdavis.edu/pdflib/CROS/CROS_82010.pdf.

Simmons, J. R. (1938). *Feathers and fur on the turnpike*. Boston, MA: Christopher Publishing House.

Smith, M. (2009). Road kill: Remembering what is left in our encounters with other animals. In M. Smith, J. Davidson, L. Cameron, & L. Bondi (Eds.), *Emotion, place, and culture* (pp. 21–34). Farnham, UK: Ashgate.

Smith, T. W., Marsden, P., Hout, M., & Kim, J. (2013). *General social surveys, 1972–2012*. Retrieved from http://www3.norc.org/GSS+Website/Download/STATA+v8.0+Format/.

Soron, D. (2011). Road kill: Commodity fetishism and structural violence. In J. Sanbonmatsu (Ed.), *Critical theory and animal liberation* (pp. 55–69). Lanham, MD: Rowman & Littlefield.

StataCorp. (2013). *Stata statistical software: Release 13*. College Station, TX: StataCorp LP.

Stern, P. C., Dietz, T., & Guagnano, G. A. (1998). A brief inventory of values. *Educational and Psychological Measurement, 58*, 984–1001.

Trombulak, S. C., & Frissell, C. A. (2000). Review of ecological effects of roads on terrestrial and aquatic communities. *Conservation Biology, 14*(1), 18–30.

Vollum, S., Buffington-Vollum, J., & Longmire, D. R. (2004). Moral disengagement and attitudes about violence toward animals. *Society & Animals, 12*(3), 209–235.

Chapter Ten

Animals and the Law

Maintenance of the Status Quo

Stuart M. Collis

INTRODUCTION

Laws reflect the values and interests of the society that created them at the moment in time that the laws were created. Because laws reflect a society's core values, most societies adopt rules that restrict the ability to change the law. In America's judiciary, the doctrine of *stare decisis* was implemented for this purpose. Thus, the judiciary generally only has the power to interpret the law consistent with how legislation was written, as well as deciding cases based upon precedent interpreting legislation and common law.

Animals are no exception within the law. Most American law is based on Judeo-Christian belief systems. Therefore, it is little surprise that the treatment of animals within the law is based upon Biblical foundations. Genesis specifically granted people dominion "over the fish of the sea, and over the fowl of the air, and every living thing that moveth upon the earth" (Genesis 1:28, New International Version). This proclamation of ownership relegated animals to the status of property.

In ancient civilization, identifying animals as property made sense. Animals were trained to be used as tools to assist in working the land. Others were tools trained to assist in hunting animals, for transportation, or to carry messages. Animals, not used as tools to obtain food, either had their byproducts, such as milk and eggs, consumed as food or became food themselves. Therefore, it was not difficult for our ancestors to think of an animal in the same way that one thought of a table or chair.

As civilization progressed, society began to see animals as living and breathing creatures that required some protection. Therefore, animal cruelty laws were drafted (Beers, 2006). Competing interests in the fields of lab animal medicine and animal husbandry resisted the implementation of laws, obtaining exemptions for their industries (Beers, 2006). The law has become further complicated by the emerging issue of pet owners' greater attachment to their animals and their demands for greater rights associated with the injury or death of their animals. The balancing of all of these competing interests continues to create and modify our current understanding of the law.

This chapter will give an overview of the current treatment of animals in the law. While Federal laws are uniform across the nation, state laws are not. Where differences between state laws and legal decisions are significant, they will be discussed. Furthermore, this chapter will discuss current trends and emerging issues within the law.

ANIMAL CRUELTY

Historically, people have been concerned with the well-being of animals. The Bible instructed people to treat animals well. God commanded that working animals, like people should be allowed to rest on Sabbath (Exodus 20:10 and Deuteronomy 5:14, NIV). Angels scolded people when they beat their ass (Numbers 23:23, NIV). The Bible also prohibited plowing with an ox and ass together, presumably to not unduly burden the ass or cause pain to it from the relatively harder workload (Deuteronomy 23:10, NIV). Animals struggling from a load were required to have their burden removed (Exodus 23:5, NIV). Furthermore, the Jewish people were required to kill animals they ate in a way that minimized an animal's suffering (Deuteronomy 12:21, NIV & Eisenberg, 2004).

However, the first law in America actually prescribing a punishment for animal cruelty was created by the Pilgrims in 1641. They adopted a set of laws called the "Body of Liberties." Liberty 92 specifically stated that, "No man shall exercise any tirranny or crueltie towards any bruite creature which are usuallie kept for man's use." The first law with definitive penalties for animal cruelty in America was not created until 1821 in Maine. It provided a fine between $2 and $5 and up to thirty days in jail for a person that cruelly beat any horse or cattle. [1]

Today, every state in the nation and the District of Columbia have laws preventing cruelty to animals. [2] Most of these state laws have exemptions for hunting, fishing, research and veterinary care. Also, normal farming and husbandry acts are commonly exempt from animal cruelty laws. [3] The Federal Government's anti-animal cruelty statutes are limited to the Humane Methods of Slaughter Act, The Twenty-Eight Hour Law, and the Animal Welfare Act. The Humane Methods of Slaughter Act applies to "cattle, calves, horses, mules, sheep, swine, and other livestock" and specifically requires that animals be rendered insensible to pain before being killed.[4] It also recognizes that the Jewish ritual method of killing animals for food is humane.[5] The Twenty-Eight Hour Law only applies to the resting of live-stock being transported to slaughter.[6] The Animal Welfare Act provides rules and provisions for regulations for the treatment of animals in research facil-ities, animal exhibitions, certain pet dealers, and prohibits the sponsoring or exhibiting animals in fighting ventures.[7] Since the laws vary between the states and the Federal laws are constructed to deal with animals in commerce, actions that may be considered animal cruelty in one place may not be in another. Consequently, the discussion of animal cruelty in America must be analyzed generally.

Animal cruelty laws are often attacked for being unconstitutionally vague or overbroad. If a law is vague or overbroad, it cannot be enforced. For example, a law cannot be enforced if, while on its face is neutral in content, it is used to prohibit ritual animal sacrifice in violation of the First Amend-ment's prohibition on the freedom to exercise a particular religion.[8] Similar-ly, a law created to prevent depictions of animal cruelty was deemed uncon-stitutionally vague and overbroad when it could be interpreted to prohibit the Freedom of Speech on legal activities such as hunting or the humane killing of animals.[9] However, undefined or broad terms in animal cruelty statutes such as "reasonable," "fair," "competent," "proper," or "unjust" have been determined to be constitutional.[10] Similarly, the words, "proper care and attention" of an animal, have been held to be non-vague.[11]

When a law has survived a Constitutional challenge, the court must deter-mine whether the Defendant's *mens rea* (or guilty mind) meets the threshold to be convicted under an animal cruelty statute. The law has two different types of *mens rea* crimes: general intent crimes and specific intent crimes. General intent crimes are committed when one merely intends to do a prohib-ited act.[12] However, specific intent crimes require not only the act, but also the intent to cause a specific result.[13] This distinction is important as there are numerous defenses to specific intent crimes, such as: intoxication, a defendant's diminished capacity short of insanity, or mistake. To date, most courts have found that anti animal cruelty statutes only require general in-tent.[14]

Acts that may seem cruel to the common person may lack intent to form a crime in the eyes of the law. For example, beating a horse to train was held not to be an unnecessary infliction of pain in violation of animal cruelty laws under a New Hampshire statute.[15] That case, which was decided under a statute that required specific intent, would not likely have the same result under New Hampshire's current statute.[16] Yet, Kentucky, still exempts peo-ple from prosecution under its animal cruelty laws for injuries or death of an animal when training horses, cats and dogs for sport or show.[17]

Furthermore, intent may be irrelevant to other acts towards animals be-cause a statute exempts the acts from animal cruelty statutes. Good husband-ry acts or common industry practices are generally exempt from animal cruelty.[18] Thirty-four states specifically exempt commonly accepted animal husbandry practices such as dehorning, castrating and branding.[19] Twenty-three states exempt animal slaughter from anti-cruelty statutes, though some specify that only humane killings are exempt.[20] Iowa and Utah exclude live-stock from the definition of the word, "animal," which completely omit livestock from the cruelty statutes.[21] Legal hunting, fishing, and trapping acts generally are excused from anti-cruelty statutes.[22] Surprisingly, only thirty-one states exempt traditional veterinary medical practices from animal cruel-ty statutes.[23] Scientific research is exempted in twenty-one states.[24] Perhaps more surprising is that only twenty-one states specifically exempt the killing of insects, vermin, rodents and like pests from their animal cruelty statutes.[25] Although, a possible explanation for the lack of other states not specifically exempting the killing of insects may be because most states narrowly define the word "animal" to exclude insects, vermin and other pests. Fourteen states exempt rodeos from animal cruelty laws.[26] And four states exempt zoos and circuses from animal cruelty laws.[27]

Numerous states also exempt the killing of dogs that are threatening an owner's livestock or property.[28] However, if the dog is not caught in the act of harassing, injuring, attacking, or killing the livestock, one is not exempt from animal cruelty laws if the dog is injured or killed.[29] Furthermore, the person that injures or kills the dog in such a circumstance could be held civilly liable to the dog owner.[30]

The Fourth Amendment protects the public from unreasonable searches and seizures. Since animal cruelty is a criminal offense, suspects accused of cruelty are afforded the same Constitutional protections as any other defen-dant. That means a warrant, which requires probable cause of the crime, is generally needed for police to investigate criminal activity on private proper-ty.[31] All evidence obtained in violation of the Constitution is inadmissible in a state or Federal Court.[32] However, where there are exigent circumstances, police may make warrantless entries into a home for the purpose of a search or arrest.[33] Such a case of exigent circumstances existed when police re-ceived a tip that a dog was malnourished and required medical attention.[34]

Another exception to the warrant requirement is the doctrine of "open fields." Essentially, the Supreme Court has ruled that areas, which can open-ly be seen by the public have no expectation of privacy and thus are exempt from warrant requirements.[35] Therefore, Indiana police were entitled to walk onto an individual's property to find dead horses on the property after receiv-ing an anonymous tip.[36]

Once a defendant is charged with a crime, a court must define the appli-cable duty of care. While the words of a statute define the parameters of what cruelty may be, statutes often use indefinite words such as "unreasonable," "unjustly," or "improperly." Because the words are undefined, each case is fact driven. For example, in a Washington D.C. case, what proper shelter or protection might be required for one breed of dog may not be for another. [37] Thus, the court has to determine what the standard of sufficient care is in a case prior to finding a defendant guilty of animal cruelty. [38] However, animal deaths caused by dehydration or starvation provides sufficient evidence of recklessness or the intent to commit the crime of animal cruelty. [39] The abandonment of a sick animal in an open field with nobody to take care of it, even if the animal was not owned by the person who abandoned it, is guilty of animal cruelty. [40] Defendants also cannot use willful or negligent ignorance of the basic needs of food, water or shelter needs of an animal as a defense to an animal cruelty charge. [41]

Cases of starvation or malnutrition are usually simple for determining whether cruelty exists. However, other cases are more complicated. Animal restraint cases are more difficult because many cities and states have leash or animal containment laws. [42] An owner who fails to maintain their animal (usually a dog) on a leash or enclosed on their property may be guilty of a crime. [43] Furthermore, owners could be civilly liable for their animal damaging another's property. [44] Therefore, an animal owner must restrain and contain his animal.

However, the owner cannot restrain or contain an animal in such a way that it falls within the parameters of an animal cruelty statute. Consequently, the courts refuse to apply strict liability to cruelty in animal restraint cases and each case must be measured by its independent facts. Electronic collars used with invisible fences can be considered animal cruelty if the collar burns a dog. [45] Collars which are embedded into an animal's skin has been held to be animal cruelty. [46] One court ruled that when a dog was tied to a chair on a porch, had tangled itself in a way that it could not reach its water, and no owner could be found for at least seven hours, that cruelty existed. [47] However, another court held that a dog that was tied to a tree that could not reach shade and died from overheating was not cruelty because the defendant lacked the requisite *mens rea* to show that he was acting in way that was reckless because he had tied the dog to the tree numerous times over eighteen months without ill effect. [48]

Courts inspecting anti-cruelty statutes have more difficulty when determining when the lack of veterinary care becomes animal cruelty. Several states have determined that animal owners have an affirmative duty to provide veterinary care for their animals. [49] New York has what may be perceived as a split within its own state regarding the requirement of veterinary care. In *People v Arroyo*, a New York court declared that the cruelty statute was void for vagueness as applied to the specific facts of an owner who failed to give veterinary care to a terminally ill animal. [50] The court vacated the conviction for animal cruelty and dismissed the case. [51] However, in *People v Mahoney,* a case decided less than a year later, another New York court stated that the word "sustenance" in the animal cruelty statute necessarily included veterinary care, which appears to be a direct contradiction to the holding on the same word in the first case. [52] However, in *Mahoney*, the defendant had taken the animal to the veterinarian and was told to follow up to see if the animal's tumor was operable. [53] Rather than return to the veterinarian, the owner left the animal in his basement to die. [54] Some may argue that *Mahoney* supersedes *Arroyo*. However, it is possible that the New York courts can reconcile the cases, carving out a "confirmed terminally ill exception" whereby an owner would not have to medically treat an animal when a veterinarian confirmed that was nearly certain to die.

The duty to treat an animal could work an incredible hardship on an individual who cannot afford the required veterinary care. Only two states have addressed the issue of economic distress. The Texas Court of Appeals reluctantly held that economic hardship is not a defense to the duty to provide veterinary care and upheld the conviction of an elderly woman who tried home remedies to cure her animal. [55] The Court nearly went as far as to admonish the prosecution for bringing the case in its footnote stating, "In my view, anyone visiting this home should have realized Martinez, poor, isolated, and elderly needed assistance. . . . Perhaps she could have been educated without the rigors of a full courtroom experience – nothing more than a helpful follow-up visit – for the benefit of the other, healthy dogs. . . . She did what she could short of calling for the dog's removal." [56] Washington, however, has taken a different approach and specifically legislated that economic distress is an absolute defense to the duty to provide veterinary care to an animal. [57]

The inability to care for one's animals, financially or otherwise, may result from the sheer number of animals. Animal hoarding has been recognized as mental disorder. [58] Yet, the law fails to recognize this disorder as a defense as it does not fit within the legal definition of insanity. The law has punished animal hoarders criminally, usually citing the failure to provide necessary shelter, food and water or the necessary veterinary care for the animals. [59] In addition to being criminally charged, some states also authorize the seizure of the animals. [60] Such seizures have been upheld as Constitutional under the Fifth Amendment. [61] Hawaii has gone further, codifying animal hoarding as a misdemeanor. [62]

FEDERAL LAWS REGULATING ANIMALS

Early state laws prohibiting animal cruelty caused a push for laws at the Federal level. One of the first laws that was created has become known as the

Twenty-Eight Hour law. This law provides that animals being transported by rail, express carrier or common carrier (other than water or air carrier) cannot be left without water, food or rest. [63] Sheep may be confined without food, water or rest for thirty-six hours. [64] Before the twenty-eight hours expire, the animals are required to be unloaded for at least five consecutive hours in to pens that allow for food, water and rest. [65] However, there are numerous exceptions within the statute to animals being given food, water and rest. First, the twenty-eight hours can be extended to thirty-six hours if the owner of the animals requests it in writing. [66] Second, food, water and rest do not have to be given if there were accidental or unanticipated occurrences that would prevent a careful person from giving the required food, water and rest. [67] Finally, the law does not apply at all if the animals are transported in pens that give adequate room for food, water and rest. [68]

The Supreme Court has held that the exceptions should be construed in the transporter's favor while also giving effect to the humanitarian purposes of the statute. [69] "Room to rest" means that all of the animals in the pen must have the ability to lie down, regardless of the likelihood that all animals will not lie down at the same time. [70] The reason for the opportunity to rest is because when animals are being transported, they are subjected to severe nervous and muscular strains that the animals would never experience in a stable or open field. [71]

As previously stated, the statute also allows for accidental and unavoidable causes to be exempted from the twenty-eight hour rule. "Accidental and unavoidable cause" are occurrences which a reasonable person exercising due diligence and foresight, would not ordinarily anticipate under similar circumstances and would ordinarily avoid. [72] The breaking of drawbars that caused delay to a shipment of animals exempted a train from compliance with the twenty-eight hour rule. [73] Similarly when a twenty-eight hour violation was caused by a hot box and a leaky engine, the violation was excused. [74] Stormy weather also will excuse a carrier from strict compliance with the twenty-eight hour rule. [75]

It does not matter whether the animals arrive at their destination in good condition. [76] The violation and penalties accrue once the time limit is exceeded barring accidental or unavoidable cause. [77] When a carrier violates the Twenty-Eight Hour law, the carrier is liable to the United States for a civil penalty between $100 and $500. [78] The fine is not calculated per animal or per pen. [79] The fine is calculated per time period violation of the statute. [80] Therefore, only two violations occurred when a rail carrier violated the twenty-eight hour law and also failed to get an eight hour extension. [81]

While the $100-$500 fine may have been a huge penalty when the law was created in the early 1900s, today it is *de minimis*. Therefore, one might ask what incentive a carrier has to comply with the Twenty-Eight Hour law.

A person who willfully violates the law and damages property could be found guilty of a crime and sentenced up to ten years in prison. [82]

The Humane Methods of Livestock Slaughter Act governs the slaughtering of livestock. [83] The word "livestock," includes cattle, calves, horses, mules, sheep, and swine. [84] However, it excludes chickens. [85] Two methods of slaughtering are deemed to be humane under the law. The first is the rendering an animal insensible to pain by a single blow, gunshot, or electrical, chemical or other means that is rapid and effective. [86] The second is the slaughtering in accordance with the ritual requirements of the Jewish laws of kashrut or any other religious faith that requires slaughter where the animal loses consciousness by anemia of the brain from simultaneous and instantaneous severance of the carotid arteries with a sharp instrument. [87] The Act further permits the Department of Agriculture to research methods to determine other humane ways to slaughter animals that would be quick and effective with modern technology. [88]

Research is at the heart of the Animal Welfare Act ("AWA"). It was created for three stated purposes: 1) to insure that lab animals, exhibition animals, and pets receive humane treatment; 2) to prevent the theft of pets for use in research; and, 3) to assure humane treatment in the transportation of animals. [89] Exhibition animals are those that are involved in carnivals, circuses, zoos and animal acts but excludes retail pet stores, purebred dog and cat shows, rodeos, county fairs and livestock shows. [90] Sponsoring or exhibiting animal fighting or causing someone under the age of sixteen to witness animal fighting is expressly forbidden by the AWA. [91] However, if a state allows bird fighting, the AWA exempts the sponsor or exhibitor from the ban against animal fighting. [92]

The AWA defines the word "animal" to exclude rats, horses that are not used for research, non-warm blooded animals, and farm animals, including livestock and poultry. [93] Therefore, animals not regulated by the AWA receive no protection from cruelty and have no regulations with regard to research or experimentation on them.

Research facilities only may purchase their animals from licensed dealers or exhibitors. [94] No agency of the United States is exempt from that requirement either. [95] All research animals must be marked to insure compliance. [96] The dealers and exhibitors are required to keep accurate records regarding the purchase, sale, identification, and previous ownership of the animals they handled. [97]

The Department of Agriculture is responsible for creating regulations for the "handling, housing, feeding, watering, sanitation, ventilation, shelter from extremes of weather and temperatures, adequate veterinary care, and separation by species where . . . [it is] necessary for humane handling, care, or treatment of animals." [98] Veterinarians must advise the Department of Agriculture with recommendations on the exercise of dogs and the psychological well-being of primates covered under the AWA.[99] The Department of Agriculture also must create additional standards for research facilities.[100] The standards must address animal care, treatment, and practices in experiments that minimize an animal's pain and distress.[101] The standards must include adequate veterinary care and instruct the principal researcher to consider alternatives to a procedure that will cause pain or distress to an animal.[102] If a planned experiment will likely cause pain to an animal, a licensed veterinarian must be consulted in planning the procedure for the use of tranquilizers, analgesics and anesthetics, pre and post-surgical care; and only withholding tranquilizers, anesthesia, analgesia or euthanasia when scientifically necessary.[103] No animal is permitted to be used in more than one major operative experiment without recovery time, except when scientifically necessary or if the Department of Agriculture permits it.[104]

Each research facility must create a Research Facility Committee to assess animal care, treatment and practices in the facility's experimental research.[105] The Chief Executive Officer of the research facility appoints the committee.[106] The Committee must be composed of at least three members, one of which must be a licensed veterinarian.[107] Another member must not be affiliated with the facility, a member of the immediate family of anyone affiliated with facility, and provides representation for general community interests.[108] If the Committee is more than three people, only three may come from the research facility.[109] This Committee must make a semiannual report regarding all facilities of the research facility and review the condition of the animals at the facility and practices regarding animal pain.[110] Furthermore, it must file an inspection certification report which is signed by a majority of the Committee involved in the inspection.[111] The report must include reports of violations of any standards and deviations from originally approved research proposals, minority views of the Committee and any other pertinent activities of the Committee.[112] None of these reports can be made available to the public and the AWA states that the purpose for this is to protect trade secrets and commercial and financial information regarding the research facility.[113]

While the AWA portends to protect animals, numerous loopholes exist. First, since a research facility picks its committee, there is little incentive to pick anyone that will go against the research facility's desires. Second, there seems to be no set criteria as to when causing pain to an animal is necessary. Therefore, it is up to the research to set the parameters of pain and distress caused to an animal as long as the researcher consults with a veterinarian (Francione, 1995; 1996). Third, the statute itself only permits the Department of Agriculture to oversee the facilities. Consequently, private parties cannot challenge research or practices at research facilities.[114] However, state laws may supplement and strengthen the intentions of the AWA.[115]

Animal rights activists have been distraught with decisions that only the Department of Agriculture can enforce, interpret and create regulations for the AWA. Consequently, some animal rights activist groups took the matter into their own hands, broke into research facilities, freed animals, videotaped conditions and in some cases damaged research facilities. To prevent such behavior, Congress created the Animal Enterprise Protection Act.[116] Animal rights activist have attempted to challenge the Act on Constitutional grounds, such as vagueness, but the challenges were unsuccessful.[117]

The Act protects commercial and academic enterprises, zoos, aquariums, animal shelters, pet stores, breeders, furriers, circuses, rodeos, lawful competitive animal event, and fairs to promote agricultural arts and sciences from break-ins and other unlawful interference.[118] It has varying levels of punishments and fines depending on the harms that an individual or group causes.[119] A person or group convicted under this law must pay restitution, including the cost of repeating any experimentation that was invalidated or interrupted, loss of food production or farm income, and any other economic harm caused by the offense.[120]

Federal law similarly protects hunters due to animal rights activists interfering with hunts. The Recreational Hunting and Preservation Act makes it illegal for anyone to engage in physical conduct which interferes with a lawful hunt.[121] States can and have supplemented hunting harassment laws with their own.[122] Someone that chooses to interfere with a lawful hunt is subject to a civil fine under the Act, as well as injunctive relief and any other civil penalties or criminal penalties under Federal or state law.[123] Furthermore, all provisions in the Recreational Hunting and Preservation Act must be construed in a way to preserve peaceful Freedoms of Speech and Assembly guaranteed under the First Amendment.[124]

Because the Recreational Hunting and Preservation Act only protects lawful hunts, certain hunts are prohibited. These vary at the state level but are uniform at the Federal level. Hunting and fishing are permitted in National Wildlife Refuges, as approved by the Secretary of the Interior.[125] However, airborne hunting is prohibited anywhere in the United States.[126] Also, nobody may hunt, possess, kill, purchase, sell, barter or transport Bald or Golden Eagles.[127] Unless one is an Eskimo, Indian, or Aleut or has been permitted to do scientific research by the Secretary of Commerce, nobody may kill, hunt or harass North Pacific Fur Seals.[128]

However, the most restrictive Federal legislation regarding animals is the Endangered Species Act.[129] Under the Endangered Species Act ("ESA"), only the Secretary of Commerce has the ability to determine whether a plant, fish or other wildlife meets the criteria for a threatened or an endangered species.[130] The Secretary of Commerce, in evaluating whether a species is endangered or threatened, must analyze the present or threatened destruction or modification of habitat, overutilization, disease or predation, the inadequacy of other regulations affecting the species' existence, and how manmade or other factors affect its continued existence.[131] However, the Secretary of Interior has to concur with the Secretary of Commerce to remove the threatened or endangered designation.[132]

Once a species has been identified as threatened or endangered, the Secretary of Commerce must create a recovery plan. That plan must include site specific management actions to preserve the species, objective and measurable criteria that would cause a species to be removed from the list, and estimates of the time and cost to attain the goal of removal from the list.[133] To accomplish the goal of the recovery of the species, land may be purchased by the United States to safeguard the species.[134] Also, the Secretary may enlist assistance from states, including paying states, to assist with conservation efforts.[135] Every two years, the Secretary of Commerce must prepare a report detailing the status of the recovery process for the species and its current status.[136]

If a person wishes to be exempt from the ESA, that person must submit an application to the Endangered Species Committee.[137] The Committee consists of the Secretary of Agriculture, the Secretary of the Army, the Chairman of the Council of Economic Advisors, the Administrator of the Environmental Protection Agency, the Secretary of the Interior, the Administrator of the National Oceanic and Atmospheric Administration, and one representative from each state affected, who is appointed by the President of the United States.[138] Applications must be approved or rejected within thirty days of submission.[139]

Violations of the ESA are punished harshly. Inadvertent violations are assessed civil penalties of $500 per violation. A person who knowingly violates the ESA can be assessed, depending on the section of the ESA, up to $12,000 or up to $25,000 per violation. In addition to the civil penalties, people that knowingly violate the ESA can be ordered to pay criminal costs of up to $25,000 or $50,000 and be sentenced up to six months or a year in jail depending upon the section of the ESA that is violated.

Unlike much of the Federal laws regarding animal interests, citizens may sue to enforce the ESA.[140] Citizens are specifically authorized to sue the United States or any of its agencies and to obtain injunctive relief against them.[141] Citizens also can file suits to compel the Secretary of Commerce to create regulations to protect endangered or threatened species.[142]

CURRENT TRENDS AND EMERGING ISSUES

The law can only rule over people and property. Since animals are not people, they are deemed to be property.[143] As property, animals cannot own property of their own or bring a suit on their own behalf. Because the animal cannot sue, neither animals nor their owners cannot recover for the animal's pain and suffering.[144] Because animals are deemed to be property, animals generally are valued no differently than a chair, table, or door in the eyes of the law. In many cases, this makes perfect sense within the law. For example, if someone was to kill livestock, the law would simply order that the killer give the owner the value that the livestock could have brought him at market, if it was in excess of the value of its replacement. Or, perhaps the actor killed an acclaimed race horse. In that case, the owner of the race horse might be able to recover for siring fees, loss of future earnings on races that the horse could have participated in, and any other income the race horse, reasonably and foreseeably could have earned its owner.

However, what if the animal is not a race horse or livestock? What if the animal has no real market value, as in the case of a pet? Traditionally, if an object (or in this case, an animal companion) has no fair market value, then the owner cannot recover any monetary damages associated with its loss.[145]

That is a result that would likely outrage many of the nation's pet owners. In an agrarian society, cats might have had the purpose of ridding barns of mice or other disease causing rodents or dogs might have had the purpose of safety and assistance in hunting. Today, however, the United States is largely an urban society. Dogs, cats, birds and other animals are kept not for a utilitarian purpose but for companionship and love (Sife, 1993). In fact, many pet owners see their animals as members of the family.[146] Consequently, owners go through similar stages of grieving when their pet dies (Sife, 1993). Given these new realities, state courts and legislatures are struggling with determining the proper monetary value to award an owner when a companion animal is harmed.

There is a modern trend for pet owners to court seeking emotional distress damages, recovery for the pain and suffering of the animals and loss of companionship when their animal is killed. However, historically the law will not allow for such awards, as property can merely be repaired or replaced.[147] After all, if someone broke a homeowner's window, the homeowner might be upset. But, as long as the homeowner was made whole by receiving the money to repair or replace the window, one would not expect the homeowner to have lingering psychological distress over the original window's loss. Therefore, animal owners in these states can expect that they will not be able to recover any non-economic losses associated with any harm or death to their pet.[148]

Most states also will not allow for emotional distress damages for pet owners who had their animal harmed or killed by the negligence of a defendant. This means that if a veterinarian committed malpractice, the veterinarian would be immune from paying emotional distress damages to the pet owner.[149] The requirements for recovery under the legal theory of negligent infliction of emotional distress normally bar non-economic damages for the death or injury of a pet. To recover for the negligent infliction of emotional distress, one must witness the injury or death of someone else emotionally close to the bystander, usually a spouse or other family member.[150] A court might also require that the bystander have received or been threatened with the same harm as the person who was injured or killed.[151] If the injury or death is not personally witnessed, then there is no liability for negligent infliction of emotional distress.[152] Witnessing a close friend's death has been held to not create liability against the negligent killer.[153] Thus, it is hardly a surprise that a pet, which is considered property, would not give rise to a suit for negligent infliction of emotional distress.[154] However, at least one state allows for emotional distress recoveries associated with the negligent destruction of any property, including pets.[155]

Cases sometimes come out differently regarding the recovery of emotional distress damages when the killing of a pet is intentional.[156] The general rule for recovery under the theory of intentional infliction of emotional distress requires that someone shows extreme and outrageous conduct by a defendant that is intentional or reckless and causes severe emotional distress.[157] Conduct is not "extreme and outrageous" if it is merely insulting, threatening, or annoying.[158] Extreme and outrageous conduct must exceed all possible bounds of decency and be extreme to the point of being atrocious and utterly intolerable based on community standards.[159] The standard of "extreme and outrageous," is a very high hurdle and not easily overcome. For example, derogatory comments about one's gender or religion may not overcome the standard of "extreme and outrageous" conduct.[160] Similarly, when a veterinarian performed surgery based on another animal's x-ray, no recovery was permitted under the legal theory of intentional infliction of emotional distress.[161]

However, a police officer that trespasses on one's land and intentionally and unlawfully kills a pet dog was held liable for intentional infliction of emotional distress.[162] When police wrongfully kill a wandering pet, it is a violation of the seizure clause of the Fourth Amendment and thus could entitle a person to damages for intentional infliction of emotional distress.[163] Shooting unlicensed dogs and then depositing the dead dogs' bodies on the owner's property met the "extreme and outrageous" threshold.[164] Selling another's horses for slaughter under the guise of permitting the horses to stay in pasture on a "free-lease agreement" was held to be sufficiently extreme and outrageous conduct giving rise to a claim for intentional infliction of emotional distress.[165]

However, Wisconsin takes a very narrow view of permitting recovery under the theory of intentional infliction of emotional distress.[166] The courts there state that conduct, no matter out intentional, extreme and outrageous must also be intended to cause the severe emotional distress.[167] The natural byproduct of distress from a wrongful action is insufficient.[168] Thus, the mere killing of a pet is insufficient to meet the threshold for recovery without proving that the killing was done for the purpose of causing severe emotional distress to another. [169]

Despite the fact that in the majority of states, emotional distress damages are not permitted, the law has allowed for additional recoveries associated with the injury or loss to a pet. Each court starts from the premise that when property is damaged, one is only entitled to the fair market value of the object or the cost to repair it, whichever is less. [170] If the cost to repair is greater than the fair market value of the property, then the fair market value is the cap of recovery. [171] However, the law recognizes an exception to this rule, the uniqueness theory. [172]

For the uniqueness theory to apply, an item must have nominal or no fair market value. [173] The item must have an intrinsic value, unique to itself. For example, an old watch might have no value in of itself, but if it is an heirloom that has been passed within a family for several generations, there is a value to that owner that is greater than most anyone else in the world. The same would hold true for items like family portraits or trophies.

Courts that have utilized the uniqueness theory have recognized that companion animals have a similar intrinsic value. [174] Generally sentimental value and loss of companionship may not be used in calculating the intrinsic value to the owner. [175] The court must look to the animal's qualities, characteristics, usefulness, services, and pedigrees in setting a value on damages. [176] This may include an animal's potential loss of income to the owner. [177] One court liberally utilized this theory to allow for $2,500 in veterinary expenses when a replacement dog would be worth $500 because the court found the pet itself had no actual market value. [178]

CONCLUSION

Analyzing the animal cruelty laws, Federal laws, and the current trends in court decisions regarding companion animals reveal that as a culture, people have paradoxical views regarding animals. On one hand, people want to create laws that recognize that animals are living, breathing creatures that have the capacity to feel pain and animals should be treated in such a way that such harm is avoided. Simultaneously and contrarily, laws reflect that when the animal has a human utility, whether as a food product, a tool for research, or for sport in hunting, rodeos, or other displays, animals are much more likely to be construed as objects. However, these paradoxical views are not new. After all, the Bible simultaneously gave man the dual responsibilities to care for the animals, not act cruelly towards them, and at the same time use animals for all of man's needs.

This observation leads to the obvious question: how does one reconcile these apparently opposing views? The answer is that these views are not entirely contradictory. Overall, laws affecting animals have been created for the purpose of giving humans the greatest possible utility of animals. Our laws for research, give us permission to use animals, with few restrictions, for any purpose to advance science.

In a similar manner, we protect hunters from having their right to hunt, fish, and trap, protecting our interest in using animals for food and clothing. The Endangered Species Act may protect certain animals from being slaughtered out of existence. However, the reason for that is that we have no idea what effect the extinction of an animal or species would have on people. Furthermore, the purpose of the statute is to restore the animal or species, presumably so we can hunt, kill, trap or otherwise utilize the animals again in the future for our benefit.

Livestock are used for food and the law only gives them naked protection. In most cases, livestock and poultry are immune from the cruelty statutes. These animals are permitted twenty-eight hours without rest before slaughter. The supposedly assure a humane slaughter, as well. However, the protection is meaningless, as only the Federal government can enforce the regulations for the "animals' benefit" by causing the carrier to be fined or sanctioning the slaughterhouse.

Animal cruelty laws were created for the purpose of preventing pain to animals. However, while the laws were created with a humanistic purpose, they serve a utilitarian purpose. There is a correlation between animal abuse and abuse of people. Stecker, N. (2004). Many of the animal cruelty statutes state that a person convicted of animal abuse may not own an animal and is required to go through psychological counseling. The animal cruelty laws, in effect, are an early detection device to catch potential human abusers and get them the psychological care that these individuals require. Therefore, these laws clearly have a utility to humans beyond altruistic purposes.

Even pet ownership laws have a utilitarian purpose. As discussed earlier, animals are considered property. If an animal had unique rights of its own, would it want to be owned as a pet? Would humans be able to afford veterinary care for their pet? If animals had greater rights, could veterinarians afford to practice medicine, given greater risk for malpractice claims? These are the very same questions that lead courts to prevent owners from the recovery of emotional distress damages because it would open the courts to an uncontrollable flood of litigation. By not permitting animals some sort of status other than property, we free people to own and love animals without fear of infringing on an animal's right. Pet ownership often requires licensing and animal containment rules that further reinforce an animal's property status.

Another effect of animals being property is that they do not have the ability to bring suit. They cannot litigate. They rely on humans to do it for them. Consequently, barring a human interest, an animal can never assert or enforce its desires. Therefore, while laws and societal views may change, laws regarding animals will continue to be created and refined in a way that can provide the best utility to people.

REFERENCES

Beers, D. (2006). *For the prevention of cruelty: The history and legacy of animal rights activism in the United States*. Athens, OH: Swallow Press.

Collis, S. (1997). Awards for pain and suffering: The owner's or the patient's. *Michigan Veterinary Medical Association News & Views,* 8–8.

Eisenberg, R. (2004). *The jps guide to Jewish traditions*. Philadelphia, PA: Jewish Publication Society.

Francione, G. (1996). *Rain without thunder: The ideology of the animal rights movement*. Philadelphia, PA: Temple University Press.

Francione, G. (1995). *Animals, property, and the law*. Philadelphia, PA: Temple University Press.

Sife, W. (1993). *The loss of a Pet*. New York, NY: Macmillan.

Stecker, N. (2004). Domestic violence and the animal cruelty connection. *Michigan Bar Journal, 83*, 36–36.

NOTES

1. Me. Laws ch. Iv, § 7 (1821).

2. Ala. Code § 13a-11-14 (2014); alaska stat. § 11.61.140 (2014); ariz. Rev. Stat. § 13-2910 (2014); ark. Stat. Ann. § 5–62–103 (2014); cal penal code § 597 (2014); colo. Rev. Stat. § 18-9-202 (2015); conn. Gen. Stat. § 53-247 (2015); del. Code tit. 11, §1325 (2014); d.c. code § 22-1001 (2012); fla. Stat. § 828.12 (2015); ga. Code § 16-12-4 (2014); haw. Rev. Stat. § 711-1109 et. Seq. (2014); idaho code § 25-3504 (2015); ill. Rev. Stat. Ch. 510 § 70/3.01 (2014); ind. Code § 35-46-3-12 (2014); iowa code § 717b.2 (2015); kan. Stat. § 21-6412 (2014); ky. Rev. Stat. § 525.130 (2014); la. Rev. Stat. Ann. § 102.1 (2014); me. Rev. Stat. Tit. 17, § 1031 (2014); md. Code ann. Art. 27, § 10-604 (2014); mass. Gen. Laws ch. 272, § 77 (2014); mich. Comp. Laws § 750.50 (2015); minn. Stat. § 343.21 (2015); miss. Code ann. § 97-41-1 (2014); mo. Rev. Stat. § 578.009 (2014); mont. Code ann. § 45-8-211 (2015); neb. Rev. Stat. § 28-1009 (2014); nev. Rev. Stat. § 574.100 (2014); n.h. rev. Stat. Ann. § 644:8 (2014); n.j. rev. Stat. § 4:22-17, 26 (2015); n.m. stat. Ann. § 30-18-1 (2014); n.y. agric. & mkts. Law § 353, 353-a (2015); n.c. gen. Stat. § 14-360 (2014); n.d. cent. Code § 36-21.2-03 (2013); ohio rev. Code ann. § 959.02 (2014); okla. Stat. Tit. 21, § 1685 (2014); or. Rev. Stat. § 167.315 (2015); 18 pa. Cons. Stat. § 5511 (2014); r.i. gen laws § 4-1-2 (2014); s.c. code ann. § 47-1-40 (2014); s.d. codified laws ann. § 40-1-2.4 (2014); tenn. Code. Ann. § 39-14-202, 212 (2014); tex. Penal code ann. § 42.09 (2014); utah code ann. § 76-9-301 (2014); vt. St. Ann. Tit. 13, § 352 (2014); va. Code ann. § 3.2-6570 (2014); wash. Rev. Code § 16.52.205 (2015); w. Va. Code § 61-8-19 (2015); wis. Stat. § 951.02 (2015); wyo. Stat. § 6-3-203 (2014).

3. *See* linn county v. Andrews, 739 n.w.2d 504 (iowa ct. App. 2007).

4. 7 u.s.c. § 1902 (2014).

5. *Id.*

6. 49 u.s.c. § 80502 (2014).

7. 7 u.s.c. § 2131 *et. Seq.* (2014).

8. Church of lukumi babalu aye v. City of hialeah, 508 u.s. 520 (1993).

9. United states v. Stevens, 559 u.s. 460 (2010).

10. *See* people v. Allen, 657 p.2d 447 (colo. 1983), analogizing commonly understood words in animal cruelty statutes to those under child abuse and neglect statutes and people v. Bunt, 462 n.y.s.2d 142 (1983), stating that "unjustifiably" is not unconstitutionally vague.

11. People v. Untiedt, 116 cal. Rptr. 889 (cal. Ct. App. 1974).

12. People v. Langworthy, 331 n.w.2d 171 (mich. 1983).

13. *Id.* And people v. Beaudin, 339 n.w.2d 461 (mich. 1983).

14. People v. Alvarado, 23 cal. Rptr.3d 391 (cal. Ct. App. 2005) and people v fennell, 677 n.w.2d 66 (mich. Ct. App. 2004); but *see* commonwealth v. Askins, 761 a.2d 601 (pa. Super. Ct. 2000) requiring specific *mens rea* of recklessness.

15. State v avery, 44 n.h. 392 (1862).

16. N.h. rev. Stat. Ann. § 644:8 (2014).

17. Ky. Rev. Stat. § 525.135(3)(d) (2014).

18. *See* westfall v. State, 10 s.w.3d 85 (tex. Ct. App. 1999) and linn county v. Andrews, 739 n.w.2d 504 (iowa ct. App. 2007).

19. Ariz. Rev. Stat. § 13-2910(c) (2014); colo. Rev. Stat. § 18-0-201.5, 202(2)(a.5)(vii) (2015); conn. Gen. Stat. §53-247(b) (2015); fla. Stat. § 828.125 (2015); idaho code §25-3514 (2015); ill. Rev. Stat. Ch. § 70/13(2014); ind. Code § 35-46-3-5 (2014); iowa code § 717b.1; kan. Stat. Ann. § 21-6412 (2014); la. Rev. Stat. Ann. § 14:102.1.c (2014); md. Code crim. Law, § 10-603 (2014); mich. Comp. Laws § 750.50 (2015); mo. Rev. Stat. § 578.007 (2014); mont. Code ann. § 45-8-211 (2015); neb. Rev. Stat. § 28-1013 (2014); nev. Rev. Stat. § 574.100 (2014); n.j. stat. Ann. §574.0550; n.j. stat. Ann. § 4:22-16 (2015); n.m. stat. Ann. § 31-18-10 (2014); n.d. cent. Code § 36-21.2-03 (2013); ohio rev. Code ann. § 959.13(b) (2014); or. Rev. Stat. §167.335 (2015); 18 pa. Cons. Stat. §5511 (2014); s.c. code ann. § 47-1-40(c) (2014); s.d. codified laws ann. § 40-1-17 (2014); tenn. Code ann. § 39-14-202(e)(1) (2014); tex. Penal code ann. § 42.09, 42.092 (2014); utah code ann. §76-9-301(1)(b)(ii) (2014); vt. Stat. Ann. Tit. 13 § 351b, 352(a)(3) (2014); va. Code ann. § 3.1-796.122(c) (2014); wash. Rev. Code § 16.52.185 (2015); w.va. Code § 61-8-19(e), 7-10-4 (2015); wis. Stat. § 951.14 (2015); wyo. Stat. § 6-3-203(f) (2014).

20. Ariz. Rev. Stat. § 13-2910(c) (2014); cal. Penal code § 599(c) (2014); colo. Rev. Stat. Ann § 18-9-202 (2015); conn. Gen. Stat. §53-247(b) (2015); del. Code ann. Tit. 11 § 1325(b) (2014); ga. Code § 16-12-4(c) (2014); idaho code § 25-3514 (2015); ill. Rev. Stat. Ch. 510 § 70/13 (2014); ind. Code. § 35-46-3-5 (2014); ky. Rev. Stat. §525-130(2)-(3) (2014); md. Code crim. Law, § 10-603 (2014); mich. Comp. Laws § 750.50 (2015); neb. Rev. Stat. § 28-1013 (2014); n.m. stat. Ann. § 31-18-10 (2014); n.d. cent. Code § 36-21.2-03 (2013); ohio rev. Code ann. § 959.13(a)(2) (2014); or. Rev. Stat. § 167.315(2), 167.320(2), 167.335 (2015); r.i. gen. Laws §4-1-5 (2014); s.d. codified laws ann. § 40-1-17 (2014); utah code ann. §76-9-301(1)(b)(ii) (2014); wash. Rev. Code § 16.52.180 (2015); w.va. Code § 61-8-19(e), 7-10-4 (2015); wis. Stat. § 951.015 (2015).

21. Iowa code ann. § 717b.1 (2015); utah code ann. § 76-9-301(11)(b)(ii) (2014).

22. Alaska stat. § 11.61.140(b) (2014); ariz. Rev. Stat. § 13-2910(c) (2014); cal. Penal code § 597d(5), 599c (2014); colo. Rev. Stat. Ann § 18-9-201.5, 18-9-202(2)(a.5)(vii) (2015); del. Code ann. Tit. 11 § 1325(f) (2014); ga. Code ann § 16-12-4(c) (2014); idaho code § 25-3515 (2015); ill. Rev. Stat. Ch. 510 § 70/13 (2014); ind. Code. § 35-46-3-5 (2014); iowa code § 717b.2 (2015); kan. Stat. Ann. § 21-6412 (2014); ky. Rev. Stat. Ann. § 525.130(2)-(3) (2014); la. Rev. Stat. Ann. § 14:102.1.c (2014); me. Rev. Stat. Ann. Tit. 7 §4011 1-a, 2, tit. 17 §1032(3) (2014); md. Code crim. Law, § 10-603 (2014); mich. Comp. Laws § 750.50 (2015); mo. Rev. Stat. § 578.007 (2014); mont. Code ann. § 45-8-211 (2015); neb. Rev. Stat. § 28-1013 (2014); n.j. stat. § 4:22-16 (2015); n.m. stat. Ann. § 31-18-10 (2014); n.c. gen. Stat. § 14-360 (2014); n.d. cent. Code § 36-21.2-03 (2013); or. Rev. Stat. § 167.335 (2015); 18 pa. Cons. Stat. § 5511 (2014); r.i. gen. Laws § 4-1-5 (2014); s.c. code ann. § 47-1-40(c) (2014); s.d. codified laws § 40-1-17 (2014); tenn. Code ann. § 39-14-201 (2014); tex. Penal code ann. § 42.09, 42.092 (2014); utah code ann. § 76-9-301(11)(b)(ii) (2014); vt. Stat. Ann. Tit. 13 § 351b (2014); wash. Rev. Code § 16.52.180 (2015); w.va. Code § 61-8-19(e), 7-10-4 (2015); wis. Stat. § 951.015 (2015); wyo. Stat. § 6-3-203(f) (2014).

23. Alaska stat. § 11.61.140(b) (2014); colo. Rev. Stat. § 18-9-201.5, 18-9-202(2)(a.5)(vii) (2015); conn. Gen. Stat. § 53-247(b) (2015); del. Code tit. 11, § 1325(b) (2014); fla. Stat. §

828.12(3) (2015); haw. Rev. Stat. § 711-1109 (2014); idaho code § 25-3514 (2015); ind. Code §35-46-3-5 (2014); iowa code § 717b.2 (2015); kan. Stat. Ann. § 21-6412 (2014); ky. Rev. Stat. Ann. § 525.130(2) (2014); la. Rev. Stat. Ann. § 14:102.1.c (2014); me. Rev. Stat. Tit. 7, § 4011 1-a, 2, tit. 17 § 1031, 1001(20) (2014); md. Code crim. Law, § 10-603 (2014); mich. Comp. Laws § 750.50 (2015); mo. Rev. Stat. § 578.007 (2014); mont. Code ann. § 45-8-211 (2015); neb. Rev. Stat. § 28-1013 (2014); n.h. rev. Stat. Ann. § 644:8(v) (2014); n.m. stat. Ann. § 31-18-10 (2014); n.d. cent. Code § 36-21.2-03 (2013); ohio rev. Code ann. § 959.02 (2014); or. Rev. Stat. § 167.335 (2015); 18 pa. Cons. Stat. § 5511 (2014); s.c. code ann. §47-1-40(c) (2014); s.d. codified laws ann. § 40-1-17 (2014); tenn. Code ann. § 39-14-202(b) (2014); utah code ann. § 76-9-301(7) (2014); vt. Stat. Ann. Tit. 13 §351b, 352b (2014); va. Code ann. § 3.2-6506 (2014); wis. Stat. § 951.02, 951.06 (2015).

24. Alaska stat. § 11.61.140 (2014); colo. Rev. Stat. Ann § 18-9-201.5, 18-9-202 (2015); conn. Gen. Stat. §53-247(b) (2015); del. Code tit. 11, § 1325(b) (2014); haw. Rev. Stat. § 711-1109 (2014); idaho code § 25-3514 (2015); iowa code § 717b.2 (2015); kan. Stat. Ann. § 21-6412 (2014); ky. Rev. Stat. Ann. § 525.130(2) (2014); la. Rev. Stat. Ann. § 14:102.1.c (2014); md. Code crim. Law, § 10-603 (2014); mich. Comp. Laws § 750.50 (2015); mo. Rev. Stat. § 578.007 (2014); neb. Rev. Stat. § 28-1013 (2014); n.j. stat. Ann. § 4:22-16 (2015); n.m. stat. Ann. § 31-18-10 (2014); n.d. cent. Code § 36-21.2-03 (2013); or. Rev. Stat. § 167.335 (2015); utah code ann. § 76-9-301(7) (2014); vt. Stat. Ann. Tit. 13 §351b, 352b (2014); w.va. Code § 61-8-19(e), 7-10-4 (2015);

25. Colo. Rev. Stat. § 18-9-201.5, 18-9-202(2)(a.5)(vii) (2015); haw. Rev. Stat. § 711-1109 (2014); idaho code § 25-3514 (2015); ill. Rev. Stat. Ch. 510, § 70/13 (2014); ind. Code. § 35-46-3-5 (2014); iowa code § 717b.2 (2015); kan. Stat. Ann. § 21-6412 (2014); me. Rev. Stat. Tit. 7, § 4011 1-a, 2, tit. 17, § 1031 (2014); md. Code crim. Law, § 10-603; mich. Comp. Laws § 750.50 (2015); mo. Rev. Stat. § 578.007 (2014); neb. Rev. Stat. § 28-1013 (2014); n.j. stat. § 4:22-16 (2015); n.m. stat. Ann. § 31-18-10 (2014); n.d. cent. Code § 36-21.2-03 (2013); or. Rev. Stat. § 167.335 (2015); 18 pa. Cons. Stat. § 5511 (2014); s.d. codified laws ann. § 40-1-17 (2014); vt. Stat. Ann. Tit. 13, § 352b, 362 (2014); wash. Rev. Code § 16.52.190(3) (2015); wis. Stat. § 951.06 (2015).

26. Ariz. Rev. Stat. § 13-2910.04 (2014); colo. Rev. Stat. § 18-9-201.5, 18-9-202(2)(a.5)(vii) (2015); idaho code § 25-3514 (2015); kan. Stat. Ann. § 21-6412 (2014); mo. Ann. Stat. § 578.007 (2014); mont. Code ann. § 45-8-211 (2015); neb. Rev. Stat. § 28-1013 (2014); nev. Rev. Stat. § 574.100 (2014); n.m. stat. Ann. § 31-18-10 (2014); n.d. cent. Code § 36-21.2-03 (2013); or. Rev. Stat. § 167.335 (2015); utah code ann. § 76-9-301(1)(b)(ii) (2014); wash. Rev. Code §16.52.185 (2015); wyo. Stat.§ 6-3-203(f) (2014).

27. Mich. Stat. Ann. § 750.50 (2015); mo. Rev. Stat. § 578.007 (2014); n.d. cent. Code § 36-21.1-02(7) (2013); utah code ann. §76-9-301(1)(b)(ii) (2014).

28. Cal. Food & agric. Code § 31103 (2014); fla. Stat. § 767.03 (2015); idaho code § 25-2806 (2015); iowa code § 351.27 (2015); ky. Rev. Stat. § 258.235 (2014); me. Rev. Stat. Ann. Tit. 12, § 12404 (2014); mich. Comp. Laws § 287.289 (2015); minn. Stat. § 347.03 (2015); n.c. gen. Stat. § 67-14 (2014); ohio rev. Code § 955.28 (2014); 3 pa. Cons. Stat. § 459-704 (2014); tex. Health & safety § 822.013 (2014).

29. People v. Pope, 383 n.e.2d 278 (1978); state v. Smith, 72 s.e. 321 (n.c. 1911).

30. Trautman v. Day, 273 n.w.2d 712 (n.d. 1979); johnson v. Mcconnell, 22 p. 219 (cal. 1889); *but see* mcdonald v. Bauman, 433 p.2d 437 (kan. 1967) where a jury found no liability on the part of a farmer who pursued and shot a dog he found attacking his hogs.

31. *See* united states v. Leon, 468 u.s. 897 (1984).

32. Mapp v. Ohio, 367 u.s. 643 (1961); wolf v. Colorado, 338 u.s. 25 (1949).

33. Payton v. New york, 445 u.s. 573 (1980).

34. Trimble v. State, 842 n.e.2d 798 (ind. 2006).

35. *See* oliver v. United states, 466 u.s. 170 (1984).

36. Baxter v. State, 891 ne2d 100 (ind. Ct. App. 2008).

37. Jordan v. United states, 269 a.2d 848 (d.c. 1970).

38. *Id.*

39. State v. Schott, 384 n.w.2d 620 (neb. 1986).

40. Mcdonald v. State, 64 s.w.3d 86 (tex. Ct. App. 2001); *see also* brewer v. State, 133 p.3d 892 (okla. Crim. App. 2006) where a partner in a business was convicted of animal cruelty when the business partners left animals starve in a field.

41. State v. Klammer, 41 n.w.2d 451 (minn. 1950).

42. Ala. Code § 11-47-110 (2014); ariz. Rev. Stat. § 9-240, 11-1005, 11-1012 (2014); ark. Code ann. § 14-54-1102, § 20-19-310 (2014); colo. Rev. Stat. § 25-4-610 (2015); conn. Gen. Stat. § 7-148(c)(7)(d), § 22-364 (2015); del. Code ann. Tit. 9, § 908 (2014); d.c. code § 1-303.41 (2012); ill. Comp. Stat. Ch. 55, § 5/5-1071 (2014); ill. Comp. Stat. Ch. 65, § 5/11-20-9; ill. Comp. Stat., ch. 510, § 5/14 (2014); iowa code § 351.37 (2015); ky. Rev. Stat. § 258.265 (2014); la. Rev. Stat. Ann. § 3:2731, 3:2771 (2014); me. Rev. Stat. Tit. 7, §3901, 3948; mass. Gen. Laws. Ch. 131, § 82, 140, 167, 174b (2014); mich. Comp. Laws § 67.1, 91.1, 287.262 (2015); minn. Stat. § 347.14, 365.10 (2015); miss. Code ann. § 21-19-9 (2014); mo. Rev. Stat. § 79.400 (2014); mont. Code ann. § 7-23-102, 2108, 4101 (2015); neb. Rev. Stat. § 17-526, 54-607, 608 (2014); n.h. rev. Stat. Ann. § 47:17, 466:31, 33 (2014); n.j. rev. Stat. § 40:48-1 (2015); n.m. stat. Ann. § 77-1-12 (2014); n.y. agric. & mkts. Law § 121, 122 (2015); n.c. gen. Stat. § 67-12 (2014); ohio rev. Code ann. § 955.221 (2014); okla. Stat. Tit. 4, § 43 (2014); okla. Stat. Tit. 74, § 2217 (2014); or. Rev. Stat. § 609.060 (2015); 3 pa. Cons. Stat. § 459-305 (2014); 53 pa. Cons. Stat. § 23143 (2014); r.i. gen. Laws § 4-13-15-1 (2014); s.c. code ann. § 47-3-50, 51-3-145 (2014); s.d. codified laws ann. § 40-34-4, 5 (2014); tenn. Code ann. § 44-8-413 (2014); tex. Health & safety code ann. § 822.007, 012, 031 (2014); va. Code ann. § 3.2-6522, 6539 (2014); wash. Rev. Code § 16.08.030, 35.27.370 (2015); wis. Stat. § 174.042 (2015); wyo. Stat. § 11-31-301 (2014).

43. Ala. Code § 9-11-305 (2014); n.c. gen. Stat. § 67-12 (2014); s.d. codified laws ann. § 41-17-18.1 (2014).

44. Ala. Code §3-1-1 (2014); mich. Comp. Laws § 287.280 (2015); minn. Stat. § 347.01 (2015); mo. Rev. Stat. § 273.020 (2014); s.d. codified laws ann. § 40-34-2 (2014).

45. Parcher v. Invisible fence of dayton, 798 n.e.2d 1121 (ohio ct. App. 2003).

46. Ziegelmair v. State, 997 s.w.2d 764 (tex. Ct. App. 1999).

47. Commonwealth v. Askins, 761 a.2d 601 (pa. Super. Ct. 2000).

48. State v. Bergen, 700 n.e.2d 345 (ohio ct. App. 1997).

49. Martinez v. State, 48 s.w.3d 273 (tex. Ct. App. 2001), people v. Sanchez, 114 cal. Rptr. 437 (cal. Ct. App. 2001); state v. Dresbach, 702 n.e.2d 513 (ohio ct. App. 1997); biggerstaff v. State, 435 n.e.2d 621 (ind. Ct. App. 1982); people v. Olary, 170 n.w.2d 842 (mich. 1969).

50. 777 n.y.s.2d 836 (n.y. crim. Ct. 2004).

51. *Id.*

52. 804 n.y.s.2d 535 (n.y. sup. Ct. 2005).

53. *Id.*

54. *Id.*

55. Martinez v. State, 48 s.w.3d 273 (tex. Ct. App. 2001).

56. *Id.*

57. Wash. Rev. Code § 16.52.207(4) (2015).

58. Amer. Pysch. Assoc., diagnostic and satistical manual of mental disorders, 301.4(5) (4th ed. 2000).

59. State *ex re* gregan v. Koczur, 947 a.2d 282 (conn. 2008), 46 cats in a 950 square home with feces, urine and vomit everywhere and moldy cat food in the microwave and insufficient food in house for cats resulted in seizure of the cats; state v. Walder, 952 so.2d 21 (la. Ct. App. 2006), 123 convictions of animal cruelty; state v. Mcdonald, 110 p.3d 149 (utah ct. App. 2005), 58 cats in a trailer without proper ventilation for shelter or proper veterinary care resulted in 58 convictions for animal cruelty; people v. Speegle, 62 cal.rptr.2d 384 (cal. Ct. App. 1997), 229 dogs with no obvious food or water, the dogs having excessive health issues, and feces everywhere resulted in numerous convictions for animal cruelty.

60. Scott v. Jackson county, 403 f. Supp.2d 999 (d. Or. 2005), *aff'd in part, rev'd in part,* 297 fed. Appx. 623 (9th cir. 2008).

61. *Id.*

62. Haw. Rev. Stat. § 711-1109.6 (2014) requires knowing or reckless possession of more than 15 dogs or cats and failing to provide the necessary sustenance to each of the animals.

63. 49 u.s.c. § 80502 (2014).

64. *Id.*

65. *Id.*

66. *Id.*

67. *Id.*

68. *Id.*

69. United states v. Illinois cent. R. Co., 303 u.s. 239 (1938).

70. United states v. Boston & m.r.r., 117 f.2d. 424 (1st cir. 1941); united states v. New york cent. & h.r.r. co., 191 f. 938 (c.c.w.d.n.y. 1911); united states v. Erie r. Co., 191 f. 941 (c.c.n.y. 1911).

71. Northern pac. Ry. Co. V. Finch, 225 f. 676 (d. N.d. 1915).

72. Chicago, b. & q.r. co. V. United states, 194 f. 342 (8th cir. 1912).

73. United states v. Boston & maine r.r., 99 f.2d 635 (1st cir. 1938).

74. United states v. Boston & m.r.r., 228 f. 915 (d. Mass. 1915).

75. United states v. Chicago, st. P., m. & o. Ry. Co., 245 f. 179 (n.d. iowa w.d. 1917).

76. United states v. Railway express agency, inc., 10 f. Supp. 259 (s.d. n.y. 1934).

77. *Id.*

78. 49 u.s.c. § 80502 (2014).

79. Baltimore & ohio southwestern railroad co. V. United states, 220 u.s. 94 (1910).

80. *Id.*

81. *Id.*

82. 49 u.s.c. § 80501 (2014).

83. 7 u.s.c. § 1901 (2014).

84. 7 u.s.c. § 1902 (2014).

85. Levine v. Conner, 540 f. Supp.2d 1113 (n.d. cal. 2008), *vacated and remanded on other grounds with instructions to dismiss*, 587 f.3d 986 (9th cir. 2009).

86. 7 u.s.c. § 1902 (2014).

87. 7 u.s.c. § 1902 (2014).

88. 7 u.s.c. § 1904 (2014).

89. 7 u.s.c. § 2131 (2014).

90. 7 u.s.c. § 2132 (2014).

91. 7 u.s.c. § 2156 (2014).

92. *Id.*

93. 7 u.s.c. § 2132 (2014).

94. 7 u.s.c. § 2137 (2014).

95. 7 u.s.c. § 2138 (2014).

96. 7 u.s.c. § 2141 (2014).

97. 7 u.s.c. § 2140 (2014).

98. 7 u.s.c. § 2143 (2014).

99. *Id.*

100. *Id.*

101. *Id.*

102. *Id.*

103. *Id.*

104. *Id.*

105. *Id.*

106. *Id.*

107. *Id.*

108. *Id.*

109. *Id.*

110. *Id.*

111. *Id.*

112. *Id.*

113. *Id.*

114. Animal legal defense fund, inc. V. Epsy, 23 f.3d 496 (d.c. 1994); int'l primate protection league v. Inst. For behavioral research, inc., 799 f.2d 934 (4th cir. 1986), *cert. Denied*, 481 u.s. 1004 (1987), *reh'g denied*, 482 u.s. 909 (1987).

115. Kerr v. Kimmell, 740 f. Supp. 1525 (d. Kan. 1990).

116. 18 u.s.c. § 43 (2014).

117. Blum v. Holder, 744 f.3d 790 (1st cir. 2014), *cert. Denied*, 135 s.ct. 477 (2014); united states v. Fullmer, 584 f.3d 132 (3rd cir. 2009).

118. 18 u.s.c. § 43 (2014).

119. *Id.*

120. *Id.*

121. 16 u.s.c. § 5201 (2014).

122. Ariz. Rev. Stat. § 17-316 (2014); ill. Rev. Stat. Ch. 720, § 5/48-3 (2014); md. Code ann. Art. 27, § 10-422 (2014); mich. Comp. Laws. § 324.40112 (2015); n.d. cent. Code § 20.1-01-31 (2013); n.y. envtl. Conserv. Laws. § 11-0110 (2015).

123. 16 u.s.c. § 5202-5204 (2014).

124. 16 u.s.c. § 5206 (2014).

125. 16 u.s.c. § 668dd (2014).

126. 16 u.s.c. § 742j-1 (2014).

127. 16 u.s.c. § 668-668c (2014).

128. 16 u.s.c. § 1151-1154 (2014).

129. 16 u.s.c. § 1531 *et. Seq.* (2014).

130. 16 u.s.c. § 1533 (2014).

131. *Id.*

132. *Id.*

133. *Id.*

134. 16 u.s.c. § 1534 (2014).

135. 16 u.s.c. § 1535 (2014).

136. 16 u.s.c. § 1533 (2014).

137. 16 u.s.c. § 1536 (2014).

138. *Id.*

139. *Id.*

140. 16 u.s.c. § 1540 (2014).

141. *Id.*

142. *Id.*

143. Roman v. Carroll, 621 p.2d 307 (ariz. App. 1980); ten hopen v. Walker, 55 n.w. 657 (mich. 1893).

144. Womack v. Von rardon, 135 p.3d 542 (wash. Ct. App. 2006); oberschlake v. Veterinary assoc. Animal hosp., 785 n.e.2d 811 (ohio ct. App. 2003); gluckman v. American airlines, inc., 844 f. Supp. 151 (s.d.n.y. 1994).

145. *See* sentell v. New orleans & c.r. co., 166 u.s. 698 (1897).

146. *See* bennett v. Bennett, 655 so.2d 109 (fla. Dist. Ct. App. 1995).

147. Price v. High pointe oil co., inc., 828 n.w.2d 660 (2013).

148. *Id.*; sawh v. Lino lakes, 823 n.w.2d 627 (2012); scheele v. Dustin, 998 a.2d 697 (ver. 2010); carbasho v. Musulin, 618 s.e.2d 368 (w.va. 2005); mitchell v. Heinrichs, 27 p.3d 309 (alaska 2001); johnson v. Douglas, 723 n.y.s.2d 627 (n.y. sup. Ct. 2001); koester v. Vca animal hosp., 624 n.w.2d 209 (mich. Ct. App. 2000); nichols v. Sukaro kennels, 555 n.w.2d 689 (iowa 1996); jason v. Parks, 224 a.d.2d 494 (n.y. app. Div. 1996); fowler v. Ticonderoga, 131 a.d.2d 919 (n.y. app. Div. 1987).

149. Kaufman v. Langhofer, 222 p.3d 272 (ariz. 2009); kennedy v. Byas, 867 so. 2d 1195 (fla. Dist. Ct. App. 2004); oberschlake v. Vet. Assocs. Animal hosp., 785 n.e.2d 811 (ohio ct. App. 2003); koester v. Vca animal hosp., 624 n.w.2d 209 (mich. App. 2000), *appeal denied*, 631 n.w.2d 339 (mich. 2001); fackler v. Genetzky, 595 n.w.2d 884 (neb. 1999); zeid v. Pearce, 953 s.w.2d 368 (tex. Ct. App. 1997); jankowski v. Preiser animal hosp., ltd., 510 n.e.2d 1084 (ill. App. Ct. 1987); *see also* altieri v. Nanavati, 573 a.2d 359 (conn. Super. Ct. 1990). Florida is currently in a state of conflict as two other cases from the 3rd district appellate court in florida have permitted pain and suffering awards in cases of pet injuries or death associated

with the gross negligence of a veterinarian. *See* johnson v. Wander, 592 so. 2d 1225 (fla. Dist. Ct. App. 1992) and knowles animal hosp. V. Wills, 360 so. 2d 37 (fla. Dist. Ct. App. 1978).

150. Nugent v. Bauermeister, 489 n.w.2d 148 (mich. App. 1992).

151. Carrol v. Rock, 469 s.e.2d 391 (ga. Ct. App. 1996); langford v. Emergency pet clinic, 644 n.e.2d 1035 (ohio ct. App. 1994); soucek v. Banham, 503 n.w.2d 153 (minn. Ct. App. 1993); gill v. Brown, 695 p.2d 1276 (idaho ct. App. 1985); little v. Williamson, 441 n.e.2d 974 (ind. Ct. App. 1982).

152. Roman v. Carroll, 621 p.2d 307 (ariz. Ct. App. 1980).

153. Nugent v. Bauermeister, 489 n.w.2d 148 (mich. App. 1992).

154. Schrage v. Hatzlacha cab corp., 788 n.y.s.2d 4 (n.y. app. Div. 2004); krasnecky v. Meffen, 777 n.e.2d 1286 (mass. App. Ct. 2002); lockett v. Hill, 51 p.3d 5 (or. Ct. App. 2002); harabes v. The barkery, inc., 791 a.2d 1142 (n.j. super. Ct. App. Div. 2001); carrol v. Rock, 469 s.e.2d 391 (ga. Ct. App. 1996); rowbotham v. Maher, 658 a.2d 912 (r.i. 1995); roman v. Carroll, 621 p.2d 307 (ariz. Ct. App. 1980).

155. Campbell v. Animal quarantine station, 632 p.2d 1066 (haw. 1981).

156. Washington has an action for malicious injury to pet. Womack v. Von rardon, 135 p.3d 542 (wash. Ct. App. 2006). No elements have been set forth for this cause of action and it is unclear whether this is something between negligent infliction of emotional distress and intentional infliction of emotional distress.

157. Atkinson v. Farley, 431 n.w.2d 95 (mich. App. 1988); dickerson v. Nichols, 409 n.w.2d 741 (mich. App. 1987).

158. Tope v. Howe, 445 n.w.2d 452 (mich. App. 1989).

159. Grochowalski v. Detroit auto inter-ins. Exch., 430 n.w.2d 822 (mich. App. 1988).

160. Meek v. Michigan bell tel. Co., 483 n.w.2d 407 (mich. App. 1991).

161. Daughten v. Fox, 539 a.2d 858 (pa. Super. Ct. 1988).

162. Garland v. White, 368 s.w.2d 12 (tex. Ct. App. 1963).

163. Brown v. Muhlenberg twp., 269 f.3d 205 (3d cir. 2001).

164. Katsaris v. Cook, 225 cal. Rptr. 531 (cal. Ct. App. 1986).

165. Burgess v. Taylor, 44 s.w.3d 806 (ky. Ct. App. 2001).

166. Rabideau v. City of racine, 627 n.w.2d 295 (wis. 2001).

167. *Id.*

168. *Id.*

169. *Id.*

170. Sawh v lino lakes, 823 n.w.2d 627 (2012); leith v. Frost, 899 n.e.2d 635 (ill. App. Ct. 2008).

171. *Id.*; strzelecki v. Blaser's lakeside indus. Of rice lake, inc., 348 n.w.2d 311 (mich. App. 1984).

172. It should be noted that the author believes that this is the correct method of analyzing damages for the injury or death of a pet and stated it as a possibility in another article. Collis, s. (1997). While animal rights activists seek emotional distress damages associated with the loss of an animal, this theory essentially may be able to awards a similar value without the necessity of creating a special category for companion animals, opposed to livestock, racehorses or other income producing or high fair market value animals.

173. *See* sherman v. Kissinger, 195 p.3d 539 (wash. Ct. App. 2008); mcdonald v. Ohio state univ. Vet. Hosp., 644 n.e.2d 750 (ohio ct. Of claims 1994).

174. Medlen v. Strickland, 353 s.w.3d 576 (tex. 2013); petco v. Schuster, 144 s.w.3d 554 (tex. Ct. App. 2004); paguio v. Evening journal ass'n, 21 a.2d 667 (n.j. sup. Ct. 1941); wilcox v. Butt's drug stores, 35 p.2d 978 (n.m. 1934); mccallister v. Sappinfield, 144 p. 432 (or. 1914); klein v. St. Louis transit co., 93 s.w. 281 (mo. Ct. App. 1906); hodges v. Causey, 26 so. 945 (miss. 1900); bowers v. Horan, 53 n.w. 535 (mich. 1892).

175. Medlen v. Strickland, 353 s.w.3d 576 (tex. 2013); petco v. Schuster, 144 s.w.3d 554 (tex. Ct. App. 2004); mcdonald v ohio state univ. Vet. Hosp., 644 n.e.2d 750 (ohio ct. Of claims 1994); wilcox v. Butt's drug stores, 35 p.2d 978 (n.m. 1934); mccallister v. Sappinfield, 144 p. 432 (or. 1914). But see klein v. St. Louis transit co., 93 s.w. 281 (mo. Ct. App. 1906) which permitted loss of dog's company as part of the calculation for intrinsic value.

176. Medlen v. Strickland, 353 s.w.3d 576 (tex. 2013); petco v. Schuster, 144 s.w.3d 554 (tex. Ct. App. 2004); paguio v. Evening journal ass'n, 21 a.2d 667 (n.j. super. Ct. 1941); wilcox v. Butt's drug stores, 35 p.2d 978 (n.m. 1934); mccallister v. Sappinfield, 144 p. 432 (or. 1914); klein v. St. Louis transit co., 93 s.w. 281 (mo. App. 1906); hodges v. Causey, 26 so. 945 (miss. 1900); bowers v. Horan, 53 n.w. 535 (mich. 1892).

177. *See* mcdonald v ohio state univ. Vet. Hosp., 644 n.e.2d 750 (ohio ct. Of claims 1994); paguio v. Evening journal ass'n, 21 a.2d 667 (n.j. super. Ct. 1941).

178. Hyland v. Borras, 719 a.2d 662 (n.j. super. Ct. App. Div. 1998).

Appendix

SELECTED HORSE ORGANIZATIONS ILLUSTRATING
SPECIALIZATION AND INSTITUTIONALIZATION
OF THE ROLE OF THE HORSE

US Polo Association (nee Polo Association), established 1890: The Polo Association, now the US Polo Association, was created in 1890 "to help American polo players improve their skills and compete in the 'Game of Kings'" (http://uspolo.org/about/uspa/).

US Jockey Club (Regulating Organization for Thoroughbred Racing Industry; Thoroughbred Registry), established 1894: Achieved incorporation by 8 "racing leaders [to] not only . . . Encourage the development of the thoroughbred horse, but to establish racing on such a footing that it may command the interests as well as the confidence and favorable opinion of the public" (http://www.jockeyclub.com/default.asp?section=About&area=0). It is an international organization that maintains The American Stud Book and is a founding member of The International Stud Book Committee "which serves to coordinate the policies and practices of more than 60 stud book authorities around the world to harmonize the rules of different jurisdictions in order to facilitate cross-border commerce . . . . Over the course of the past 25 years or so, The Jockey Club has created and developed a group of commercial, for-profit subsidiaries and a commercial partnership, each with a twofold purpose: to serve specific segments within the industry using highly efficient, state-of-the-art technology platforms and to generate profits that are used to support important industry initiatives" (http://www.jockeyclub.com/default.asp?section=About&area=0).

Horses in the (II) Olympiad, established 1900: Disappeared until 1912 but has been part of every summer Olympics since.

American Morgan Horse Association (nee The Morgan Horse Club), established 1909: The Morgan Horse Club is formed at the Vermont State Fair in 1909; the first register of Morgan Horses was published in 1894. In 1927 The Morgan Horse Club incorporates and begins to issue certificates of registration, and becomes the American Morgan Horse Association, Inc. in 1971. Breed based Morgan Horse Shows recognized by the AHSA, now the USEF in 1952 (http://www.morganhorse.com/upload/photos/245History.pdf).

United States Equestrian Federation (USEF) Originally the American Horse Shows Association (AHSA), established 1917: Established by a Vanderbilt and others in 1917 as a framework to support leisure activities with horses. The AHSA became the USEF in 2003 by merging with the USET after operating as USA Equestrian since 2001. The USEF supports 12 different Breed-shows and is the National Governing Body for equestrian sport in the US. It includes USHJA, the USDF, and the USEA (http://en.wikipedia.org/wiki/United_States_Equestrian_Federation).

Federation Equestre Internationale (FEI); in the US, called the International Equestrian Federation (still FEI), established 1921: The FEI provides all the rules and regulations for international eventing, dressage, driving, and the original show jumping, vaulting, and now Western Reining (a total of 7 distinct high performance equine sports) and thereby controls the World Equestrian Games and equine events in the Olympics. Founding countries include: Switzerland, France, the USA, Sweden, Japan, Belgium, Denmark, Norway and Italy (http://www.fei.org/fei/about-fei/history/history-of-the-fei). The current and all past presidents of the FEI are members of European Royal Families.

Professional Rodeo Cowboys Association (PRCA); also goes by Pro Rodeo and Professional Rodeo Association, established 1936: Coordinates Professional Rodeo Events and thereby serves as umbrella organization for other (professional) rodeo organizations. "The PRCA's nearly 4 million loyal attendees across the U.S are about .49 percent male and 51 percent female; 63 percent have household income of $50,000 or more and 50 percent have children in the household. In surveys, 81 percent report that they have had a soft drink in the previous 30 days, 50 percent have had a beer in the previous 30 days and 95 percent have eaten at a fast food restaurant in the previous 30 days. ProRodeo fans come from all walks of life, but as a group, they are demographically similar to NASCAR fans, and are likely to also enjoy hunting, fishing and camping." (ProRodeo.com/demographics).

United States Trotting Association, established 1939: Coordinating organization for harness-racing, specifically trotters.

American Quarter Horse Association (breed Association), established 1940: The World's largest equine breed and membership organization established with "the support of individuals with the power, influence and money to transform Denhardt's concept into reality such as Dan and Jack Casement of Kansas and Colorado, Bert Benear of Oklahoma, J.E. Browning of Arizona, and a raft of Texans: George Clegg, Bob Kleberg of the King Ranch, Jack Hutchins, Raymond Dickson, L.B. Wardlaw, W.B. Warren, Walter Hudgins and Jim Minnick." The group met, proposed and fine-tuned a charter, and bought stock in a new organization that they incorporated as the American Quarter Horse Association. Denhardt later wrote, "We doubted if there were over 300 horses of the type we wanted to be registered in Texas, and probably less than a thousand in the country. We were trying to preserve a nearly extinct line. ... We misjudged what the future would hold for the Quarter Horse." (http://www.aqha.com/About/Content-Pages/About-the-Association/History.aspx).

National Cutting Horse Association (NCHA), established 1946: The first cutting "shows" and exhibitions were in 1898 at the Cowboy Reunion and added to the Stock Show in Fort Worth, Texas in 1919.

US Cavalry dissolves (as does the UK's), 1948: Horses were no longer a vital part of military prowess and power; replacement of cavalry with mechanized alternatives served as catalyst for formalization of 3-day eventing as a discipline as well as other horse show rules and regulations governing equine sports.

United States Equestrian Team (USET) now Foundation (since 2003) supporting 8 disciplines (indicated with * in this list), established 1950: A foundation supporting High Performance Equine Sports (specifically Olympic level) now supports 8 disciplines (all those supported by the FEI including the paraequine sports). The United States Equestrian Team became the United States Equestrian Team Foundation in 2003 after the USET and the United States Equestrian Federation (USEF founded in 1917 as the American Horse Shows Association (AHSA)), signed an agreement making the foundation the unified governing body which included oversight of the Olympic equestrian disciplines in the US. Its Board of Trustees (as of September 2014) reads like a who's who of the rich and famous, horsey or not including Lyle Lovett, Bertram R. Firestone, Jane Forbes Clark, Misdee Wrigley Miller, Patti Scialfa Springsteen, Abigail S. Wexner, and Jacqueline B. Mars, as well as at least 5 others whose names are recognizable to many horse people (www.uset.org/about.php). "The United States Equestrian Team, or USET, was founded in 1950 at the Coates estate on van Beuren Road in Morristown, New Jersey, and is the international equestrian team for the United States. With the assistance of financier and philanthropist Finn M. W. Caspersen (1941-2009) and Beneficial Corporation, the USET relocated to its current headquarters *Hamilton Farm* in Gladstone, New Jersey" (http://en.wikipedia.org/wiki/United_States_Equestrian_Team).

Europe regulates Eventing as international sport, circa 1950: "Eventing competition that resembles the current three-day were first held in 1902, at the Championnat du Cheval d'Armes in France, but were not introduced into the Olympic Games until 1912. [Three-day eventing includes] Dressage . . . . Cross-country . . . . [and] . . . stadium jumping . . . . The Olympic eventing competition was originally open only to male military officers in active duty, mounted only on military charges. In 1924, the event was open to male civilians, although non-commissioned Army officers could not participate in the Olympics until 1956. Women were first allowed to take part in 1964; equestrian sports are one of the few Olympic sports in which men and women compete against one another" (http://en.wikipedia.org/wiki/Eventing).

US Pony Club (following Europe beginning in 1928, informally in US by 1930), established 1954: "U.S. Pony Clubs started in 1954 to teach the English style of riding and the proper care of horses. It is an offshoot of the British Pony Club, which was created in 1929 as a junior branch of the Institute of the Horse. Since then, Pony Club has expanded to many countries around the world. The main purpose is to promote sportsmanship, stewardship and leadership through horsemanship" (http://www.ponyclub.org/?page=aboutus).

U.S. Eventing Association (as of 2001; nee the U.S. Combined Training Association (USCTA),* established 1960: Combined Training is the formal name for Eventing or 3-Day Eventing; the heritage and goals of this organization come directly from the training and preparing of Calvary Horses for War. International 3-Day events (also called "CCI'" events) are sponsored by companies that cater to members of affluence social groups; the Rolex, an annual 3-Day event in Kentucky, is so named because of its long established sponsorship by the watch maker, Rolex. The 2014 Rolex was sponsored by Land Rover. The Rolex, in existance only since 1998, was the first 3 and four star 3-Day Event in the US, only the 3rd outside of England, when it started.

National Reining Horse Association* (FEI 2000), established 1966: "The National Reining Horse Association is the standard-setting body of the sport of Reining. NRHA, with their International Headquarters in Oklahoma City, is responsible for promoting the sport of Reining and working to ensure the highest standards of competition. NRHA strives to educate its members and the public about Reining" (https://www.facebook.com/nrhareining/info?tab=page_info).

American Endurance Ride Conference, established 1972: "The American Endurance Ride Conference (AERC) was founded in 1972 as a national governing body for long distance riding. . . . it has developed a set of rules and guidelines . . . to provide a standardized format and strict veterinary controls . . . . to avoid the rigidity and complexity. . . characteristic of many other equine disciplines. . . . The AERC sanctions more than 700 rides each year throughout North America. In 1978 the Federation Equestre Internationale (FEI) recognized endurance riding as an international sport . . . In 1993 Endurance became the fifth discipline under the (USET). . . . the AERC encourages the use, protection, and development of equestrian trails, especially those with historic significance. . . . The founding ride of endurance riding, the Western States Trail Ride or "Tevis," covers 100 miles of the famous Western States and Immigrant Trails over the Sierra Nevada Mountains (AERC) rides promote awareness of the importance of trail preservation for future generations and foster an appreciation of our American heritage" (http://www.aerc.org/About.aspx).

United States Dressage Federation (USDF),* established 1973: Although dressage was supported by the AHSA and the USET, by the 1970s, "dressage enthusiasts were concerned that the AHSA, the governing body for dressage, could not give the discipline of dressage the attention it needed to flourish. There was a need to establish uniform standards for the sport, and to provide education to dressage judges, instructors, and trainers. . . . . [Given] a lack of nationwide communication, interaction, and cohesiveness amongst these groups . . . . the time was ripe to establish a national organization for the sole purpose of furthering dressage in the United States." (http://www.usdf.org/about/about-usdf/history.asp).

American Driving Society,* established 1974: "There are two carriage driving organizations in the U.S.–the Carriage Association of America, known as the CAA and the American Driving Society, the ADS. The CAA was the first . . . founded in 1960 by twelve people . . . [for] the preservation, restoration and exhibition of antique carriages, . . . and the history of horse drawn vehicles. In the early seventies, a number of members of the CAA wished for better guidelines and consistency in the judging of pleasure shows . . . to form an organization–the ADS–patterned after the BDS (the British Driving Society) . . . . [with about 35] Founding Members . . . [who] contributed money to start the [American Driving] Society. . . . Charles Kellogg, became the volunteer editor of the WHIP, the official publication of the ADS. . . . [and] the glue that kept the fledgling membership together and growing.

These Founding Members devised Pleasure Driving rules that created "working classes" which emphasize the horse, and 'reinsmanship classes' with emphasis on the good driver, so that not only the most expensive harness and antique turnout would always win. Driving Patterns, precursors of the driven dressage tests were developed. There were guidelines to driving in the AHSA (now USEF) rulebook, but they largely pertained to show ring breed driving, so an ADS committee was formed to revise these rules and to submit them to the AHSA for their 1975/76 rule book. A Licensed Officials Committee was established to help make judging more uniform, a handbook was published to spell out some of the requirements for a fair competition. And thus the seeds for competitive driving in this country took root and began to grow" (http://www.americandrivingsociety.org/history.asp).

United States Hunter Jumper* Association (USHJA), established 2004: Established after the reorganization of the AHSA into the USEF to provide the third leg of the "English" Equine Sport Organizations of the USEF. Hunters and Jumpers had been the primary focus of the AHSA which made the existence of a unique organization unnecessary until the reorganization that produced the USEF in the early 2000s.

About the Contributors

Jessica Bell is a Ph.D. student in Sociology, with specializations in Animal Studies, Environmental Science and Policy, and Conservation Criminology, at Michigan State University. She holds a Bachelor of Science in Human Development and a Master of Arts in Psychology from Northwestern University and developed her interest in interdisciplinary research at the Social Neuroscience Laboratory at the University of Chicago. Jessica's research interests include scientific representations of animal behavior and mind, the impact of visual and discursive representations of wildlife on conservation, the sociopolitical dynamics of conservation initiatives, and conservation crime (e.g. wildlife poaching). Her publications include a book chapter on wolf reintroduction (in *A Fairytale in Question: Historical Interactions Between Humans and Wolves*, 2015, White Horse Press), an article on the conservation claims and repercussions of circuses (in press at *Society & Animals*), a book chapter on elephant tourism and the ivory trade in Thailand (in *Conservation Criminology: The Nexus of Crime, Risk and Natural Resources*, 2016, Wiley-Blackwell), and encyclopedia articles on elephants and the ivory trade (in *Humans and Animals: A Geography of Coexistence*, 2016, ABC-CLIO Press). She has received research fellowships from Kellogg Biological Station at Michigan State University and the Animal Welfare Trust, and has presented her work at numerous international conferences, including the International Society of Anthrozoology, the American Sociological Association, the International Wolf Symposium, and the Australian Animal Studies Group.

Stuart Collis is an attorney licensed in Michigan and New York. He has been a speaker on issues of animal law at the Michigan Veterinary Medical Association's semi-annual conference and a speaker and moderator for Michigan's Institute of Continuing Legal Education. Mr. Collis has taken on animal law cases involving ferrets, birds, dogs, swans, and horses. Excerpts of one of his briefs was published on the cover of the Michigan State Bar's Animal Law section's newsletter. Also, he has had numerous articles published in the Michigan Veterinary Medical Association's News and Views and republished in the American Avian Association's news.

Erin M. Evans is a Ph.D. Candidate in Sociology at the University of California, Irvine and will graduate in 2016. Erin was a grassroots activist for over 15 years before pursuing a career in academia, and now specializes in social movements, mass media, institutionalization, animal rights, and culture. Her recent work on legal, policy, and mass media outcomes of animal advocacy can be found in *Social Movement Studies (2015)*, *Society & Animals (2010)*, and *Sociological Perspectives (2016)*. Erin's primary research program examines whether small political gains activists receive, represent an ineffective cooptation of movement influence, or whether these small gains provide a foothold for growing influence. Using regulatory oversight of animals used in research as a case study, one phase of this project used interviews with scientists, ethnographic fieldwork, and archival research to interrogate the long-term effects of the Animal Welfare Act on the institution of science. The first article from this project will be in *Sociological Perspectives* in 2016. Erin is grateful for research support from the Newkirk Center for the Social Studies of Science, the Animal Welfare Trust, Public Responsibility in Medicine and Research, the Sociology Department at UC Irvine, and the Dean's and Associate Dean's offices of the School of the Social Sciences at UC Irvine. Erin continues to be a contributing editor for Mobilizing Ideas, a blog site for social movement's research. Please visit www.emevans.com for further information on her work.

Linda Kalof, Ph.D., is Professor of Sociology and Founding Director of MSU's interdisciplinary graduate specialization in Animal Studies (http://animalstudies.msu.edu). She has published more than 50 articles and book chapters and ten books including *Making Animal Meaning* (MSU Press, 2011), *A Cultural History of the Human Body in the Middle Ages* (Berg 2010), *A Cultural History of the Human Body in the Renaissance* (Berg 2010), *Introduction to Social Statistics* (Wiley/Blackwell, 2009), *Essentials of Social Research* (McGraw-Hill 2008), *Looking at Animals in Human History* (University of Chicago/Reaktion 2007), *A Cultural History of Animals in Antiquity* (Berg 2007), *The Animals Reader* (Berg 2007), *The Earthscan Reader in Environmental Values* (Earthscan 2005), and *Evaluating Social Science Research* (Oxford University Press 1996). She has served as General Editor for the multi-volume *A Cultural History of Animals, A Cultural History of the Human Body,* and *A Cultural History of Women.* She is currently editor of *The Oxford Handbook of Animal Studies* (Oxford University Press) and *The Animal Turn* (Michigan State University Press). Dr. Kalof has received two outstanding scholarship awards (the *Choice* Award for Outstanding Academic Title for *A Cultural History of Animals* and the ASA Outstanding Paper Award from the Animals & Society Section) and three outstanding teaching awards (State University of New York, George Mason University and Michigan State University). She has served on the National Academy of Sciences' National Research Council Committee to review the US wild horse and burro management program; appointed to the Advisory Board for the Detroit Zoo's Center for Zoo Animal Welfare; appointed to the Steering Panel of the Dama International Project, University of Nottingham, UK, to examine the European fallow deer as a medium for understanding the evolution of European Society 6000 BC to AD 1600; and appointed to the Advisory Board of the National Museum of Animals & Society. Her current research project, "Picturing Animals in 125 Years of National Geographic," is funded by the National Science Foundation.

Andrea Laurent-Simpson is a Ph.D. Candidate in Sociology at Texas Woman's University. She specializes in Social Psychology and Stratification. Currently, her work examines the development of the parent identity in companion animal owners that do not have human children.

Shawn McEntee, Ph.D., is Associate Professor of Sociology at Salisbury University where she teaches a range of courses: Introduction to Sociology, Introduction to Global Sociology, Race Relations in Global Perspective, Sociology of Conflict and Non-Violence, Globalization and Social Change, Population Studies, and Women and Development. Shawn adopted the label 'global sociologist' in graduate school stemming from a chronic tendency to see the 'big picture.' Her teaching focuses on helping students make connections to apply sociology to their daily lives and encourage the development of sociological imagination. Dr. McEntee grew up in Franklin County, the center of Ohio, which then had more horses per square mile than any other county in the US and now lives in Maryland, the state that has more horses per square mile than any other in the country. Horses have been a part of Shawn's daily life almost continuously since she was 9; she met her equine partner (of now 15 years) when Countess was 3 days old.

Daniel Moorehead, Ed.D., is Assistant Professor of Sociology at Frostburg State University where he continues to teach a range of courses: Animals in Human Society, Criminology, Introduction to Sociology, Juvenile Delinquency, Marriage and Family, Sociology of Deviant Behavior, Sociology of Education, and Social Problems. Dr. Moorehead strives to create a "learning community" in his classrooms, promoting engagement in the learning process by sharing information, ideas, and experiences. His course "Animals in Human Society" was nominated for the 2015 Award for Outstanding Course on Animals & Society "*The Clifton Bryant Animals & Society Course Award.* " He was recently awarded the Dean's Merit Award for Professional Achievement in the College of Liberal Arts. In addition, he recently published an article with several of his colleagues entitled "Invisible Faculty:" Department chairs' perceptions of part-time faculty status in Maryland four-year public and private higher education institutions. *The Delta Kappa Gamma Bulletin: International Journal of Professional Educators*, *81*(4), 102-119. He is a member of the American Sociological Association and Southern Sociological Society and active in varied social and animal organizations. He earned his doctorate degree from West Virginia University, Morgantown, WV.

Richard Ravalli, Ph.D., is Assistant Professor of History at William Jessup University in Rocklin, California. His work on sea otter history has been published in the journals *Asia Pacific Perspectives*, *Pacific Northwest Quarterly*, and *International Journal of Maritime History*. A native of the California Central Valley, Professor Ravalli credits his interest in sea otters in part to many family trips to the coast as a child. He is currently developing a manuscript with University of Nebraska Press tentatively titled *Sea Otters: A History*.

Stephen Vrla is a Ph.D. student in the Department of Sociology at Michigan State University. Within the department, he is specializing in environmental sociology. He is also pursuing interdepartmental specializations in animal studies and environmental science and policy. In August, he will present his paper "Something to See Here: Looking at Road-killing and Road-killed Animals" at the American Sociological Association Annual Meeting. In addition to his coursework, he works as a research assistant on Dr. Linda Kalof's "Picturing Animals in *National Geographic*, a National Science Foundation-funded, three-year-long project exploring representations of animals in *National Geographic* magazine issues from the past 125 years. He is a co-author on the paper "On the Coexistence of Humans with Liminal Animals: Cultural Representations in the Northern Environment over the Twentieth Century," in preparation for publication in *Urban-Rural-Wilderness: The Co-living of Humans and Animals in the North since the Nineteenth Century*, a forthcoming anthology edited by Taina Syrjämaa, Helena Ruotsala, and Tuomas Räsänen.

Andrew Woodhall, a final year AHRC-funded Ph.D. student at the University of Birmingham. His thesis focuses on anthropocentrism within ethics, specifically the sub-section referred to as 'nonhuman ethics', and argues for a clarified explanation of anthropocentrism and a new, non-anthropocentric approach to non-human ethics. I show how this can be achieved and why such an approach would be better for non-humans and the aim of non-human ethics. Andrew presented at the MANCEPT workshops conference on anthropocentrism and citizenship theory in 2013 and the anthropocentric problems arising from using political and ethical theories in resolving nonhuman issues in 2014. He is am co-organizing the 2015 nonhuman ethics panel at MANCEPT which is focused on intervention for non-human animals. He also presented on anthropocentrism at the Minding Animals Conference 3 in New Delhi, India, January 2015, and in April 2015 and co-organized an international conference on the contemporary ethical and political approaches to non-human issues, supported by the *Society for Applied Philosophy*, *Mind*, and the *Aristotelian Society*. Andrew is presently working on his first journal publications, two on anthropocentrism, a paper on the relation of aesthetics and ethics and a paper on Incest and Bestiality, and another more general ethical paper, as well as currently organizing two volumes on non-human issues which he will be co-editing. He has published a book review on Anna L. Peterson's *Being Animal* in *Ethical Theory and Moral Practice*, and currently working on a review of Tony Milligan's *Animal Ethics: The Basics*. Andrew has been awarded five prizes in philosophy at the University of Aberdeen, taught five courses on philosophy since beginning his Masters in 2011, and has been invited to speak on philosophy across the UK. He is also co-founder of the Saving Nonhumans Initiative.

Cameron Thomas Whitley is a Ph.D. candidate in the department of Sociology at Michigan State University. He strives to be well rounded by focusing on three core principles: research, teaching and service. Cameron is currently engaged in research addressing risk perceptions, state-based policy initiatives and environmental justice/exposure to hydraulic fracturing, with a particular focus on how new energy technologies impact domestic, wild and liminal animals. He is also working on a National Science Foundation (NSF) funded project exploring the use of animal representations in popular science venues with Dr. Linda Kalof. Additionally, Cameron has received numerous fellowships and recognitions for his innovative teaching techniques, which often employ student driven photography and film. Beyond teaching and research, Cameron is interested in public sociology, or the ways in which we can take our work into the community. With a focus on assisting animals, he has engaged in domestic volunteer work such as working with the local humane society to international endeavors like assisting with turtle relocation on the island of St. Croix. Cameron's research and work has been published in numerous book chapters and journals. His work has appeared in *Teaching Sociology*, *Sociological Perspectives*, *International Journal of Sociology*,

American Emergency Medicine and the *Proceedings of the National Academy of Sciences (PNAS)* among others.

Ms. Corey Wrenn is a Lecturer of Sociology with Monmouth University and a Ph.D. student (ABD) in Sociology at Colorado State University. She received her M.S. in Sociology in 2008 and her B.A. in Political Science in 2005, both from Virginia Tech. She is a council member of the American Sociological Association's Animals & Society section (2013-2016) and contributes to the *Human-Animal Studies Images* and *Cinema* blogs for the Animals and Society Institute. She is the author of *A Rational Approach to Animal Rights: Extensions in Abolitionist Theory*, published by Palgrave Macmillan in 2015, and she has been published in several peer-reviewed academic journals including the *Journal of Gender Studies*, the *Journal of Agriculture & Environmental Ethics*, *Food, Culture & Society*, and *Society & Animals*. In July 2013, she founded the Vegan Feminist Network, an academic-advocacy project that seeks to raise intersectionality awareness in animal rights spaces.